General Printing

Request · Read · Return

...Your Library. Delivered.

Engraved Stone

Manuscript Writing

Gutenberg Press

First Linotype

Stages in the Development of the Graphic Arts as Shown in Murals in the New York Public Library
Painted by Edward Laning

Courtesy, New York City Public Library

GENERAL PRINTING

GLEN U. CLEETON
Dean of the School of Printing Management
Carnegie Institute of Technology
Pittsburgh, Pennsylvania

CHARLES W. PITKIN
Vice President and Director of Manufacturing
Doubleday & Company, Inc.
New York City

Revised By
RAYMOND L. CORNWELL
Formerly, Professor and Coordinator of Graphic Arts
State University of New York, College at Oswego

McKNIGHT & McKNIGHT PUBLISHING COMPANY
BLOOMINGTON, ILLINOIS

REISSUED BY
Liber Apertus Press
SARATOGA, CALIFORNIA

Reissued September 2006
ISBN 0-9785881-4-2

Liber Apertus Press

P.O. Box 261, Saratoga, CA 95071 USA
www.LiberApertus.com
info@LiberApertus.com

2006 Foreword

by David S. Rose

At its peak in the mid-twentieth century, printing was the sixth largest industry in the United States ... and virtually all of it was done using the letterpress process. This technology, originally perfected by Johann Gutenberg in 1451, brought to life newspapers, fine books, circus posters and everything in between. In the years following Gutenberg, thousands of inventors, machinists and businessmen worked to improve the mechanics of laying down ink on paper from relief printing surfaces, and the results of their efforts ranged from miniature business card presses to five-story tall newspaper behemoths.

The march of technological progress is inexorable, however, and the postwar years in the twentieth century saw the rapid commercialization of photo-offset lithography, which began to render obsolete five hundred years' worth of equipment and procedures. With the new technology, phototypesetting machines replaced large banks of metal type and flexible offset plates replaced giant stereotype plates. "Stonehands" who had spent their careers learning to impose large forms of type and cuts were replaced by "paste-up men." This new generation used waxers and blue pencils to assemble the same pages in a fraction of the time. But the pace of change was accelerating, and where metal type had lasted over half a millennium, "cold type" lasted less than half a century. The digital revolution made phototype completely obsolete, and now in the twenty-first century the technology to generate unlimited amounts of the highest resolution type is available to the most impecunious amateur.

But history is full of twists and turns, and today a new generation has discovered the allure of letterpress technology. What began as a motley assortment of avant garde artists, historically-minded scholars and "gentleman printers" has turned into an international movement of tens of thousands of people who find their creative outlet (and often careers) in reviving this classic printing process. Letterpress printers today encompass professional stationery craftspeople, publishers of fine art books, proprietors of private presses, and hobbyists who delight melding graphic design with hands-on production.

The problem for today's printers, however, is finding training resources for this wonderful, archaic practice. In 1683, the publication of Joseph Moxon's *Mechanick Exercises* for the first time revealed the secrets of the Black Art. From that point forward, letterpress printing manuals were written and re-written at a breakneck pace for over 250 years, with some of the more popular ones going through several dozen successive editions. This came to a crashing halt with the demise of the commercial letterpress industry, and every letterpress manual ever written was out of print by the late 1970s. During the past 25 years, only three new books[*] have been published on the subject, but two of them are highly specialized and the third is a very simplified introductory text.

The book you hold in your hand, *General Printing* by Glen U. Cleeton and Charles W. Pitkin, is generally regarded by experienced printers as being the best all-around manual for traditional letterpress printing. Originally intended as the course text for a college-level audience, this manual covers all of the steps from typesetting to finishing, and is profusely illustrated with detailed and useful photographs. It is the manual most recommended on the Letpress Internet mailing list of over a thousand experienced

---

[*]Rummonds, *Printing on the Iron Handpress*, Oak Knoll Press, 1997

Lange, *Printing Digital Type on the Hand-Operated Flatbed Cylinder Press*, Bieler Press, 2001

Maravelas, *Letterpress Printing: A Manual for Modern Fine Press Printers*, Oak Knoll Press, 2006

printers, and its popularity (and scarcity) has made it one of the top ten most sought after out-of-print books (of any kind!) for two years in a row.

This edition is an exact reproduction of the original release of *General Printing*, and should occupy a prominent place on the shelf of every letterpress printer. It will serve as the next best thing to an apprenticeship at the feet of a master printer, and is certain to be used as a handy reference throughout your printing journey.

For pointers to a wide range of additional resources that will help you get started establishing a letterpress print shop of your own—including a lengthy bibliography of other printing and design manuals—be sure to check out the Introduction to Letterpress Printing, at *www.fiveroses.org/intro.htm*.

Good luck with your future printing!

David S. Rose
New York, NY
August, 2006

David S. Rose, a letterpress printer and book collector with one of the world's largest collections of letterpress printing manuals, is President of the Typophiles and Proprietor of the Five Roses Press. He maintains the Getting Started Guide for the Letpress mailing list and is the author of the Introduction to Letterpress Printing.

Suggestions to Students

By studying the lessons in this book three things can be accomplished: (1) You will become reasonably proficient in the mechanical details of type composition and simple presswork; (2) You can learn many new and interesting facts about the history of printing and develop an understanding of the importance of the graphic arts to the progress of civilization; (3) You can learn to judge the quality of printed jobs and develop appreciation for good printing.

Your teacher will assist and direct you in your study; but, with the help of the lessons contained herein, you should be able to accomplish a great deal by studious self-direction. No one can do your learning for you; it is strictly your individual problem. The more attention and effort you devote to the study of graphic arts, the more you will accomplish.

Study each lesson as it is assigned by your teacher. Don't fall behind in your work. Even better, read a few assignments in advance. When studying an assignment, make certain that you know *what* you are supposed to do and *how* you are supposed to do it before starting to work. If you have difficulty in understanding the explanations given in the book, do not go to your teacher with the general statement, "I do not understand this lesson." Rather, study the particular assignment, step by step, until you have found the specific part in your textbook which you do not understand; then ask your teacher to explain the troublesome items. By following these suggestions, you will save time, and your progress will be more rapid. If all members of your class work together to save time, all will be able to complete the work in the time that is allotted and everyone will profit from the course.

Always try to connect the special instructions given by your teacher with the explanations in the book. When a demonstration is given, relate it in your thinking to the information in the text and to your previous learnings. The steps, or operations, in printing, are closely connected and are about equal in importance. By doing one step improperly, the whole job may be spoiled. Every mistake you make will waste your time and the time of your teacher. To develop ability in printing, you must learn to plan carefully and to think things out for yourself.

Study examples of printing in books, magazines, and advertising materials. Learn to judge the *quality* of printed jobs and to know what is *good* or *bad* in printed pieces. Examine jobs to see if they meet the requirements of good spacing, legibility, balance, proportion, suitability of type face and paper, general attractiveness, and quality of presswork. Learn to recognize various printing, duplicating and art processes, as well as the kinds of paper on which they are printed. Collect samples of each.

Be critical of your own work. First of all, learn to compose your job to meet high standards of neatness and accuracy. Then, as you progress, learn to build into your work all of the desirable qualities which a fine piece of printing should have. Do not be discouraged if your teacher suggests ways in which they can be improved. He must occasionally criticize your work if you are to improve your abilities. You will learn from experience that all printing jobs must be proofread carefully and corrected several times. Books and magazines are proofread and corrected four to six times before they are printed. Bibles and dictionaries may be read and corrected as many as fifteen to twenty times.

The study of printing will give you an excellent opportunity to use your knowledge of arithmetic. You will learn that typesetting requires a special system of measurement. You must also learn to be careful about spelling, punctuation, word division, capitalization, and grammar. Mistakes in English are exposed for the whole world to see if put in print. New and important facets of history will be learned by studying printing, because the history of printing has closely paralleled the history of the world during the past five hundred years.

Graphic materials should be of interest to all students of printing. Some of the more important facts about type faces, paper, ink, and type metals have been included as lessons in this book. If you do not learn all that you would like to know about these materials from the lessons, the bibliography in the back and your teacher can suggest sources of additional information. Special reports written by members of your class on various topics dealing with graphic arts would be a good way to collect such information.

It is not likely that all members of your class will wish to enter the graphic arts industries as a means of earning a livelihood. But we hope that all students who use this book will study various vocations in printing before choosing an occupation. You will experience something of the work of compositors and pressmen in your study of this course. But there are many other occupations relating to the planning, production, and selling of printing. Then, too, there are important closely related fields, such as advertising and publishing, office duplicating, and the manufacture of machinery and materials, such as printing presses, ink, and paper. Printing, publishing, and the related graphic arts make up the leading custom manufacturing industry in the United States today, when measured by the number of persons gainfully employed. Although you may never be engaged in the printing business, you will be a user of printing throughout your entire life. Any occupation you might select will use printed materials. Furthermore, it is quite possible that several members of your class will find in printing an interesting hobby.

Acknowledgments

Many of the photographs dealing with graphic arts procedures were produced by Charles W. Pitkin while he was an assistant professor of printing at Carnegie Institute of Technology. Technical direction of photography for instructional units was provided by L. H. Miller of the Tech operations staff. Several photographs and original materials used as general illustrations were contributed by Professor Homer E. Sterling, a member of the instructional staff of Carnegie School of Printing Management.

The charts used to illustrate Unit 93 originally appeared in *Graphic Design*, by Leon Friend and Joseph Hefter, who graciously granted permission for their use. Grateful acknowledgment is also made to the many authors whose works were consulted in preparing the text. Thanks of the authors are hereby extended to Dorothy McCarroll, whose assistance in collecting materials and preparing the manuscript made possible the second edition of the book.

Manufacturers of printing equipment generously supplied photographs to be used in connection with the related information units. Acknowledgments in this respect are due to the Mergenthaler Linotype Co., Harris-Intertype Corp., Lanston Monotype Machine Co., Ludlow Typograph Co., American Type Founders, Inc., Miehle Co. and Dexter Co. of Miehle-Goss-Dexter, Inc., Miller Printing Machinery Co., The Chandler & Price Co., Brandtjen & Kluge, Inc., Heidelberg Eastern, Inc., Commercial Controls Corp., Fairchild Graphic Equipment, Davidson Products Div. of Fairchild Camera & Instrument Corp., Cronite Co., Inc., The Challenge Machinery Co., Bostitch, Harris-Seybold Co., Addressograph-Multigraph Corp., International Business Machines Corp., Champlain, Inc., and T. W. & C. B. Sheridan Co.

International Paper Company furnished a series of drawings from *Pocket Pal*. The Hammermill Paper Company supplied a series of illustrations dealing with the process of papermaking. Printing Industry of America and Printing and Publishing Industries Division of U. S. Dept. of Commerce furnished data of the industry. The *Graphic Arts Monthly* gave permission to reproduce layouts of a spread from their magazine.

The frontispiece photographs were secured from the New York City Public Library. They show a series of murals executed by Edward Laning. The authors not only gratefully acknowledge permission to use reproduction of the murals, but also commend Mr. Laning on the insight with which he has depicted the progress of printing.

Several specimens of type faces shown in Units 94-102 were reproduced through permission of Harvard University Press, the publishers of *Printing Types: Their History, Forms, and Use*, by D. B. Updike. Illustrations of early printing presses, used in Unit 103, were reproduced through the courtesy of the board of editors of *The Dolphin*, publishers of *A History of the Printed Book*, by Lawrence C. Wroth. The chart of the letter "g," shown on page 132, and the chart of the letter "d," on page 136, were reproduced through the courtesy of the late Frederic W. Goudy.

Foreword to the Third Edition

The first two editions of General Printing have been well accepted and are widely used in many kinds of schools. This edition retains this time-tested approach to teaching basic techniques while showing modern equipment.

A broad overview of graphic arts processes has been added to the introductory section. Many concepts have been compressed into this section which identifies the entire scope of modern graphic arts. It is suggested that this overview be used first as an introduction to printing, and later as a summary of work covered. Much of the information will take on increased meaning after working with type, paper and ink.

With this edition, Dr. Raymond L. Cornwell becomes an additional co-author and will aid in a continuing revision of content. New materials reflect content he has developed while teaching in Racine, Wisconsin, at Stout State College, at State University College at Oswego, New York, and from experience gained in commercial printing.

Contents

Printing and the Graphic Arts

Printing has been a basic factor in shaping civilization. The general cultural development of a country can be determined by the amount of paper (mostly printed) it uses per person each year (examples for 1959: U.S. 437.8 pounds, Russia 32.6 pounds, Congo 3.9 pounds). The invention of printing was man's first experience with mass production methods. The spread of printed products helped put an end to the dark ages, and prompted the discovery and exploration of the new world. Democracy depends on enlightened voters, and the United States government runs the largest printing plant in the world. Totalitarian powers rigidly control printing and the spread of information. Besides governmental uses, printed material is basic to educational and religious institutions. Advertising and packaging are major uses of printing. Business depends also on paper records, forms, and data systems.

When you read a book, a magazine, or a newspaper, you are using printing. Look about you during the day and observe the number of times you must depend on printing to obtain the information which you need. If you make a telephone call, make a purchase at a store, prepare your lessons, answer an advertisement, select a breakfast food, find the date on a calendar, or do any of a hundred other things, printing guides your actions. As a user of printing, therefore, you should have an interest in the way printing is done.

What Is Printing

The purpose of printing is to record messages on paper or other surfaces *graphically* by making a *number of copies* of pictorial, typographical, lined, or decorative arrangements. In the basic historical printing process (letterpress) there are four main stages of work: (1) a design or *layout* is planned to serve the needed use, (2) type is assembled or *composed* into lines according to the layout, and locked into a form, (3) the form is placed in a *press,* the type is inked, and an impression is made on paper, (4) printed sheets are folded,

Designing a Printing Job

Setting the Type

Printing a Job

fastened, cut, counted, packaged, or otherwise processed in the *bindery*. These four basic stages in printing a job are known as layout, composition (and preparatory), presswork, and bindery.

It would be interesting to stop for a moment and note some of the specific printed products you have used today. Books, magazines, and newspapers come to mind first. But don't forget all the printed forms, tickets, licenses, passes, stamps, and paper money necessary to business and government operation. In homes are framed art prints, photographs, wallpaper designs, printed textiles, plastic counter or floor coverings, toothpaste tubes, can labels, and cereal packages. In school or office are stationery, duplicated memos, mimeographed tests, dittoed instructions, or any typing for that matter. Almost anything manufactured has some printing on it — for example a pencil, a razor blade, or a clock. All these have one thing in common — they are printed.

What Are the Graphic Arts

From such a diverse list you can see that modern printing needs are extremely varied. Today, many methods of printing are used to put images on a wide variety of surfaces. All of these processes, together with such related fields as photography, papermaking, and ink-making, are called the *graphic arts*. Graphic arts implies broader content than printing. It also puts more emphasis on printing design. Even though the word printing can be used in a broad sense, it sometimes is interpreted as meaning only the printing *trade*, or just *commercial* printing, or even just commercial *letterpress* printing (printing from type or raised surfaces formed from type).

The term *graphic arts* also has some limited, specialized meanings. In television and motion pictures, graphic art refers to the design of titles, credits, and captions which appear at the beginning, the end, and on graphs or charts. Artists sometimes speak of art work for advertising or publications as *graphic art* (as opposed to *fine* art), and the *graphic arts* as hand processes to produce a number of art prints from a plate or block. The *graphic arts*, as defined broadly, are the subject of this overview.

Three Classes of Graphic Reproduction

Actually there are three classes of graphic arts processes: commercial printing, office duplicating, and art processes.

Printing

Printing or *commercial printing* describes the work of specialists whose business it is to produce books, stationery, or any of the many printed products we need. Some plants do a variety of work and are known as commercial *job printers*. Other printers work in *publication plants* producing a single product such as newspapers. Some work for *specialty houses* where printing is limited to business forms, calendars, decals, tags, or some other specialty.

Duplicating

Office or in-plant duplicating uses simplified techniques to reproduce letters, forms, business systems, instructional materials, working drawings, and similar materials. These materials are commonly used in business firms or schools.

Larger offices usually have a separate duplicating department to reproduce letters, forms, drawings and similar printed work quickly on their own premises. Workers in such departments become quite specialized and their skills may become similar to those of commercial printers. Usually their training period is much shorter and their equipment is smaller and built lighter than that of a commercial printer.

Examples of duplicating processes include office photocopying (Verifax or Thermofax), stencil duplicating (Mimeograph), spirit duplicating (Ditto), offset duplicating (Multilith), and blueprinting (Ozalid). Nearly everyone has needs for typewriting and a knowledge of these duplicating techniques.

Many office machines have their own printing system built in to make a permanent visible record. Examples can be found in cash registers, adding machines, computers, and data processing equipment. In fact, a major problem now is that many machines can record data and think faster than they can print, so quicker print-out methods are being sought.

Also closely related to duplicating is marking and industrial printing. *Marking* uses various rubber or steel stamps and dies. Rubber stamps, daters, tape markers, adjustable stencils, steel letter punches, and credit cards are examples of marking equipment. In *industrial printing*, the product is usually made of a material other than paper, with instructions, nameplates, or other information printed during manufacture. Nearly any graphic arts process can be adapted to a specialized purpose. Rulers, etching on metal, radio dials, and printed electronic circuits are a few examples of industrial printing.

So, in a broad sense, duplicating includes typing and carbon copies, office reproduction, in-plant duplicating, printing devices on office machines, marking, and industrial printing. Some of these duplicating processes are taught in business and office practice courses, but a broad study of the graphic arts makes them more easily understood.

Art Processes

Art processes are those techniques by which artists make multiple art prints: etchings, wood or linoleum block prints, lithographs, and screen process prints (silk screen, seriographs, or mitography). Making art prints is a common hobby and means of self expression. These processes are usually taught in art courses, but printing experience can improve the quality of prints made from the blocks or plates.

Historically, art processes were the source from which more complex printing processes (as well as the simplified duplicating processes) evolved. Wood and metal engravings were used for art prints a hundred years before the discovery of America. Printing was first perfected by Johann Gutenberg about fifty years later. The first office duplicating process, (the Mimeograph, meaning "copy-print") was developed by Thomas A. Edison and Albert B. Dick in the late 1880's.

What You Should Learn

A broad introductory study of graphic arts should help you understand all of these three classes: printing processes, duplicating processes, and art processes. You should learn how to do layout, composition, presswork, and bindery work — and the interdependence of each. You should learn about such related areas as paper, ink, history of graphic arts, the graphic arts industry today, and careers in graphic arts.

This book contains most of the information you will need. You are also encouraged to visit a newspaper or printing plant, to talk to people who do printing or duplicating, and to read elsewhere about printing. The Bibliography at the back of this book lists many references, topics to check in encyclopedias or indexes, and organizations which may have recent data.

Using this book you will learn to perform the basic operations of typesetting and presswork for letterpress printing. These are covered very thoroughly and give the book its primary emphasis in the general printing area. The knowledge thus developed forms the basis for an excellent understanding of duplicating, art processes, and the modern graphic arts industry. The skills you will acquire will be a firm foundation for advanced study. The units on materials, history, and equipment should be studied along with the work units.

Running a Duplicator (A. B. Dick)

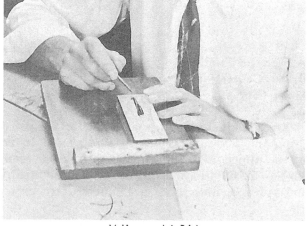

Making an Art Print

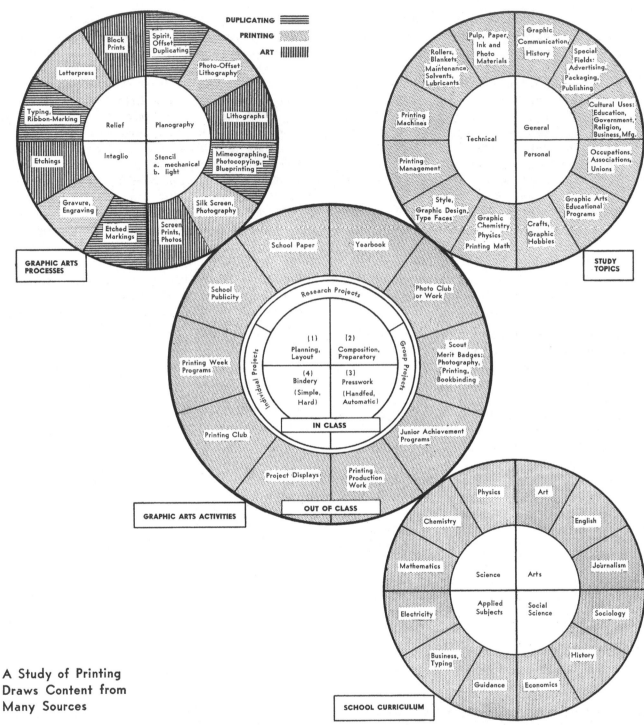

DUPLICATING ≡
PRINTING ▦
ART ▥

GRAPHIC ARTS PROCESSES

Block Prints
Spirit, Offset Duplicating
Letterpress
Photo-Offset Lithography
Typing, Ribbon-Marking
Relief
Planography
Lithographs
Etchings
Intaglio
Stencil a. mechanical b. light
Mimeographing, Photocopying, Blueprinting
Gravure, Engraving
Silk Screen, Photography
Etched Markings
Screen Prints, Photos
Screen Prints, Photos

STUDY TOPICS

Pulp, Paper, Ink and Photo Materials
Graphic Communication, History
Rollers, Blankets, Maintenance, Solvents, Lubricants
Special Fields: Advertising, Packaging, Publishing
Printing Machines
Technical
General
Cultural Uses: Education, Government, Religion, Business, Mfg.
Printing Management
Personal
Occupations, Associations, Unions
Style, Graphic Design, Type Faces
Graphic Arts Educational Programs
Graphic Chemistry Physics Printing Math
Crafts, Graphic Hobbies

GRAPHIC ARTS ACTIVITIES

School Paper
Yearbook
School Publicity
Photo Club or Work
Research Projects
(1) Planning, Layout
(2) Composition, Preparatory
Individual Projects
Group Projects
Printing Week Programs
(4) Bindery (Simple, Hard)
(3) Presswork (Handfed, Automatic)
Scout Merit Badges: Photography, Printing, Bookbinding
IN CLASS
Printing Club
Junior Achievement Programs
Project Displays
Printing Production Work
OUT OF CLASS

SCHOOL CURRICULUM

Physics
Art
Chemistry
English
Mathematics
Science
Arts
Journalism
Electricity
Applied Subjects
Social Science
Sociology
Business, Typing
History
Guidance
Economics

A Study of Printing Draws Content from Many Sources

An introductory study of printing can draw from the several graphic arts processes listed at the upper left. Your activities in class (center) will be those required to complete any printed job, and there are many extracurric- ular activities which are related. Most of your school subjects (bottom) are also closely related. The topics at the upper right suggest some of the information to obtain by studying, reading, and working in the library.

Basic Methods of Printing

There are four basic methods of printing, classified by the surface used: *relief, intaglio, planographic,* and *stencil.* All printing, duplicating and art processes use one of these four basic surfaces. Probably all future methods will simply be new variations, adaptations, or combinations of these. This unit briefly describes these basic surfaces.

Relief Processes

In relief printing the printing surface is raised above the non-printing surface (the white areas). This is shown in Fig. A.

Forming a Relief Surface

The relief surface can be obtained by *cutting* away the white areas with hand tools (as in block printing), by machine *routing* (wood type), by *burning* or melting of plastic (Fairchild halftones), by *acid etching* of metal (photoengraving), by light hardening and a water wash-out (Dycril plates), by *casting* from a carved or punched matrix (foundry type and Monotype), by casting from a *series of assembled punched matrices* (Linotype and Ludlow), by casting from a *duplicate paper mold* of an original relief form (stereotyping), by *electroplating* on a duplicate plastic mold (electrotyping), by *molding* or vulcanizing on a duplicate mold (rubber stamps, rubber or plastic plates), by *die-forging,* die-casting, heat treating (steel stamps, typebars on business machines and typewriters), by *embossing* of plastic or metal sheets (addressing plates and credit cards), or in a recent development by *electrically raising* small needle-like sections to form the image (high-speed computer printer).

Printing a Relief Surface

Historically, relief printing is the oldest of all methods. Usually *ink* is placed on the raised surface and pressed against paper. Other processes strike through an *inked ribbon* or carbon paper. In credit card machines the relief surface presses against the back side of the sheet. An *inked pressure roller* is passed over the top so that ink is rubbed off over the high areas of the printing surface. (A light smudge may be left over the rest of the area.) Relief surfaces can be heated to transfer *heat-sensitive foil* (about 250-300°F) as in gold stamping. Relief surfaces can be used to leave an image on special *heat or pressure sensitive paper.* Hot dies are used to *burn* an image in wood or for branding of animals. And, of course, hard dies can be used to *blind stamp* softer materials by leaving only an impression with no ink or color.

Characteristics of Relief Printing

There usually is a sharp image in relief processing using ink. Ink does tend to spread slightly, forming a heavier ring around each letter. Nicks or scratches leave a void in the image (show white). There is usually some denting of the printed surface. These characteristics are easily seen through a magnifying glass.

Intaglio Processes

Intaglio (in-tal'-yo) processes use lines, or wells, which are *depressed* below the surface of the plate to carry the ink to form the image. See Fig. B. This is the exact reverse of relief processes. The sunken image can be formed

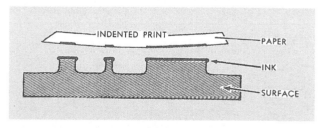

Fig. A. Relief Surface

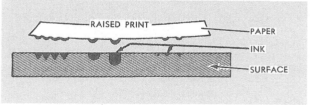

Fig. B. Intaglio Surface

either by means of a *sharp tool* (as in dry point art prints and in copperplate engravings), or by *acid etching* (as in art etchings or photogravure).

Printing an Intaglio Plate

In printing, ink is placed over all the plate and then scraped or wiped from the surface. This leaves ink trapped in wells that vary in depth as well as width. Intaglio thus is capable of the best tonal rendition because it is the only basic method capable of transferring infinite variations in the thickness of the ink film at different parts of the image. Unlike relief there is no spreading of the image and no ridge of ink. Details can be extremely sharp.

Characteristics of Intaglio Printing

Under a magnifying glass the printed image seems to stand up above the sheet. In fact this raised image may often be felt or seen with the naked eye. The printed sheet may show the outline of the entire plate or parts of it. The back side may be slightly roughened or pushed forward into lines of the image, but never embossed outward as from relief surfaces. Scratches print lines across white areas.

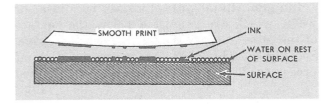

Fig. C. Planographic Surface

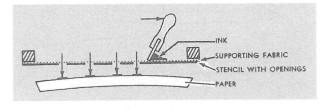

Fig. D. Mechanical Stencil

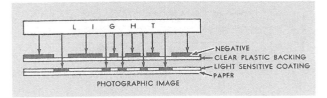

Fig. E. Light Stencil or Negative

Planographic Processes

Planographic processes print from a plane or *flat* surface. See Fig. C. Both the image and the white area come from the same level. This may be done by depositing enough of the image-forming ink or dye on a surface so that a number of prints can be made from it. This technique has several duplicating applications such as Verifax (4 to 10 photocopies), Hektograph (50 copies), or Ditto (250 copies). In these duplicating processes each print gets lighter than the one preceding.

The Lithographic Principle

For a practical printing process, it is necessary to apply ink before making each print without inking the non-image areas. In lithography, this is achieved by using a grease-base ink and water. The total plate area is kept dampened with water. Water will not adhere to the grease-attracting image and greasy ink adheres only to the image. This dampening procedure is used in the various lithographic processes.

Most printing processes transfer ink directly from the printing surface to the paper. In *offset lithography*, the inked plate prints onto an intermediate rubber blanket. The blanket in turn transfers the ink to the paper, and is thus itself a planographic surface. Plates for offset must be *right-reading* (that is not a mirror image or *wrong-reading* or reversed from left to right as is type or a rubber stamp). This is because the image is reversed in being transferred to the blanket, and then reversed back again when transferred to paper. Offset allows better printing of fine detail on rough papers.

Lithography literally means *stone printing*. The process was discovered in 1796 when Alois Senefelder was writing on a piece of limestone with a greasy crayon. He found that if he dampened the stone he could roll ink over the entire area and it would adhere only to the crayon lines. Artists still use stones for art prints. Today, however, most lithographic surfaces are made of thin sheets of aluminum, zinc or paper treated to retain moisture as well as the ink attracting image. Thin sheets can be handled easily, curved into a circle for fast rotary printing, and compactly stored for re-running.

The Photogelatin Principle

Collotype is a rather uncommon planographic process which prints from a flat *gelatin* surface. It has the unique capability of holding varying amounts of water at different parts of the photographic image. Dry areas accept a heavy layer of ink, wet areas take none, and there are varying degrees of density in between. This is the only process capable of using black ink to reproduce the various tones of gray without screening into a multitude of dots.

Characteristics of Planography

As the pressure of printing from flat surfaces is distributed over both the image and the non-image areas, there is very little image spread, no ridge of ink around the image and no embossing or denting of the surface. Planographic processes often do not quite achieve the image density found in intaglio, relief, or stencil processes, and are usually characterized by soft shading of tones. A scratch or defect on the plate may show across both image and non-image areas. As planography is chemical as well as mechanical, considerable skill is needed for top quality work, yet satisfactory duplicating is accomplished by novices.

Stencil Processes

Stencil processes print through the openings in a mask which form the image areas. These openings can be actual holes in *mechanical stencils,* or transparent sections of negatives in *photographic* processes. See Figs. D and E.

Mechanical Stencils

In the simplest form of stenciling an opening of the desired shape (such as a circle) is cut in tough paper and laid over the surface to be stenciled. Pigment can then be brushed, sprayed, or forced through the opening. If a letter "O" is needed rather than the solid ball, then a center area must be left in the stencil. Usually the letter is divided slightly so that two or more *ties* are left holding the center to the body of the stencil. This forms a distinctive style for open-link stencil lettering. This is often used on mail boxes, packing cases, personal and sports equipment.

More refined mechanical stencils incorporate many minute almost invisible ties that leave no breaks in the design. These ties are in the supporting woven fabric in the various silk screen processes, and in the tissue fibers in stencil duplicating (Mimeographing). Breaks in the stencil would allow ink to leak into white areas. Dried ink tends to clog openings causing voids in the image.

Nonmechanical Stencils

In photographic processes, *a film negative* is a light stencil with the tones reversed from normal — whites are opaque and the blacks are clear. See Fig. E. When the negative is photographically printed it becomes a *positive* — a positive *print* if on paper, and a *film* positive if on transparent film. Such prints may be made with the negative in direct contact with the film or paper *(a contact print),* or the negative may be projected through a lens to enlarge or reduce it, or otherwise modify it.

Tone sensitivity may be of two different types. In *contrast* processes, the negative is either completely opaque or it is clear — all or nothing. In *continuous-tone* processes the negatives (and resulting positives) have intermediate shades between black and white.

Light-Sensitive Chemicals

Photographic processes depend on light-sensitive chemicals which change after being exposed to light and subsequent developing solutions. Such development removes the unexposed light-sensitive chemical and fixes it so that it becomes permanent. Photographic films usually contain a *silver halide* (such as silver bromide) which darkens to metallic silver. Blueprints, bluelines, vandykes, carbon tissue, and gelatin processes make use of *potassium bichromate* (or similar chemicals) which develops out in water but may require chemical fixing.

Diazo dyes are used in many variations, but all contain two molecules of nitrogen (azote) called a *dye parent.* By themselves they are nearly colorless and easily destroyed by light. When exposed diazo materials are developed in various *dye couplers,* the image formed by light can be permanently dyed most any color and made either positive or negative by changing dye couplers. Diazo coatings are used in Ozalids or white prints, which are positive working (form a positive from a positive). The diazo compound is decomposed in white areas by exposure to light. The developer is an alkaline solution or an exposure to ammonia fumes. Diazo compounds are also used on pre-sensitized plates for photo-offset lithography. *Diazo films* can have an image in most any transparent color on a clear background. These films are used for projection, overlays, and proofs of negatives for color printing.

Color Photography

All photographic processes named thus far are *monochromatic* — black and white processes which record *tones* but not color. Most *color* films have three layers, each sensitive to only one of the three *additive primary colors* of light (in simple terms: orange, violet, green).[1] Each layer becomes a negative of the tones for its color. Additional processing with proper dye couplers results in a view of the original scene in full color. Color films may be positive or negative working. A *color negative* is reversed both in tone and in color—dark colors are light, reds are green, etc. It must be printed on negative material to again reverse these to their normal tones and colors. Colored film positives are called *transparencies*. These are viewed by projecting them onto a screen or holding the transparency in front of a light.

Color films are used to make photographs or transparencies, but are not used in making their printed reproductions. Printers must again separate the colors into the three *subtractive primary colors* of inks and dyes. These pigments have color because they reflect only part of white light seen as the color and subtract the rest (the complimentary color). The subtractive primaries are: *yellow* (or white minus violet), *red* (or white minus green), and *blue* (or white minus orange), and sometimes a corrective black.[2] These separations are made on monochromatic films because tones for only one color are being recorded. In printing, one color at a time is superimposed on the others.

Uses of Photography

Photographic techniques are often used in conjunction with most other processes. Today, photography is used in almost every stage of a printed job, and in most methods of graphic reproduction. Photographs are a common form of illustration. Much hand art work is prepared with the aid of photographic techniques, such as tracing around projected images in laying out enlargements or reductions. There are photo-lettering and photo-typesetting processes. Photo-imposition (or photo-composing) repeats an image many times on one plate so that larger sheets result in shorter runs. Plates, stencils, and masters can be made photographically for all methods of printing.

Variations of Nonmechanical Stencils

There are two variations of light energy stencils which are not photographic. *Thermographic* processes (Thermofax) react to the *heat* of infrared light rather than to the light itself. *Electrostatic* processes use electrically charged surfaces rather than chemically sensitive surfaces. Both surfaces are sensitive to the energy of light.

Stencils can be classified as follows:

1. Mechanical Processes
   a. *Open link* — hand or machine cut
   b. *Tieless* — mimeograph and silk screen
2. Non-Mechanical Radiant Processes
   a. *Photographic* — film, blueprints, diazo
   b. *Thermographic* — Thermofax copying
   c. *Electronographic* — Xerox, electrostats.

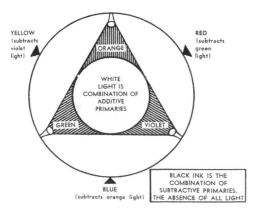

Fig. F. Additive Primary Colors of Light (inside the circle), Subtractive Primary Colors of Ink (outside). Mixing Any Two Primary Colors Produces the Color Between Them

[1] The true colors are a little clockwise of the simple names shown in Fig. F. Additive primaries actually are a reddish orange, a bluish violet, and a yellowish green, commonly called red, blue and green.

[2] Subtractive primaries actually are a violet-red, a greenish blue and yellow, called magenta (minus green), cyan (minus red), and yellow (minus blue). The simple terms used above are quite descriptive, and are easier to remember.

Major Printing Processes

Three *classes* of graphic reproduction were identified in the preface: printing, duplicating, and art processes. You will recall, too, that four basic *methods* of graphic reproduction were described in the introduction: relief, intaglio, planographic, and stencil. These are classified and listed in Table I, along with the names of specific processes. The major printing processes will be summarized here. These are letterpress, gravure, engraving, offset lithography, and screen process printing.

Letterpress Printing

Letterpress printing applies ink directly to paper from metal type and relief plates. Most type is set by machine on Linotypes, Intertypes or Monotypes. Some is hand set from cast type or from wood type, particularly in large sizes. The Ludlow is a machine for casting display lines of type for letterpress. Here matrices for each letter are assembled by hand, cast in the machine, and immediately returned to the storage case. Type for relief plates can also be set photographically. All numbering is done by relief numbering machines.

Plates

Relief plates for letterpress can be either *original* or *duplicated* from molds. Relief plates once were hand cut in wood. This is unusual today, but printers still speak of plates for a type form as "cuts." Most original plates are *photoengravings* etched in metal, *electronic engravings* on plastic, or *Dycril* plastic plates.

These plates may be line, or halftone. *Line cuts* refer to type, pen and ink drawings, and other copy which has no shading. *Halftones* are made of photographs and shaded drawings. Halftones give the illusion of the various tones of gray even though only black ink is used on white paper. This is done by screening the image into a composite of fine dots which blend together to give the illusion of tones. *Process color* printing is in natural colors and requires a halftone for each primary color.

Duplicate plates are usually used in publication work and for long runs. This way identical plates can be put on several presses, or plates can be replaced as they wear down on long runs. The original is protected from wear and damage and can be used too in later revisions. Duplicates are made from a matrix molded from the original form. Common duplicate plates are *stereotypes* (used mostly by newspapers), *electrotypes* (common in book and periodical printing), and *plastic plates* (used where shipping weight is a factor).

Presses

There are three types of presses, see Fig. 1-A. *Platen* presses have both the type form and the paper on flat surfaces, so tremendous force is required to print the entire sheet at one instant. In (flat bed) *cylinder* presses the paper is on a cylinder which rolls over the form. As only a narrow strip is being printed at any instant, less pressure is required. In *rotary* presses the plate is also curved into a revolving cylinder so no reversing of direction of the type form is necessary This allows more speed. Platen presses print about 4000 impressions per hour (iph), cylinder presses about 5000 iph, and rotary presses about 18,000.

Web-fed presses print from rolls rather than sheets. See Fig. 1-B. Most rotary presses are web fed. *Perfecting* presses print both sides

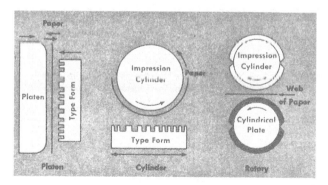

Fig. I-A. Three Forms of Presses (International Paper)

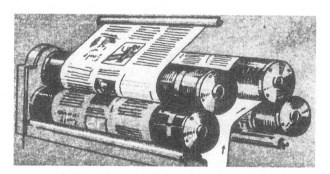

Fig. I-B. Web-Fed Perfecting Press (International Paper)

1

Table I

Processes of the Three Classes of Graphic Reproduction and the Basic Surface Used

Basic Surface	Printing	Duplicating	Art Processes

Relief	Letterpress
	  Type: Foundry, Wood,
	    Monotype, Linotype,
	    Ludlow
	    Numbering Machines
	  Photoengravings: Line,
	    Halftone; Powderless
	  Dycril Plates
	  Wrap-Around Plates
	  Stereotypes
	  Electrotypes
	  Plastic Plates
	  Brightype Conversions
	Dry Offset, Letterset
	Flexography
	Hot Stamping
	Thermography
	Die Cutting, Creasing
		Typewriting:
		  Standard
		  Proportional Spacing
		Varityper
		Justowriter
		Carbon Copies
		Multigraph (Relief)
		Addressograph
		Credit Cards
		Rubber Stamps
		Steel Stamps
		Etched Circuits
		Sign Printers
		Embossograph Signs
			Block Prints
			  Wood
			  Rubber
			  Linoleum
			  Plastic
			  Sandpaper
			Stick Prints
			Wood Engravings
			  (end grain)

Intaglio	Photogravure
	  Sheet-Fed
	  Rotogravure
	Engraving
	  Copperplate
	  Steel
	Embossing
		Etched Markings
		Routed Name Plates
		Embossed Tape Markers
			Etchings
			  Soft Ground
			  Mezzotints
			  Aquatints
			Intaglio Engravings
			  Dry Points
			  Copper Engravings

Planographic	Photo-Offset Lithography:
	  Zinc-Albumin Plates
	  Aluminum-Diazo Plates
	  Deep-Etch Zinc Plates
	Photo-Gelatin:
	  Collotype
		Offset Duplicating:
		  Direct-Image Plates
		  Photo-Transfer Plates
		    Gelatin: Verifax, Ektalith
		    Diffusion: Gevaert,
		      CopyCat, A.B. Dick
		    Electrostatic: Xerox
		Spirit Duplicating
		  Ditto, Azograph
		Gelatin Duplicating
		  Hektograph
			Stone Lithographs
			Plate Lithographs
			Crayon Stone
			Marbling

Stencil:
Mechanical
	Screen Process:
	  Cut Film
	  Direct Photographic
	  Indirect Photographic
	  Carbon tissue
	  Ektagraph
	Cut Film Negatives
		Stencil Duplicating
		  Pad Type: Mimeograph
		  Silk Screen Type: Rex,
		    Gestetner
		  Mechanical Negatives
			Screen Process:
			  Tusche-Glue
			Stenciling
			  Spatter Painting

Energy	Photo Reproduction
	  Processes
	Electrostatic Printing
	  (Onset)
	Photo Etching Resists
	Phototypesetting
	Photo Lettering
		Photocopying:
		  Transfer, Direct
		Thermal copying
		Electrostatic copying
		Blueprinting, Vandykes
		Whiteprinting (Diazo)
		X-ray Photographs
			Photographs
			Photograms

of the sheet in one run. *Color* presses have multiple units, one for each color, each with its own set of plates and inking system. Color printing is also done on single-color presses, one color at a time. Color presses are essentially several presses working together with one feed system, see Fig. 1-C. Small platen and cylinder presses may be *hand fed*, but modern commercial presses are equipped with automatic *suction feeders* to move sheets through the press. All of these are used in letterpress printing, and will be studied in more detail later.

Characteristics

In printing larger forms by letterpress, much time is used in *makeready*—adjusting the printing pressure at different points. Type and plates may be different heights, large areas require more pressure, etc. Some of this can be corrected before the job goes to press—called *premakeready*. New makeready systems have also reduced makeready time.

Letterpress printing remains the quickest, easiest, and most economical process for short runs of simple type forms such as stationery, envelopes, and programs. Corrections in standing price lists or respacing are easily done in metal type. It gives a dark print which can be recognized by a heavier ring outlining each letter and by an impression into the sheet. Letterpress books may have photographs grouped into sections and printed on slick paper. Most newspapers, magazines, and books with few illustrations are printed letterpress.

New Developments

Recently there have been several innovations in this oldest and most stable of printing processes, brought about by competition between processes. Promising developments are thin *wrap-around plates* which are light in weight, economical and have the entire form pre-positioned and made ready on one plate. New photographic platemaking techniques reduce costs of original plates to make them more competitive with duplicated molded plates and those for offset lithography. Thin wrap-around plates in low relief are being printed onto a rubber blanket and then offset onto paper. See Fig. 1-D. This is called *dry offset* (or letterset) to distinguish it from the more common use of offset in lithography. Offsetting allows finer

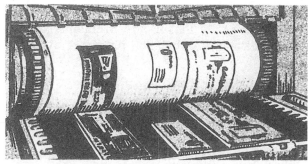

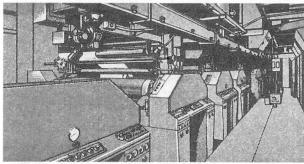

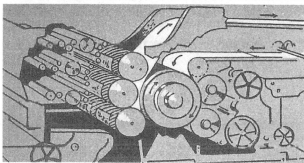

Fig. I-C. Various Letterpresses—Cylinder Press (top), Newspaper Web Press for Stereotypes (center), and Five-Color Rotary Press (bottom). (International Paper)

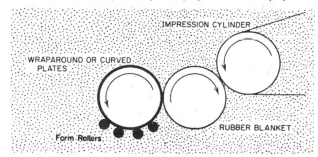

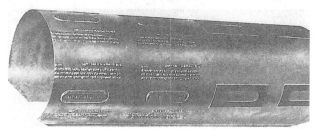

Fig. I-D. Dry Offset (top), and Wrap-Around Plate (Heidelberg)

detail on rough papers than direct letterpress, eliminates many makeready problems, and eliminates the water balance problems of lithography.

Related Relief Printing Processes

There are several relief printing processes which are related to letterpress printing.

Flexography uses relief rubber plates on a high speed rotary press. It has been called analine printing because analine dyes can be used in the ink. Flexography is typically used in the packaging industry. The flexible plates are duplicate plates molded from letterpress forms. They do not indent or weaken plastic materials, foils, paper bags, wrappings, or corrugated boxes as hard forms might. Analine dyes or bright pigments dissolved in alcohol evaporates readily—sometimes in an enclosure so the solvent can be condensed and reused. Flexography often has a slight blurred look due to the thin ink, the yielding printing surface, and the high printing speed.

Die cutting and creasing use hardened steel rules about type high. These can be cut, bent, and assembled, usually in jig-saw kerfs in ¾" plywood. See Fig. 1-E. They are much used by the packaging industry, but can be used in any strong platen or flat-bed cylinder press. Inking rollers are removed so they are not cut, and a metal jacket is placed on the platen or cylinder. Sharp rules cut one sheet of material at a time to an irregular shape or perforate small slots. Rounded rules score lines for folding. Hollow steel dies, much like cookie cutters, are another

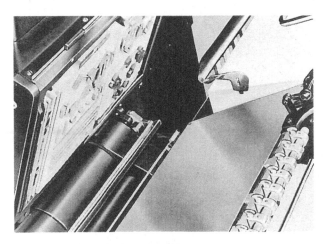

Fig. I-E. Die-Cutting Form (Heidelberg)

type used to cut out lifts of envelope stock and similar specialties.

Stamping leaves a deep impression on book covers and leather goods. *Hot stamping* uses either metalic or opaque colored foils in place of ink. Letterpress inks and unheated plates can be used. Plates are usually deeply etched in brass. The cover of this book is stamped in two colors of ink.

Thermography can be used with several printing processes, but most commonly it follows letterpress printing. Finely powdered resin is put over the wet ink immediately after printing. The excess is removed by tapping the inverted sheet or by a vacuum. Then the powder is melted with heat radiating from an electric hot plate, leaving raised printing. This is also known as artificial engraving, or "fried printing," or by the trade names of Virkotype, and Embossograph. It is cheaper than intaglio engraving, which it simulates, and is used on business cards, announcements, and stationery. It can be recognized by chipping of the resin after folding. Clear resins (gloss or dull) do not alter the original ink color. Opaque colors can also be used which cover the original color. This is one way of printing an attractive metallic or a light color over a darker one. Most printing processes (except intaglio and silk screen) have too thin a film of ink to cover well. *Stamping* with light ink on dark backgrounds is possible in two separate impressions but the design can not have fine detail.

Gravure Printing

Gravure is often called *photogravure* because the entire intaglio image is reproduced photographically by acid etching in copper. Light-sensitive carbon tissue or special Rotofilm carries an image of openings and thin spots. In etching the acid eats through this mask which protects the surface. The original type may be from photocomposition or a clean print from relief type.

The Printing Surface

In *sheet-fed gravure* the image is etched on a thin metal sheet which is clamped around a cylinder for printing on sheets of paper. *Rotogravure* prints from heavy cylinders which have been copper plated, ground, and polished before the intaglio image is etched. A web of paper is printed at high speed. Both processes give high quality work but expense usually limits use to longer runs. Sheet-fed gravure is used for shorter runs of several thousands of copies. Rotogravure cylinders may be chromium plated for runs of a million or more copies.

The fine 150-line crossline screen in *conventional* gravure serves to break the surface into a series of uniform square wells. The depth of these wells and not their size determines the thickness of the ink film transferred, and thus the tones of the picture. In printing, the screen lines nearly disappear. In the *News-Dultgen process* both the dot size and the depth vary to produce even clearer tones. This is widely used for color reproductions.

The Gravure Press

On the press, the cylinder rotates in thin ink, covering the entire surface, See Fig. 1-F. It is then scraped clean by a thin spring steel blade, not unlike an oversized razor blade the length of the cylinder. This is the *doctor blade*. Paper passes between the wiped cylinder and a rubber surfaced impression cylinder.

Characteristics

The distinctive feature for recognizing gravure is that the entire image is screened—type and line drawings as well as halftones. Small scratches from grit are a common defect. These print as fine lines in white areas. Imperfect wiping can cause a slur at the after or "tail" side of image wells. The ink is dull and often brown. Clear illustrations are possible even on cheap paper. One disadvantage is that screening small type tends to distort it.

Gravure printers usually are located only in large printing centers or in specialty plants. Typical gravure products include picture supplements for newspapers, fine advertising, sections of mail order catalogs, art reproductions, plastic counter and floor coverings, packages, and wrappings.

Steel and Copperplate Engraving

Strictly, the word *engraving* means *intaglio* engraving as used in fine stationery, business and calling cards, formal announcements, stamps, and paper money. Formerly, steel dies were engraved free-hand using burins (sharp pointed engravers). Copper, being easier to

cut, was preferred for short runs. Engravers had personal styles much like jewelry engravers. Today, a one-quarter inch steel plate is coated with asphaltum to resist the etching solution. A pantographic reducing machine traces the letters from large patterns and scratches them into the coating. See Fig. 1-G. Images can also be added by hand, photographically or by stamping from a hardened die in relief.

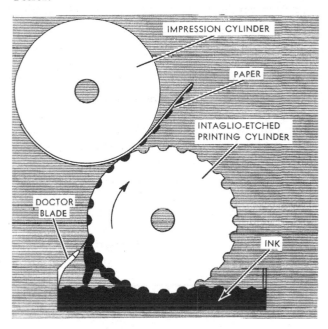

Fig. I-F. Principle of Gravure

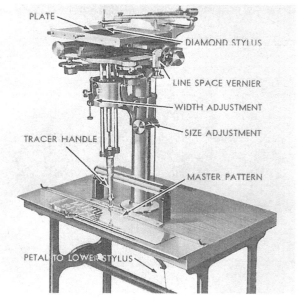

Fig. I-G. Pantographic Engraver (Cronite)

The Die-Stamping Press

After etching, the plate is run on a die-stamping press. A common size takes a 3" x 8" plate. See Fig. 1-H. A heavy cardboard counter is built up opposite the image to force the paper into the intaglio lines. The entire plate is inked with a spinning cloth-covered roller. Ink is wiped from the surface by paper from a roll, advancing after each wiping. A recent improvement is a rubber wiping belt which is later cleaned to reclaim unused ink. Drying for several hours or a quick heating is required before sheets can be stacked.

Embossing

Embossing, in which a design stands up in high relief can also be done on die stamping presses. The intaglio female die is carved, etched or machined. For deep designs a matching male die is molded from plastic. Shallow patterns can use a simple cardboard counter. *Blind embossing* has no ink or color on the design. If it is to be colored, the image usually is preprinted separately and then embossed. Heated dies and a heavy four-post press are necessary for heavily embossed designs or large areas such as book covers. Stamping foil may be used to color the design with heated dies. Engraved printed products are often embossed, as are covers for brochures and books.

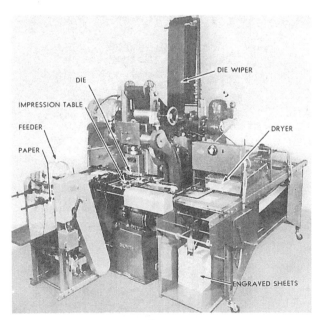

Fig. 1-H. Die-Stamping Platen Press (Cronite)

Offset Lithography

In commercial lithographic printing, all plates are made photographically and presses print indirectly from a rubber blanket, so the process is known as *photo-offset lithography*. This is usually shortened to *offset* or *offset printing*. The process has grown in the past 50 years to where it produces about a third of all printing. About half is still letterpress. (Because of growth, letterpress still has many times the volume of 50 years ago.) All other processes account for the remainder. This textbook and all others printed by the same publisher are printed by offset. Offset allows extensive use of illustrations, economically and with a minimum of press makeready.

Plates

Type for offset may be proofs of relief type which are photographed. Photographic prints or negatives or positives from phototypesetting may also be used. Type or line drawings and halftone copy are photographed separately because different techniques must be used. These must then be *stripped* (pieced) together to make a *flat*. Special effects such as *reverses* (solid backgrounds around white letters), *tint screens* (ben days), and *surprints* (type overprinting an illustration) are added on the flat. See Fig. 1-J for examples. These techniques with minor variations) are typical of photographic processes for any method of printing.

Offset plates are only .005" to .020" thick and are either *surface plates* or *deep etched*. Surface plates produce as many as 100,000 copies, deep etch more. The latter have the image etched about .0003" below the surface to get some of the advantages of intaglio plates (which have images as deep as .010"). Deep etch plates are positive working, while most surface plates require negative flats.

Until recently, grained zinc plates were the standard plate. These are given a light-sensitive albumin coating just before exposure and can be regrained and re-used. Today *presensitized aluminum* plates are more common, especially in smaller sizes. These are grained or brushed, and have a diazo light-sensitive coating. In most plants these commercial one-time plates give more dependable quality.

Offset Presses

Offset presses have three printing cylinders and two sets of rollers as shown on Fig. 1-K. The plate is clamped to the top cylinder. As it rotates it passes first under the *dampening rollers*, then *inking rollers*. The dampeners wet the plate so the non-image area will repel ink. They use a water solution made wetter by a weak acid and stickier by water-soluble gums or glycerine. The pH (acidity) is controlled to prevent unwanted reactions. Inks must be waterproof. Too much water solution on the plate keeps ink off of the image (causing a light print), curls the paper, and emulsifies on ink rollers. Too little causes toning or scumming (gray backgrounds). Finding the proper balance requires considerable skill and accounts for much of the variation in quality among lithographers. Electronic devices to simplify holding this balance have been developed recently.

The inked plate prints on the rubber blanket of the second cylinder. Paper passes between the blanket and the third cylinder. Presses have suction feeders for sheets (as large as 54 x 77) and typically run 5000 to 8000 iph. Web-fed presses may run as fast as 20,000 iph. As plates are light, presses run faster and may be constructed lighter than comparable letterpresses.

Characteristics

Typical products include advertising brochures, illustrated books, much color printing, and business forms. Offset printing can be recognized by the smooth, slightly dull print, lack of any impression or ring of ink. Dust specks cause small "doughnuts" or "hickies" in solid areas. Under a magnifying glass, some toning or specks of ink may be visible on non-image areas.

Offset Duplicators

Offset duplicators are smaller and lighter than presses and are commonly used in offices, schools, and by some printers. See Fig. 1-L. They commonly print a 10″ x 14″ area, but some are as large as 18″ x 24″. They use *direct-image plates* (masters) in addition to the photographic plates used on larger presses. These are prepared by typing, drawing or printing directly on the masters. Special ribbons, pen-

cils and inks are used which are waterproof and grease attracting. In *systems* work, varying information is typed on a preprinted plate and enough copies run for a number of uses or departments. Various direct masters can reproduce 10 to 3000 copies. Transfer photocopy machines (Zerox, Verifax, Gaevert, Ekta-

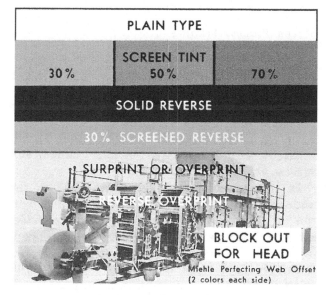

Fig. 1-J. Photographic Variations

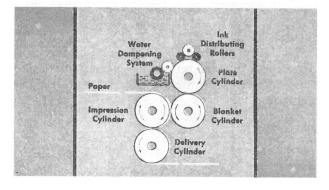

Fig. 1-K Offset Lithographic Press (International Paper)

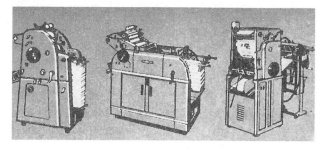

Fig. 1-L. Offset Duplicators (International Paper)

lith) can be used to transfer images to offset masters at a materials cost of about 40 cents. Direct image prints can often be recognized by letters which have hollow centers (small doughnuts for periods), caused by typing too hard. Transfer plates print a little too dark and rather unsharp, but often are clearer than mimeographing and can be printed on smoother paper.

Screen Process Printing

Screen process printing has become a mature craft only in the past 20 years. It is frequently not considered printing because workers may belong to the painters' union and often are sign painters. But it is a versatile printing process with varied uses. Until the name was standardized recently, it was usually called *silk screen printing*.

In this process, a stencil is adhered to the underside of a tightly stretched screen of cotton organdy, silk, nylon, or stainless steel mesh. Ink or paint is pulled across the openings with a rubber squeegee. See Fig. 1-M. Its features are a thick deposit of pigment, simplicity of basic equipment, economy of short runs. Many ink-like materials can be printed by this method: paint, lacquer, varnish, fluorescent colors, adhesives, dyes, abrasives, ceramic glazes, acid resists.

The latter is used in printing an acid resisting circuit pattern on a copper-plastic laminate for etched electronic circuits. After etching, the copper remains only in the strips protected from etching. These are supported on the plastic base and carry current between components easily soldered at terminal areas of the circuit board.

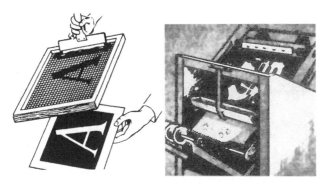

Fig. I-M. Hand Screen Process and Press (International Paper)

Various Stencils

Hand-cut stencils are made from wrapping paper or special *cutting films*. These may be lacquer- or water-base materials. The former can be used with all materials except lacquers. Water-base materials cannot be used with poster paints or dyes containing water. These pigments would dissolve the stencil. Cutting films have two layers waxed together to hold centers and intricate designs in place until they are adhered to the screen. Artists usually use a *tusche and glue stencil*. The design is drawn directly on a clean screen using a grease crayon or liquid tusche. The open areas of the stencil are then blocked out with water soluble glue. The design can then be opened up by washing the screen with a grease solvent. Unlike cut stencils, this process allows for some shading. It may be used to add texture to cut stencils.

Photographic screen stencils are in common use and can be made from any drawn or printed design. Details should not be too fine. In *indirect* photographic processes such as Ektograph or carbon tissue, the stencil is exposed to a film positive and devoloped in the dark room. It is then adhered to the screen, dried, and a supporting plastic backing removed, exposing the openings for passing the ink.

In the *direct* photo processes, the screen is given a sensitive coating, the stencil is exposed, developed and washed out on the fabric.

Equipment for Printing

Modern presses, quick-drying inks and hot air dryers allow speeds of 3000 or 4000 iph. See Fig. 1-M. Much work is screened or squeegeed by hand at a few hundred pieces per hour. Special jigs are constructed to hold solid forms for stenciling. Some allow printing on cylinders from the size of pill bottles or water glasses to 55 gallon oil drums. Special set-ups are often made for stenciling on odd shaped surfaces, or for printing huge signs and banners.

Common products are 24-sheet billboard posters, glass bottles, oversized packages, posters, counter displays, book covers, wallpaper, pennants, etc. Screen process printing can usually be recognized by the thick layer of ink and the texture of the screen on the printing.

Unit 2

Flow of Printing Production

Actual work in a beginning graphic arts course often must be limited to four simple stages of printing: planning, composition, presswork and bindery work. Advanced work and the complex industrial processes require more operations. While these vary with the different processes and classes, eight stages of work are common to most printing: 1. planning, 2. art and copy preparation, 3. composition, 4. imposition, 5. copying, 6. platemaking, 7. presswork, 8. bindery work. These stages represent the work of people with different skills, or different departments in a plant, or sometimes work which might be contracted out to specialists.

Planning

Planning usually must begin by determining the function or purpose of the printed material: Who will use it? How? What size? How many? What message? What are the standard units and storage facilities? Where would illustrations help? Would color improve it enough to pay the extra cost? What design is most attractive?

Rough sketches or *thumbnails* are made of a number of possibilities. The best ideas are incorporated into a *comprehensive layout* (and a *dummy* in multipage work). See Fig. 2-A. From this production methods are selected, costs estimated, and production scheduled. This may involve the work of many people: those in need of the printing, various committees of their company, advertising agencies, commercial artists, printing salesmen, paper salesmen, estimators, and various production superintendents and thousands of dollars. Or it simply may be a short talk between the buyer and a local job printer who has the layout on the back of an envelope.

Art and Copy Preparation

Copy preparation can mean taking the pictures, doing the drawings, lettering, decorations and writing the message called for in the layouts. This usually is done by the buyer or his agents. To the printer, the word *copy* means the manuscript from which type is to be set,

1

2

3

4

Fig. 2-A. Note Refinements as Planning Progresses From Thumbnail (1), to Rough (2), to the Comprehensive Layouts (3), and to the Final Print (4). (Graphic Arts Monthly)

Fig. 2-B. Art Preparation (above) and Copy Reading (below)

Fig. 2-C. Linotype (left) and Ludlow Typesetting Machines

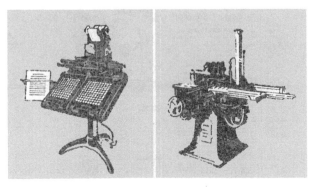

Fig. 2-D. Monotype Keyboard and Caster
(Pictures Above Courtesy International Paper)

as well as all material to be photographically reproduced. Written copy must be *copy read* (checked for spelling, grammar, capitalization, and style), usually *edited* by someone, checked for space it will occupy *(copy fitting)*, and *specifications* must be drawn up for the typesetter. Illustrations must be *cropped* (best area selected) and *scaled* (amount of enlargement or reduction computed) for size specifications. Often several kinds of art work and type proofs must be assembled in a *paste-up*, which will be photographed as a unit. Workers doing art and copy preparation include photographers, writers, journalists, artists, ad agencies, editors, layout men, and paste-up men. See Fig. 2-B.

Composition

Composition is typesetting, make-up (combining materials and spacing as required), pulling proofs (trial prints), proofreading for errors, and making corrections. Today, there are many methods of typesetting. These methods of composition are quite independent of the printing process used. In larger printing centers, type may be set in a specialized trade composition house.

Hot Type Composition

Traditionally, composition has used cast metal relief type. It can be set by hand, or by Linotype, Monotype, or Ludlow machines, see Figs. 2-C, 2-D. This is called *hot type* because the lead alloy is melted when cast. Such type forms can be printed three ways: directly, by molding duplicate plates, or by pulling reproduction proofs *(repros)* for photo reproduction.

Cold Type Composition

Cold type composition can also be used for photo reproduction. Cold type methods include phototypesetting, photo lettering, various typewriters, pre-printed letters, and lettering guides.

Some *phototypesetting machines* adapt the basic mechanisms of their counterparts for casting metal type. Photographic machines substitute a letter negative for each letter mold, but use time-tested mechanisms for keyboarding, spacing, and movements. The hot metal pot is replaced by a camera or enlarger mechanism to focus each character on film. See Fig.

2-E. Some such machines are the Intertype Fotosetter (circulating matrices), the Monophoto (characters in rows and columns on master unit), and the Hadego (handset matrices). Several phototypesetting machines select and space the letter negatives by operating a typewriter keyboard: Linofilm, A.T.F. Typesetter, Photon. These all produce a film negative or positive ready for stripping, or a print for paste-up.

Tape and Computerized Typesetting

Most typesetting machines (hot or cold) today can be operated by means of perforated paper tape less than one inch wide. See Fig. 2-F. The holes are coded much like a player piano roll. Most adapt standard office machine tape codes. These can be punched on machines having a standard typewriter keyboard faster than by keyboarding the machine directly. One of the time-consuming tasks is to decide how many words will fit on a line. Electronic computers now can be used to make these decisions at fantastically high speeds. Some even can be programmed to hyphenate words automatically.

Simple Cold Type Methods

Photo lettering devices are similar to phototypesetting machines in principle but they are manually operated. They can be used for headlines and lines of display lettering on a paste-up. Each letter in order is selected from a master negative, is positioned, exposed with a light, spaced for the next letter, and developed. Ease of operation and versatility vary among makes. Some examples are: Photo Typositor, Friden Typro, Varityper Headliner, Protype, Filmotype, Fairchild Photo Typesetter, Strip-Printer.

Typewriters using carbon ribbons sometimes achieve an image nearly as sharp as type, especially if the typing is reduced photographically. All require a second typing to justify (space out) each line to the same length. The *Varityper*, as shown in Fig. 2-G, uses a number of interchangeable faces which look much like type. They can automatically justify each line with a second identical keyboarding.

Proportional spacing electric typewriters such as the IBM Executive or Remington Rand Statesman may have one of several faces which resemble type. Individual characters and spaces vary in width. Spacing to justify lines can be added manually in a second typing. The *Friden Justowriter* is a proportional spacing electric typewriter which also perforates a control tape. This automatically operates the typewriter for a second justified typing without additional keyboarding.

Directories can be photographed directly from file cards by *automatic line photo-composing machines* such as Compos-O-Line. Corrections are typed as needed, then the entire stack of cards is run through the machine. This photographs the information in evenly spaced columns as in telephone directories.

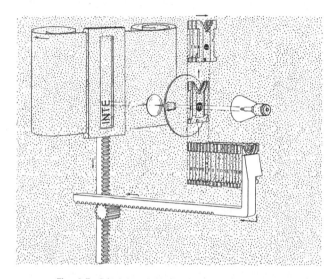

Fig. 2-E. Principle of Phototypesetting (Fotosetter)

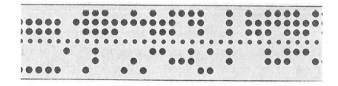

Fig. 2-F. Coded Tape for Automatic Typesetting

Fig. 2G. Varityper (left) and Paste-Down Display Type (International Paper)

While *standard typewriters* are used only occasionally in printing, they are the common form of composition for duplicating processes.

Pre-printed type, or *paste-down type* is a simple form for heads on typewriter composition, and drawings. It is frequently used by commercial artists. One style (as Artype) has letters printed on clear plastic with a waxed coating on the back. These are cut out, assembled in position, and rubbed down to make the wax stick. Another style (as Fototype) has characters printed on small cards the width of each letter. See Fig. 2-G. These are torn off of a pad, assembled in a guide, and taped together. Adhesive-backed die-cut letters are also available which can be reused if necessary.

Many forms of *lettering guides* are often used for headings and labels on drawings. The Varigraph produces letters in standard type faces with many variations. Leroy and Wrico lettering sets and simple mimeographing letterguides are sometimes used.

Imposition

Imposition is determining the position of the various units of multiple page forms so they are correct for folding and trimming. Also, any run must be in the best position for the press. Imposition may be determined when locking up a letterpress form, or on the paste-up, or in stripping the flat in photo-offset lithography.

Copying

Copying is reproducing the original image. This is done photographically or by other forms of energy such as heat, static electricity or invisible radiation. Relief forms can also be copied by molding. Typical photo-mechanical processes use a large camera, film, reversals, color separations, and stripping. See Fig. 2-H. *Modification cameras* now can change straight lines of copy into curves, circles, or prospectives, as well as reduce height and width independently.

Platemaking

Platemaking, in a broad sense, refers to making any original or duplicate surface for printing an image. Examples of platemaking are: hand-cut blocks, rubber plates or stamps, photo-engravings, stereotyping, electrotyping, offset plates, gravure cylinders, intaglio plates, duplicating masters, silk screen stencils. These techniques vary with the processes and presses described earlier.

Presswork

Presswork is *making ready* the press, then making the "run" — transferring the image to the sheets. This requires considerable mechanical skill, a knowledge of feeders, inks, rollers, paper, problems of humidity and static. The work varies considerably with the process of printing, class of work, length of run and size of sheet. It may be as simple as running a duplicator, or as complex as commanding a huge web-fed publication press printing 64 pages in five colors on each side. Some printers may do mostly presswork, hiring other specialists to do other stages of work elsewhere.

Bindery

There are two classes of bindery work. *Simple bindery* is done by most printers and reproduction departments. This includes such work as folding, punching or drilling holes, gathering sheets in order, making pads, trimming, stapling or stitching, and many other hand operations. Most of the women in the printing industry are bindery workers. Today, many new machines speed up this work.

Bookbinding in hard covers is a specialized operation usually done in trade binderies. This is called *edition binding* and includes sewing, trimming, shaping the back, reinforcing it, adding headbands, making and stamping the case (covers), and casing-in (gluing on the cover).

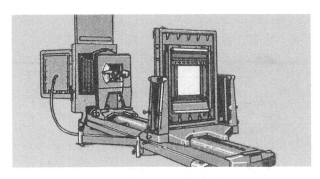

Fig. 2-H. Reproduction Camera (International Paper)

Unit 3

The Graphic Arts Industries

The printing industry is classed by the United States Bureau of Census with groups making *non-durable products*. These industries make consumables such as food, clothing, gasoline, or newspapers. Table II compares the major manufacturing industries in both durable and nondurable products. Note that the combined printing and paper industries rank fourth or fifth of those twelve.

Manufacturers of nondurable goods are less affected by business recessions than durable goods producers. When times are good, people buy more houses, cars and machinery, but these industries sometimes are forced to lay off employees when times are not so good. The demand for printed products is quite stable from season to season.

Employment in the printing, publishing, and allied industries increased twice as rapidly from 1950 to 1960 as in manufacturing as a whole. In 1900 there were about 185,000 productions workers, in 1950 about 494,000, and in 1960 about 591,000. The value of product per worker has also increased from about $2,000 per worker in 1900 to nearly $17,000 per worker in 1961. The proportion of skilled workers to other workers is about twice that of many other industries. Today there are nearly a million total employees in the printing industry.

In 1960, as in 1950, the workweek in the printing and publishing group (38.5 hours) was shorter than the average of all manufacturing industry (39.7 hours). Average hourly earnings of production workers were $2.67. This is higher than the average for nondurable goods industries ($2.05) or manufacturing as a whole ($2.26). Chicago photoengravers earned $4.50 per hour in July 1960.

Graphic Arts Centers

Almost every community has a print shop of some kind, frequently a newspaper plant which also does commercial printing. However, larger plants are usually located in large cities. One-half of the nation's printing employees are in five states: New York, Illinois, California,
Pennsylvania, and Ohio. The four top graphic arts centers have no near rivals in number of employees: New York City (150,000), Chicago (80,000), Philadelphia (38,000), and Los Angeles-Long Beach (35,000). Other centers (approximately in order) include Boston, San Francisco-Oakland, Minneapolis-St. Paul, Detroit, Cleveland, St. Louis, Cincinnati, Washington, D.C. (exclusive of government operations), Milwaukee, Baltimore. Each boasts more than 10,000 employees and hundreds, even thousands, of plants. New York City has 5,000 plants.

Employee Groups

It is difficult to obtain accurate figures for the numbers of employees working in the various stages of printing production. In smaller shops, workers often do more than one opera-

Table II

Comparison of Major Manufacturing Groups[1]

Industrial Group (by census code)	Total Employees[2] (thousands)	Average Annual Pay[2]	Value Added by Mfg.[2] (millions)
NONDURABLE GOODS			
Food, etc. 20, 21	1,782 [3]	$4878 [9]	$ 21,869 [2]
Textiles 22, 23	2,083 [2]	3378 [12]	12,310 [7]
Printing, paper 26, 27	1,497 [5]	5627 [4]	16,154 [5]
Chemicals, petroleum 28, 29	878 [8]	6459 [2]	18,205 [4]
Rubber, plastics 30	373 [11]	5431 [7]	3,929 [11]
Leather 31	350 [12]	3497 [11]	2,042 [12]
Total, Non-durables	6,965	$4750	$ 74,528
DURABLE GOODS			
Lumber, wood 24, 2511, 2512, 2521	753 [9]	$3766 [10]	$ 4,681 [10]
Metals, machinery 33, 34, 25 except wood, 35 except engines	3,603 [1]	5963 [3]	37,819 [1]
Electrical goods 36	1,367 [6]	5626 [5]	13,758 [6]
Vehicles, engines 37, 351	1,585 [4]	6715 [1]	18,509 [3]
Instruments, misc. 38, 39	902 [7]	5553 [6]	8,983 [8]
Stone, clay, glass 32	570 [10]	5173 [8]	6,336 [9]
Total, Durables	8,780	$5764	$ 90,086
Total all mfg.	16,348	$5,393	$164,614

[1]Based on *1961 Annual Survey of Manufactures*, by U. S. Bureau of the Census (M61[AS]-1).
[2]Small raised figures give rank among the 12 groups.

Fig. 3-A. Operating a Ludlow Typograph

Fig. 3-B. Mounting Color Process Halftones

Fig. 3-C. Adjusting an Offset Press

tion. Most available figures show divisions by product or process rather than by type of work performed.

It is estimated, however, that of all the employees in the printing industry, about 5% are commercial artists preparing layouts and art work, about 30% do some form of composition, make-up or imposing, 15% do photomechanical work and platemaking, about 15% are pressmen, feeders, or helpers, 20% do bindery work, about 5% are apprentices or trainees, about 5% are maintenance men, and about 5% salesmen, estimators, supervisors, and executives.

The largest group of printing craftsmen are the 180,000 composing room workers such as hand and machine compositors, make-up men, imposers, and proofreaders. Composition is used by all processes of printing and has seen many recent technological improvements. Progress in electronics, photographic innovations, and tape-operated machines are affecting the basic skills required of compositors. Because of increased productivity, this group is not expected to increase in numbers as fast as other printing occupations.

The fastest growing group are the 50,000 lithographic craftsmen: cameramen, lithographic artists (negative retouchers, etc.), strippers, offset platemakers, and pressmen. Membership in the lithographic union cuts across the usual divisions of stages of work so platemakers and pressmen are grouped together.

About 130,000 registered apprentices are being trained in skilled printing crafts. In addition there are probably another 10,000 trainees who are not registered. Many learn printing skills in small printing shops, schools, and in duplicating or reproduction services. There are numerous opportunities for young workers to enter the field. Future openings will occur because of industry growth and because of retirements or deaths. The latter will result in about 6000 to 7000 replacements each year during the 1960's.

See Units 119 and 120 for additional information about occupations. The bibliography also lists many sources of occupational information, as well as references for additional reading about various phases of the industry.

Branches of Printing and Publishing

The major branches of printing and publishing industry by kind of product are newspapers, periodicals (magazines and journals), books, and general commercial printing (custom job printing). Fig. 3-D compares the value of the products of each of these branches in 1961. Some specialty branches (such as directories, business forms, greeting cards) are not included.

Use of Processes

The values of commercial printing products are compared by printing processes in Fig. 3-E. These totals do not represent total commercial printing receipts as not all products are identified by process in data gathered by the Bureau of the Census. By subtracting figures for 1947 from those for 1958, the growth over eleven years can be computed as follows: letterpress, a $600 million increase; offset lithography, $940 million; gravure, $450 million; engraving, $32 million; screen process, $26 million. These figures show actual growth somewhat better than percentages.

The use of the various printing processes to produce some typical products is shown in Fig. 3-F. Again only selected commercial printing products are included, but the graph gives a

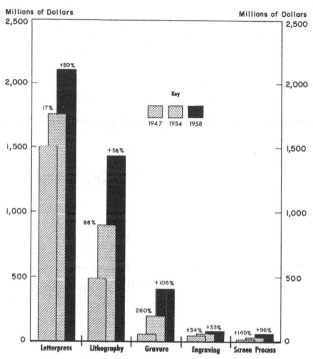

Fig. 3-E. Value of Commercial Printing by Process With Percent Change 1947-1958 (From 1958 U.S. Census of Manufactures)

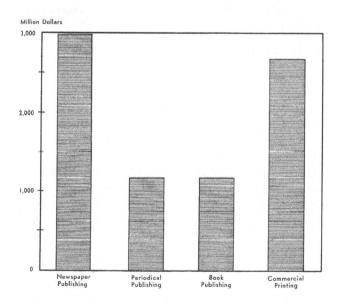

Fig. 3-D. Value Added by Manufacture in Major Branches of Printing and Publishing Industry (From 1961 Annual Survey of Manufactures)

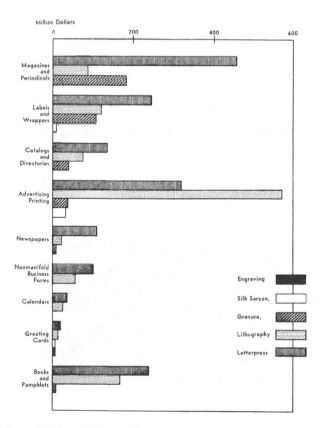

Fig. 3-F. Value of Selected Commercial Printing Products by Process (From 1958 U.S. Census of Manufactures)

good picture of uses of each process. Note that magazines are usually printed by letterpress, but advertising material is more often printed by offset. The biggest use of screen process printing is for advertising and labels. Engraving is limited to greeting cards or formal printed stationery. Gravure has a limited but important usage in several products needing fine illustrations.

Division of the Printing Sales Dollar

In industry, how money is spent is just as important as where it comes from. Fig. 3-G shows the five main slices of each dollar spent for printing production expenses: materials (36½¢), labor and factory costs (41½¢), administrative expenses (8¢), selling expenses (8¾¢), and profit before income taxes (5¢). This

Table III

Size of Industries Related to Printing

Industry (and Census Code)	No. Workers (thousands)	Value of Products (millions)
Papermaking [26]	574	$14,542
Printing Ink [2893]	8	259
Paper Machines [3554]	19	365
Printing Machines [3555]	23	429
Duplicating Machines [3579]	19	351
Photographic Materials [3861]	61	1,518
Marking Devices [3953]	6	74

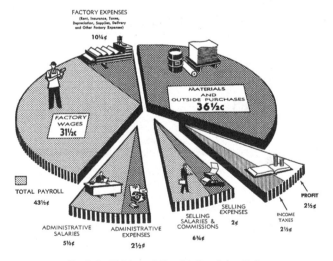

Fig. 3-G. Division of the Printing Sales Dollar (From 1962-63 PIA Ratios)

division of the dollar represents an average of many sizes and classes of printing establishments in 1962. This also suggests some of the areas related to printing: printing management, printing sales, papermaking and distribution, ink making and selling, photographic materials, and printing equipment.

Related Industries

The size of some of the industries related to printing is shown in Table III. The largest is the papermaking industry which is more than one-half the size of the printing industry. Some of the employees work in specialty paper plants which also fabricate and print such products as food containers, fiber drums, bags, etc. To some extent this results in overstating the value of paper products, since the value of this class of paper was again added into the value of the printed products to obtain the $14½ billion figure given in the table. The photographic industry includes photocopying and blueprinting equipment, as well as cameras, film, chemicals, and photographic paper.

The spread of printing methods to simplified office duplicating can be seen in the increase in duplicating machines. Sales of duplicating machines and photocopying equipment have rapidly approached those of printing presses. Duplicator sales surpassed sales of commercial presses for letterpress printing by 55% in 1958 and have nearly equalled sales of lithographic presses.

Study Questions

Here are some questions for you to think about: Why is printing a basic industry? Is the printing industry as important to the welfare of mankind as the food industries? Transportation? Clothing? Which industries would be most affected by a depression? How is it related to forestry, lumbering, or plastics? What is custom manufacturing? Why are there so many small printing plants? Why is printing production concentrated in large cities? Why has the amount of printing per wage earner increased in the past 60 years? How would this figure vary from a small to a large shop? Why? Why is specialization found in certain kinds of printing? What are the advantages of such specialization? Disadvantages?

Unit 4

The Printers' Point System

Because of the many hundreds, and sometimes thousands, of small pieces that must be fitted together in assembling even a small page of type for printing, it is necessary that you work very accurately and carefully to avoid troubles that always appear when typesetting is done in a slipshod manner. The printer works with very fine measurements. In woodworking the units of measurement are the foot and the inch, but in printing the standard units of linear measurement are the pica and the point, which are one-sixth of an inch and one-seventy-second of an inch, respectively. Frequently, you must use material that is but 1/144 of an inch in thickness.

The *pica* is the basis of the printers' point system and is .166 of an inch, or approximately one-sixth of an inch. While six picas are .004 less than one inch, this amount is so small that for practical use it is commonly accepted that six picas equal one inch. The *point* is one-twelfth of a pica or .0138 of an inch. Seventy-two points equal approximately an inch, and here again it is common practice to consider that seventy-two points are equal to one inch. When working with large sheets of paper, it is sometimes necessary for the printer to work to exact inch measurements, as the standard measurement of paper is in inches. For most work, however, the following table is accurate enough, and is used generally:

    6 points equal 1 nonpareil
    12 points equal 1 pica
    6 picas equal 1 inch
    72 points equal 1 inch
    72 picas equal 1 foot

An examination of the printers' rule, called a *line gauge* (Figure 3-A), will show that 72 picas are about 3½ points short of twelve inches. The line gauge commonly used in commercial printing offices is one foot in length, with inch gradations along one edge, and pica and nonpareil divisions along the other edge. Wooden line gauges, with the gradations printed on them, are distributed by manufacturers of printing machinery, but most printers prefer to use a more accurate gauge, made of either brass or steel, with etched scales.

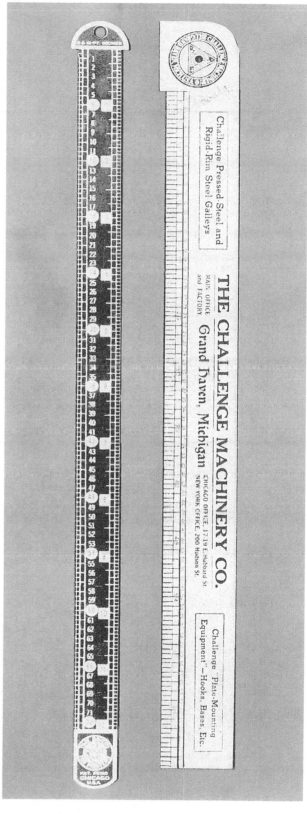

Fig. 3-A. Line Gauges — Brass and Wooden

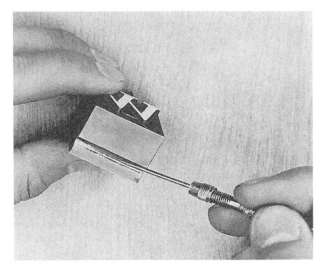

Fig. 4-A. Nick — Groove Across the Belly of a Piece of Type

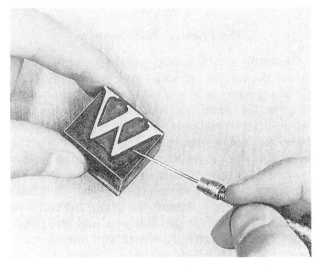

Fig. 4-D. Shoulder — Flat Part at Top of the Body

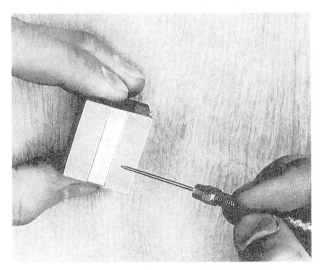

Fig. 4-B.   Feet — Present on Most Foundry Type

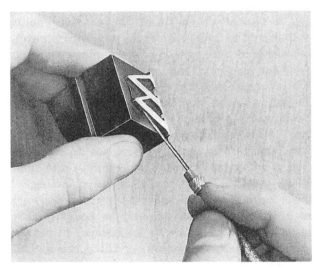

Fig. 4-E. Neck or Beard — Slanting Area from Face to Shoulder

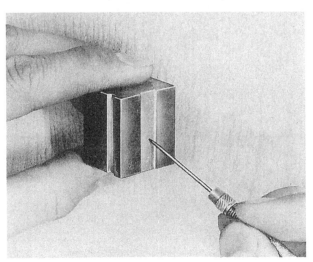

Fig. 4-C. Groove — Depressed Area Between the Feet

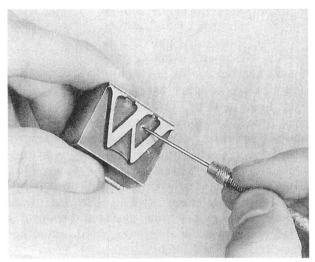

Fig. 4-F. Counter — Depressed Area Enclosed by the Character

Unit 5

The Parts of a Piece of Type

A *single type* is defined by D. B. Updike as being a right-angled prism-shaped piece of metal, having for its face a letter or character usually in high relief.

The *body* or *shank* makes up the greatest portion of the piece of type and has a back side and a front side. The front side is called the *belly* and has a groove across its surface. This groove is called a *nick*. (Figure 4-A.)

The nick is used as a guide in setting the type to show that the type is all facing in the proper direction. Foundry type usually has an extra nick near the top of the body on the small cap characters O, S, V, W, X, Z to distinguish them from the lower-case letters. The small cap I also has this nick in the old style fonts so that it may be distinguished from the Arabic figure one. A combination of nicks is sometimes used on foundry type to aid in identification.

The *feet* are the two projections at the base of the body and are formed by planing off the uneven portion left when the jet is broken off after the type is cast. (Figure 4-B. See Unit 40 for type with smooth feet.)

The *groove* is the depressed area between the two feet. (Figure 4-C, and Figure 40-A.)

The *shoulder* is the flat part at the top of the body which supports the neck and face of the type. (Figure 4-D.)

The *neck* is the beveled portion extending from the face down to the shoulder. It is sometimes called the beard. (Figure 4-E.)

The *counter* is the area enclosed by the lines of the character. (Figure 4-F.)

The *kern* is the part of the type which overhangs the body in such characters as the italic *f* and *j*.

The *face* of the type is the portion which receives the ink and makes an impression of the letter when brought into contact with the paper. (Figure 4-G.)

The *stem* is the thick stroke of the letter. (Figure 4-G.)

The *hairline* is the thin stroke of the letter. (Figure 4-H.)

The *serif* is the short cross line, or finishing stroke, at the end of the unconnected lines in the type face. (Figure 4-I.)

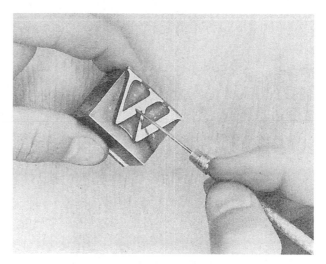

Fig. 4-G. Face — Printing Surface of the Type

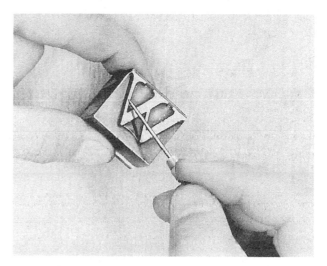

Fig. 4-H. Hairline — Thin Stroke of the Letter

Fig. 4-I. Serif — Finishing Cross Stroke of the Letter

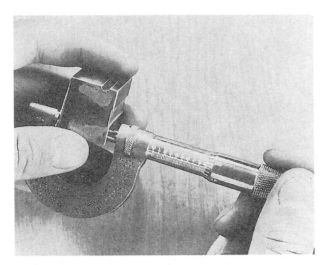

Fig. 5-A. Type High — .918 Inch is Standard from Face to Feet

Fig. 5-B. Point Size — Measured from Back to Belly

Unit 6

How to Measure Type

The American standard for "height to paper" (type high) of printing material, such as type, rules, engravings, etc., is given by some authorities as .9186 of an inch. The piece of foundry type being checked with a micrometer in Figure 5-A measures .918 of an inch, which is the height generally accepted for such material.

The cost of manufacturing printing material to a tolerance limit of only one ten-thousandth of an inch is prohibitive, and a wider tolerance is therefore chosen. (A sheet of make-ready tissue is about one thousandth of an inch in thickness.) Some of the better-managed plants attempt to keep the height of all material within one thousandth of the .918 standard. The vast majority of plants, however, use material which varies in height as much as eight thousandths — between four thousandths plus or minus from the standard. Considerable extra press make-ready is necessary to put a form of such varied height in condition for printing.

Point size (body size) of type is measured from the back to the belly, as shown in Figure 5-B. The capital W, shown, measures 6 picas. Its point size is, therefore, 72 point (6 x 12 points).

Figure 5-C shows a series of foundry Goudy Bold in the sizes commonly used in job and display composition. 120 point and 144 point are also available for large display use. Series of types used for book and magazine printing

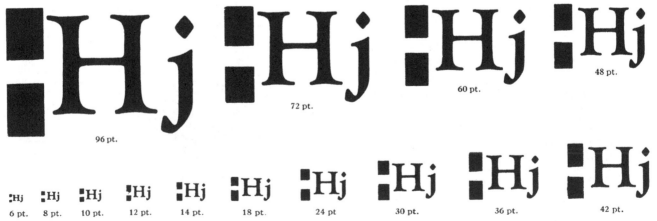

96 pt.   72 pt.   60 pt.   48 pt.

6 pt.   8 pt.   10 pt.   12 pt.   14 pt.   18 pt.   24 pt   30 pt.   36 pt.   42 pt.

Fig. 5-C. Series of A. T. F. Goudy Bold (Short Descenders) Showing Relation of Capital and Lower-case Letter to Body Size

include such sizes as 5, 7, 9, 11, 13, 16, and 22 point. A great many newspapers use 7½ and 7¾-point types cast on 8-point bodies.

Very large type, used for poster printing, is usually cut in wood and its size designated by "lines." A 20 pica wood type would be called 20-line.

Unit 7

How to Recognize Spacing Material

When a line of type is composed, *metal spaces* must be inserted between the words. Spaces are pieces of type metal that look like type, but are shorter than the type and have no character on them. When the line of type is inked and printed, a blank space is left wherever the spaces occur, as the spaces are too short to receive the ink or to contact the paper when the type is printed. (See Figure 6-A.)

There are complete sets of spaces for each size of type. The wide spaces are called *quads*. Quads are used to fill out blanks at the end of paragraphs, to center lines, and in other places where there are large areas to be blanked out in the line.

The em quad is a space which is a square. (Monotype em quads, however, are not always square. Their width varies according to the set —thickness or thinness— of the type.) The 2-em quad is twice as wide as the em quad. The 3-em quad is three times as wide as the em quad. (See Figure 6-A.)

An en quad is a space one-half as wide as the em quad. Because of the similarity of sound between "em" and "en," these quads have been given various names to avoid confusing the sounds. The em quad is frequently called a *mutton* quad. The en quad has several names. Some compositors call it a *nut* quad. Others speak of it as a *thick space,* as it is the widest space commonly used. Still others designate it as a *figure space,* because the figures in many fonts of type are made the same width as the en quad.

The other spaces are known as 3-em (a contraction from 3-to-the-em) space, 4-em space, and the 5-em space. They are respectively ⅓, ¼, and ⅕ as wide as the em quad. (See Figure 6-A.) Extra-thin spaces, called *hair spaces,* are also sometimes available.

You must learn how to recognize these spaces. Also, you must learn the relative size of the various combinations of them. Good type-setting requires careful spacing with the proper amount of space between the words.

The relative size of various spaces and their combinations can be difficult to compare. We could let the em quad equal 100% with the spaces a fraction of this. The *unit system,* however, uses the least common denominator of ½, ⅓, ¼, and ⅕ (1/60), and makes the em quad equal to 60 units with spaces a fraction of 60. This unit designation uses smaller figures and has no fractions as shown here:

em quad	$1 = 60/60$	60 units	(100%)
en quad	$\frac{1}{2} = 30/60$	30 units	(50%)
3-em space	$\frac{1}{3} = 20/60$	20 units	(33⅓%)
4-em space	$\frac{1}{4} = 15/60$	15 units	(25%)
5-em space	$\frac{1}{5} = 12/60$	12 units	(20%)

Combinations are used to give intermediate spacing widths. Here are some combinations (the first two are the most used):

two 5-em	$\frac{1}{5} + \frac{1}{5}$	24 units	(40%)
5-em and 4-em	$\frac{1}{5} + \frac{1}{4}$	27 units	(45%)
5-em and 3-em	$\frac{1}{5} + \frac{1}{3}$	32 units	(53⅓%)
4-em and 3-em	$\frac{1}{4} + \frac{1}{3}$	35 units	(58⅓%)
three 5-em	$\frac{1}{5} + \frac{1}{5} + \frac{1}{5}$	36 units	(60%)

Here is a problem to illustrate use of units. A line with six word spaces must be spaced out between words a total of 1½ em quads (90 units). What space added between words would do this? Answer: $90 \div 6 = 15$ units or an extra 4-em space between each word.

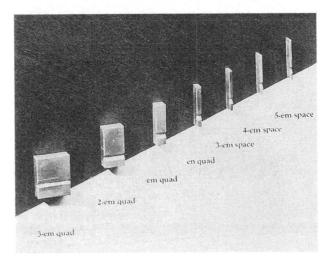

Fig. 6-A. A Set of 14-Point Spaces and Quads

Leads and Slugs

Spacing refers to separation of the words in a line. *Leading* refers to the inserting of strips of metal, *leads* and *slugs*, between the lines of type. Leads and slugs are about three-fourths of an inch high, are made from an alloy similar to type metal, and vary in thickness by points. They are usually cut to labor-saving lengths — half-pica lengths from 4 to 10 picas and pica lengths up to 40 or 50 picas.

A lead is commonly thought of as being two points in thickness. There are, however, one-point, three-point, and four-point leads.

The slug is six points in thickness. Less common, but available, are nine- and twelve-point slugs.

Unit 8

The Type Case

In the old days, when most of the typesetting was for the text or body matter of books, magazines, and newspapers, printers had to have large quantities of type and, therefore, used two cases for each size. The cases were arranged on the top of the frame, as in Figure 7-A, with the capitals in the upper case and the small letters in the lower case. This positioning of the cases accounts for the fact that we call capital letters "upper-case" and the small letters "lower-case."

Typesetting machines were perfected in the latter part of the nineteenth century, and as body matter could be set much cheaper on the machines than by hand, most printers changed over to the machine method of setting the text. The double cases are rarely found in printing offices today, as smaller fonts, required for setting occasional display lines and short texts, can be kept in a single case. (A *font* is an assortment of one size and face of type.)

A great many type cases have been developed, but the one found in general use throughout our country, at present, is the California job case, shown in Figure 8-A. The California job case has positions for the capitals, lower-case letters, figures, special characters, and punctuation marks for one size and face of type.

You will observe that this case has 89 compartments of various sizes and shapes. The largest compartment is that for the lower-case e, as this letter appears more frequently in our language than any other. Note the small size of the boxes for the k, z, and other letters which are used the least. The location of the letters in the case is called the "lay of the case," and the lay is made so that the most used letters are grouped together within convenient reach of the person working at the type case.

As the capitals are ordinarily used much less than the lower-case letters, their arrangement is not so important. They are arranged alphabetically, except for the J and U, which come after the Z. The alphabet used by the early printers had no J and U, so it was only natural that when these letters were added to our alphabet the printers *laid* them in the empty boxes following the other capitals. Had they put them in the regular alphabetical position, it would have been necessary to change the position of all the letters following the I in all the cases of type then in use.

Small capitals are often laid in *one-third* cases, three of which fit into a regular size blank case. *Quarter* cases are also sometimes used for borders, ornaments or sorts.

You should always keep the cases *clean*. A clean case has every character and space in its proper place, while a *dirty* case is one into which the characters have been carelessly distributed and are mixed up. It is almost impossible to do a good job of typesetting from a dirty case, as you will be constantly picking up wrong letters and your final job will contain many errors.

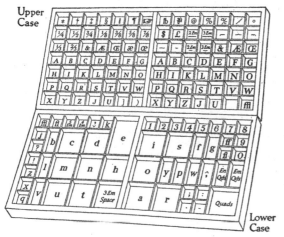

Fig. 7-A. News and Book Cases — Seldom Used Today

You must learn the lay of the case so that you can quickly find the characters you need when setting type, and also so that you can put the type back into their proper boxes when you have finished with them. Putting the type back into the case is called *distribution*.

Forty-five minutes should be plenty of time to *learn the case* by the following method:

1. Take a diagram of a blank case, or draw one, and note the three main divisions. Fill in the characters in the following order.

2. Fill in the capitals in alphabetical order except for the J and U. Note the HIK in the middle row and the TV in the next. Note the $, &, and the ffl (largest ligature).

3. Fill in the numerals in order.

4. Locate f ligatures (similars separated).

5. Quads: 2, 3 em, em, en (large first).

6. Spaces: 3-em, 4-em, 5-em (large first).

7. Learn toughies: q, x, z, (alphabetical) ! ? j.

8. Fill in points: . - ; : and ' k.

9. Fill in b,c,d,e,i,s,f,g, (be careful driving elephants into small ford garages).

10. Fill in l,m,n,h,o,y,p,w, , (let me now help out your punctuation with commas).

11. v,u,t,a,r (villains usually take a ride).

12. Trace your drawing and fill it in from memory. Check errors and practice as needed.

Unit 9

How to Work With a Type Case

Most *pied* (spilled) cases are the result of attempts to get correction characters in a hurry, or to get type from the top row of boxes in the case. Form the habit of always pulling out a supporting case before pulling out a case for any use, whether it be for a single letter, for composition at the cabinet, or to remove the case to the bank.

1. Locate the case you wish to use. (For example: 12-point Caslon Roman.)

2. Pull out, about halfway, the case immediately below the case you wish to use. (The 14-point Caslon in Figure 9-A.)

3. After the supporting case is pulled out about halfway, then pull out the 12-point case and allow it to rest on the 14-point case, as shown in Figure 9-B.

4. The 12-point case is then ready for use.

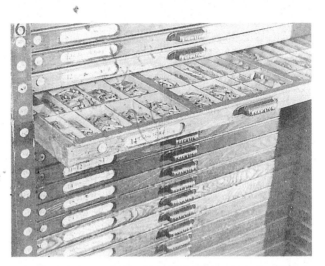

Fig. 8-A. California Job Case and its "Lay"

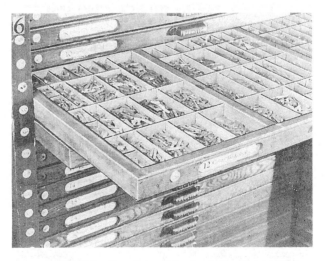

Fig. 9-A. Avoid Pling the Case — Pull Out a Supporting Case

Fig. 9-B. Case Supported — Ready for Use

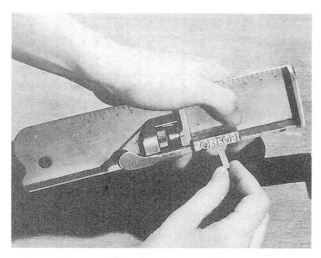

Fig. 10-A. Micrometer Composing Stick in Use

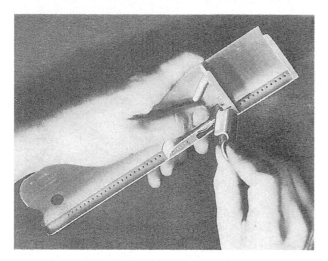

Fig. 10-B. Rouse Job Stick — Clamp Being Lifted

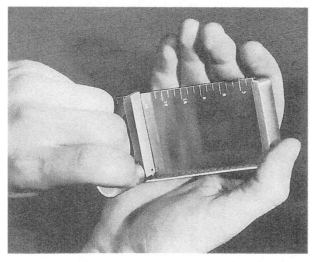

Fig. 10-C. Engaging Projections on Knee in Slots in Head of Stick

Unit 10

How to Set the Composing Stick

A *composing stick* (Figure 10-A) is used by the compositor for assembling the pieces of type into words and lines. This tool is called a stick because the early printers set their type into a carved wooden device that resembled our present stick. The early printer had to have a different stick for each length line he composed.

The modern stick is made of steel or brass. It is a great improvement over the old wooden stick, as it is easily adjustable for various lengths and is much more accurate. The composing stick is a fairly expensive precision tool, and should be handled with care as it is easily damaged by dropping or by misuse.

The stick shown in Figure 10-A is a micrometer stick and, when unclamped, is adjustable to half points by means of the micrometer screw incorporated in the knee. It is convenient for setting odd measures. A similar stick, but more finely adjustable by means of a lever in the knee, is the Rouse "quarter-point" stick.

The Rouse job stick (Figure 10-B) is a very popular model. It is adjustable to picas by means of the rectangular holes in the head of the stick. *Half-pica (nonpareil)* measures are available by turning a lever under the clamp. (See Unit 11.) The beginner should avoid using the half-pica measure, as most of the printing material is in pica lengths. Occasionally, however, the lever should be turned carefully and oiled with a light oil; otherwise, the lever may rust fast to the knee and ruin the device.

To set the job stick to any pica measure (for example, 18 picas):

1. Lift the clamp (see Figure 10-B) and disengage the projections from the rectangular slots.

2. Move the knee (the triangular piece which you unclamped) and engage the projections into the slots which will cause the flat side of the knee to fall on the 18-pica mark on the foot of the stick. (See Figure 10-C.)

3. Push the knee toward the open end of the stick so that the projections are in firm contact with the far sides of the slots. Hold it there with the left thumb.

4. Then press the clamp into position. (See Figure 10-D.)

It is important that the knee be pressed back before clamping, as there is usually considerable play or looseness in the fitting of the slots and projections. An improperly clamped knee may slip after composition is started, causing your lines to be of different lengths.

Unit 11

How to Use the Half-Pica Lever

When the flat side of the knee falls midway between the pica marks, instead of falling on one side of them, the nonpareil lever is in the half-pica position. To put it in the pica position turn the lever, as in Figure 11-A. It may be necessary to lift the end of the lever very slightly to clear the retaining holes. If it does not then turn freely, do not force it, but let your instructor set it for you. The lever may be rusty, and possibly he can loosen it with penetrating oil.

Unit 12

How to Set the Sliding Knee Stick

The Buckeye stick, shown in Figure 12-A, is of the sliding knee type. It does not have slots and projections for fixing the measure but must be clamped at the desired width by a screw arrangement.

To set the sliding knee stick for a given (15-pica) measure:

1. Loosen the clamp by lifting up on the winged-head screw. (In Figure 12-A, the wing is under the left thumb.)

2. Put a 15-pica piece of metal furniture, free of burrs, in the stick. Large foundry quads (two 72-point and one 36-point) may be used instead of the metal furniture. Do not, however, use slugs, leads, or a lot of small quads for your gauge — they are likely to give you an inaccurate measure.

3. For squeeze, insert a cardboard at the end of the furniture or quads.

4. Push the knee firmly against the gauge material with your right hand (Figure 12-A) and clamp screw firmly.

5. Remove furniture, or quads, and replace them in their proper storage location. Your stick is then ready for composition of a 15-pica measure.

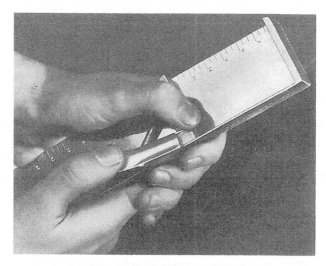

Fig. 10-D. Pushing Knee Back and Clamping

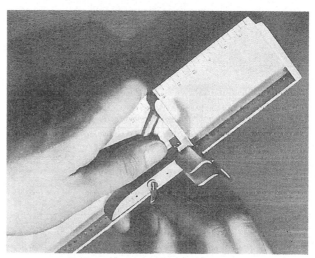

Fig. 11-A. Moving the Half-pica Lever

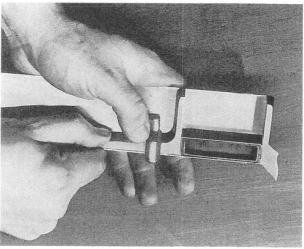

Fig. 12-A. Set Sliding Knee Against Gauge

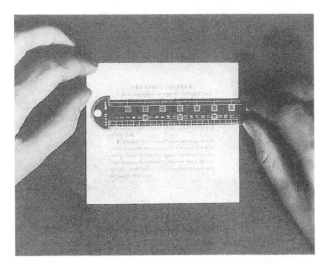

Fig. 13-A. Determining the Measure with a Brass Gauge

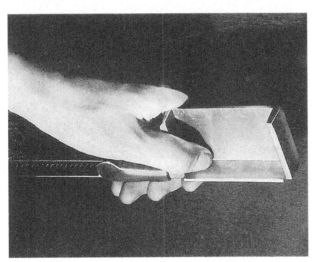

Fig. 13-B. Insert a Slug in Stick Before Starting Composition

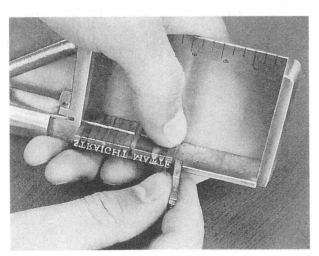

Fig. 13-C. Set Type from Left to Right, with Face Up
and Nick Showing

Unit 13

How to Center a Line

1. First determine the measure (length of type line) you are to use. Figure 13-A shows how to use the line gauge to determine the measure of reprint copy. The measure shown is 18 picas.

(The line gauge shown in Figure 13-A is of the kind which is used in magazine and newspaper printing plants. In place of the inch gradation, it has an agate scale. Columnar space in publications is measured by agate lines, the standard being 14 agate lines to the inch.)

2. Set your stick to the proper measure, making sure the knee is pressed back before the stick is clamped.

3. Insert a slug of that measure at the head of the stick (Figure 13-B). The slug should fit freely and have an end shake of about a point. The stick is manufactured with an allowance for "squeeze." A composed line is actually about a point wider than the measure.

A slug is always used, instead of a lead, at the start, as the slug is more rigid and makes it easier to remove the composed type from the stick.

4. Locate your case and pull out the case under it about halfway. (See Unit 9.)

5. Pull out your case to the working position shown in Figure 9-B. (It may be removed and placed on the top of the bank if that is the customary procedure in your shop.)

6. With the stick held properly in the left hand, as shown in Figure 13-C, pick up the types one at a time with the right hand. Place them upright against the slug at the head of the stick, with the face up and the nick showing. As you build up the word, hold the types in place against the slug and the knee of the stick with a light pressure of your left thumb.

The type will stay in place when the stick is held properly (tilted slightly so that if water were poured in the stick, it would run toward the head and to the left toward the knee). The thumb merely keeps the type from falling over as the stick is moved. Most good compositors cause the stick to "follow" the right hand, moving the stick so that the right hand does not have to travel so great a distance in bringing each piece of type to the stick.

7. As you pick up the type, spin it between your forefinger and thumb so that it will be in proper position with face up and nick out when your hand reaches the stick. This will be a little difficult to do at first but concentrate on doing it the proper way. A habit once formed is difficult to change, so do your work correctly from the start.

8. When the first word has been composed, insert a space, then set the next word. For a line of all capitals, use en quads to separate the words.

9. Do not read your composed type until you have finished the entire line.

10. Read and correct your line before justifying. This rule should never be broken. Justification is the process of making the line the proper length. It often takes longer to justify a line than it takes to set it. Therefore, it is important that the line be correct before it is justified. A correction usually makes it necessary to re-justify the line.

11. Figure 13-D shows a line being centered. Quads are inserted in pairs, one at the beginning and one at the end of the type line, until there is no longer room for a pair of quads. The remaining space is filled in the same manner with pairs of spaces placed next to the type.

The widest quads and spaces possible are used. It is better to use one 3-em quad than three 1-em quads as a less spongy line results. It is not always possible to put exactly the same amount of spacing material on each side of the words when centering a line. We can usually come very close to the exact center and can often make the line appear centered by considering the shape of the terminal characters. In the line shown in Figure 13-D, the slightly wider space could be placed next to the letter S at the beginning of the line, while the smaller space could be put after the R at the end of the line.

Do not attempt to force thin spaces down into a line, as they will probably bend. Instead, remove a quad from the end of the line, insert the thin space and then replace the quad. Trouble in inserting the last characters into a line may be caused by the type being off its feet. A remedy for this is suggested in Unit 18, on page 33.

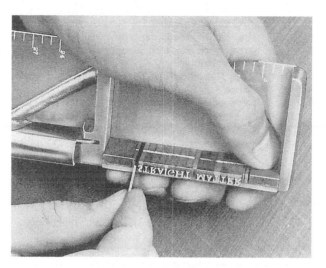

Fig. 13-D. Quads and Spaces Fill Out Blank Areas

Unit 14

How to Test Justification

Test the justification of your line as shown in Figure 14-A. A correctly justified line should be loose enough for you to push it forward with ease, but at the same time, the line should be tight enough to stand alone.

Justification must be exact. Careless justification cannot be tolerated, as it later causes damage to the type and spoilage of work.

Do not force characters and spaces into the line when justifying. Such a practice will result in springing the knee of the stick. Lines justified near the foot of a stick which has a sprung knee will be much wider than those set near the head of the stick.

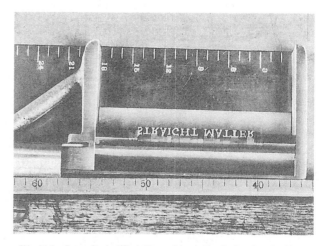

Fig. 14-A. Properly Justified Line — Moves Freely But Stands Alone

Out of this dream was born the American spirit which proved to be neither area nor population.

3   It became the incarnate   2
flame of freedom for the oppressed of the earth.

7   Today we salute this   6
Goddess of Liberty, whose   5
magic arm has pointed the
way, whose torch has blazed
the trail and whose symbol has
lighted the road.   Men have   4
10   died for her.   Patriots have
bled for her.   Nations have
sued for her hand.   She is the
greatest heiress in all the

Fig. 15-A. Poorly Spaced Front Page Editorial — Numbers Indicate Some of the Rules Violated

Practically the only live bait worth mentioning in connection with lake trout fishing is a good sized minnow of about five inches in length, and it is best to use this minnow in connection with some deep trolling rig such as the St. Lawrence or the Archer Spinners. Sometimes by fishing live minnows very deep in accordance with still-fishing methods and by trolling the rock shoals near the shore in the early morning or late evening some good fish may be taken but the best results come from trolling deep with the rigs mentioned.

Fig. 15-B. A Loosely Spaced Paragraph, Full of "Rivers" and "Lakes"

EDITOR'S NOTE: Please be brief. As a rule, 300 words should be ample. Your name and address must accompany each letter as an evidence of good faith. They will not be used or revealed unless you wish it. The Press receives many more letters than it has room to publish. Therefore, we reserve the right to reject or condense any letter.

Fig. 15-C. "Rivers" in Newspaper Composition — Note Wear on the Type Resulting From Constant Re-use of "Standing" Group

UNIFYING CAPITALS

CAP API PIT ITA TAL ALS

UNIFYING CAPITALS

Fig. 15-D. Letterspacing is Time Consuming But Improves Appearance and Legibility of All-capital Lines

Unit 15

How to Space Composition

Many printing plants throughout the United States are doing excellent jobs of type composition. They are, however, the exception, for work turned out by the average commercial shop shows a disregard of the fundamental principles of spacing, probably in the interest of speed and a cheaper product. Unfortunately, it does take longer to do the job right. The almost insurmountable handicap of a very narrow measure and a constant urge for speed results in some newspaper spacing which is atrocious and an excellent example of "How Not to Space Type." See Figure 15-A.

A properly spaced piece of type composition presents to the eye an evenly toned mass of gray. The white showing through the counters of the individual letters makes them legible. Each line is divided into words by the white showing through at the points where spaces have been inserted. The width of the space between words determines the quality of the composition.

Insufficient space between words causes them to run together and the line becomes merely a string of characters. On the other hand, too great a space between words results in "lakes" of white standing out in sharp contrast with the gray background of the type page. Streaks of white, called "rivers," caused by word spacing in several adjacent lines falling under each other, are also likely to occur in widely spaced composition. See Figures 15-A and 15-C.

Not only are these white spots and streaks unsightly, but they actually interfere with the reading of the page. Because they contrast with the gray mass of the type they are the strongest units on the page and are constantly exerting a pull upon the eyes of the reader, though he may not be conscious of it.

Spacing is relative. The ideal space to be used between words can only be determined after consideration of the design of the type face being composed. Narrow types need less space than wider ones. Long descender types have smaller lower-case letters than do short descender types, and therefore need less space between words. Differences in width and size of various types are usually reflected in the lower-case "o." That character has, therefore, been selected for use in a rule for ideal spacing.

It is customary in printing to have the lines even along the right-hand margin as well as along the left-hand side. This convention makes it difficult to achieve ideal spacing, but a careful craftsman can closely approach the ideal if he observes the rules given in this unit. Type characters are not all the same width and therefore the lines often do not come out to the proper length. When the line is too long, or too short, the space between words must be changed so that the type line will be the length wanted.

The process of making the line the proper length is called justification. Justification differs from spacing. Spacing is the adjusting of the spaces between words so that the words will appear to be the correct distance apart. Lines may be perfectly justified and yet be poorly spaced. See Figure 15-A.

Letterspacing of words composed in all capitals will often increase their legibility. To letterspace the line shown in Figure 15-D: Find, on a proof, the two letters which have the greatest space between them—CA. Cover, with two strips of paper, all but three letters in the line—CA and one adjacent. Look at the middle letter. While the serifs of the A almost touch both the C and P, the letter as a whole *appears* closer to the P. Estimate the amount of space which needs to be added to make the A appear centered. Indicate the space with a straight line for one unit, and a check for two units. Move the paper strips one character and consider the next three letters, keeping in mind the space you have added. Continue across the word; then consider other words in the line, spacing them to match the key letters. Several revisions may be necessary.

Rules for Spacing Type Composition

1. Use an em quad to start all paragraphs regardless of the measure being composed.

2. The ideal space between words in straight matter composition should be about the width of the counter in the lower-case "o."

3. Try to set your lines with the ideal space between words. When justification makes it necessary to alter the spacing, "space in" rather than "space out" the line.

4. Spacing between all the words in a line

'round the world traveler meets again the vessels of the through service from Australia to England. Tourists who omit the journey through India, and remain with the Australian steamer throughout the voyage, sail directly from Colombo, and after a course of 2,093 miles northwest across the Arabian Sea, past the Island of Socotra and Cape Guardafui, where Arab dhows in the slave trade may be seen cruising at times, reach the same port of Aden. Aden is known as the Indian Gibraltar. With this to guard the entrance to the Red Sea and the other citadel at the Pillars of Hercules to guard the Mediterranean, Great Britain controls all the great interior area of water so far as naval power is concerned. The peninsula of Aden is situated on the southeast coast of Arabia, about ninety miles from the entrance to the Red Sea. Originally it formed part of the Arabian province of Yemen, but for nearly half a century it has been included in British territory, under the governor of Bombay. The peninsula is connected with the Arabian continent on the north side by a narrow neck of land such as Gibraltar is joined to Spanish territory. The whole area of peninsula and harbor is estimated at thirty-five square miles, and the population not less than 20,000, exclusive of the garrison. The military cantonment is the place of greatest interest. There are barracks and mess-houses built of stone and mud for the accommodation of the garrison. The brigadier-general in command has under his direction a force which consists of artillery, British and Indian infantry, native sappers and miners, and a troop of native cavalry, to which camel-mounted Arabs are attached. The place is famously hot, and service on that military station is considered as exile by British officers. A notable feature of the Arabian city is the water supply. In such a climate and a large population it is not to be wondered that great care has been taken to provide a reservoir system. There are about fifty tanks in Aden with an aggregate capacity of nearly 30,000,000 gallons. The date of the original construction of some of these was as early as the year 600 A. D., and many were in fair preservation at the time of the British conquest. Not all have been fully restored, but the supply now is ample. The Red Sea is the scene of more objects of interest and of the romance of history than the casual reader is apt to remember. In the early days of civilization its waters were full of Egyptian and Arabian commerce, and the region is famous in fable as well as history. The narrow entrance to this peculiar body of water is the Strait of Babu'l Mandib, but twelve and a half miles in breadth. Just within the strait is the little island of Perim, volcanic and arid, but occupied by a small detachment of British troops and a cable station. Near by on the Arabian coasts the village of Mocha, which has given its name to a favorite brand of coffee. Two hundred miles north in the Red Sea is the little island of Kamaran, also occupied by the British government and as a cable station. On the Arabian side of this narrow sea are the cities of Yamba and Jiddah, the ports respectively of Medina

Fig. 15-E. Insertion of Quads Between Sentences Creates "Lakes" in the Composition

evident relief; so it might be said (in a spacious way) tha I had a hand in Genesis but made my exit with Exodus I would like to say here that the standard we set then wa kept up faithfully throughout the work. The over-runnin; and respacing to make required lines or lose superfluou: ones were not an easy matter or an inconsiderable labor.

❡ I have at times, in looking over the finished work wished that certain passages had been more smoothly anc evenly composed, but upon analysis I have found in almos every instance that an alteration would have produced ; worse piece of composition in some other part of the page So I venture to say that I believe this Bible, from begin ning to end, to be the finest and most consistent exampl« of composition and make-up that has been produced in ou: day. I may say this, as I had very little to do with it. It wa: done by the man at the keyboard, the man at the stone, th« man at the head of the Monotype composing room, anc the man in the proof room. And when the forms of typ« passed out of their hands to the press room the same care and skill were exercised by the head of that departmen and the man on the press. For over four years this vigilanc« was maintained, so that in the finished work no deviation i. observable from the standards of color, impression, anc register that were set in the beginning, beyond those sligh variations inevitable when printing on hand-made papei

Fig. 15-F. A Section of a Carefully Spaced Page Produced Under the Supervision of Bruce Rogers, Outstanding American Typographer

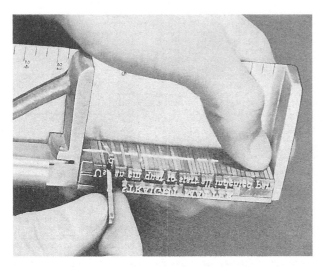

Fig. 16-A. Before Justifying — Read and Correct Your Line

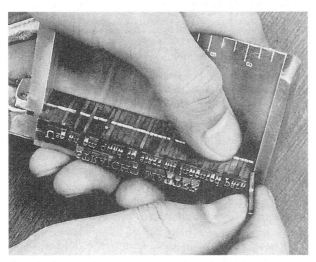

Fig. 16-B. "Spacing In" to Make Room for the Hyphen

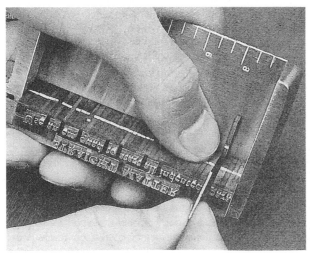

Fig. 16-C. Kick Out the Space to Be Removed

should appear equal as the eye takes in four or five words at a time. It is not always possible to make the spacing in the line appear exactly even, but with care you can make the differences so slight that they are not readily noticed.

5. Spacing of adjacent lines should vary but slightly.

6. Do not interspace words in order to fill the line, when composing straight matter.

7. Avoid using more than an en quad width in spacing straight matter composition.

8. When space must be changed between some words in order to justify the line, consider the shapes of the terminal letters of the words. Slanting letters such as y, v, w, k, open letters such as c, r, t, j, and periods and commas add space, as do certain of the capitals such as T, L, A, and others. Space may be decreased between combinations involving any of these, and if necessary, between combinations of short and tall letters such as la.

9. Use less space after commas and periods as the blanks above these punctuation marks add to the apparent space between the words.

10. The space between the period ending a sentence and the capital starting the next sentence should be decreased so that the spacing in the entire line will appear equal.

Legibility, as measured by ease and speed in reading and a balanced, pleasing appearance are qualities to be sought in spacing. Leading typographers no longer insert an extra en quad (or em quad) between sentences, because "lakes" created by extra quads make it impossible to achieve an evenly toned page (see Figure 15-E). That extra space is not needed "to show the start of a new sentence" is demonstrated by the Bruce Rogers specimen on page 29 (see Figure 15-F). A recent study shows that twenty-three out of twenty-five leading book typographers omit the extra quad.

Unit 16

How to Set Straight Matter

"Straight matter" is the name given to plain paragraph composition. To set straight matter properly, you must master the fundamentals of spacing, of justification, and of word division.

Too many people feel that printing is just a mechanical operation that anyone can do with a minimum of thinking. In order to get you to learn fundamental principles, instead of just setting the straight matter exactly as it appears in the examples, the 12-point Caslon type face, imported from England, has been used in the illustrations. It is not likely that you will have available a 12-point type which sets to exactly the same width as this Caslon. Therefore, even though you compose the copy of the example in the same measure, the spacing between words and the words in your line will probably differ from those shown.

Study the examples, learn the principles involved, and then apply them in composing the copy assigned to you. The example shown in Figures 16-A to 16-E was set in the following manner:

1. The measure (18 picas) was determined, the stick set properly, and a slug inserted. The heading was centered and a two point lead inserted below the line.

2. An em quad was put in for the indention.

3. The first line of the paragraph was set, using 3-em spaces between the words. Only "para" of the word "paragraph" would go on the line. (See Figure 16-A.)

4. Words may be divided between syllables. The division "para-graph" is correct. When in doubt about division of a word, look it up in the dictionary.

5. Read and correct the line before justifying it! Figure 16-A shows how the incorrect letter was pushed out with the correct one. The "d" was then replaced in the case.

6. Figure 16-B shows that there was not room for the hyphen at the end of the line. Space between words had to be decreased.

7. The space to be removed was tipped out against the bottom of the stick, as shown in Figure 16-C. The new space was inserted and the 3-em space replaced in its box in the case. In this line, replacing one 3-em space with a 4-em gave the space needed for the hyphen. The 4-em space was inserted after "indented" in order to get it as far away as possible from the wider spaces. Had it been inserted after "to," the eye would note the difference in width.

8. A lead was inserted after the line was justified. The lead should be inserted even though the matter is to be "set solid" (without leading) in final form. The lead gives a smooth

surface for manipulation of the line during justification. It can be removed later. Compositors used composing rules when setting type during "hand-set" days, as much of the matter was set solid. These rules are rarely seen today.

9. Note in Figure 16-D that in the first setting a 4-em space was used after the period and 3-em spaces in the rest of the line.

10. Again referring to Figure 16-D, it can be seen that there was not room for the "a" to go in the remaining space.

11. Figure 16-E shows the "a" in place. The line was justified by "spacing in." Four-em spaces replaced the 3-em ones before and after "with." (Note the slanting letter "w" and the "h l" combination and then see Unit 15, No. 8.)

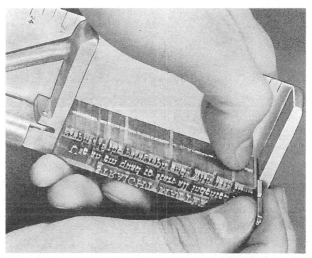

Fig. 16-D. "Space In" Whenever Possible

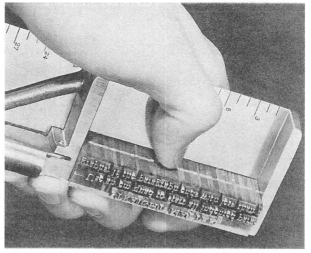

Fig. 16-E. Changing Two Spaces Allowed "a" to Go in Line

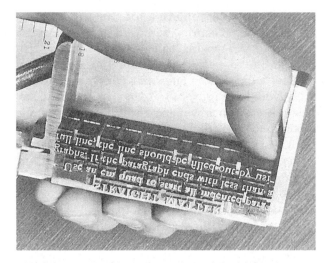

Fig. 17-A. Use Thinner Spaces After Periods and Commas

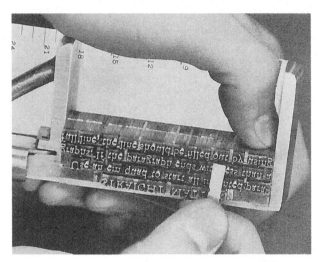

Fig. 17-B. Line Justified But Poorly Spaced

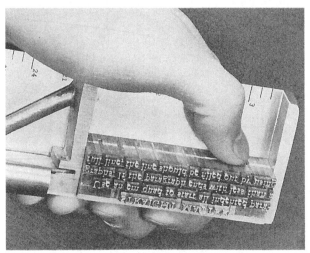

Fig. 17-C. Wider Space Inserted Between "l l"

Unit 17

How to Justify by Spacing In

Figure 17-A shows a line which could be justified by hyphenating "using" and spacing out to fill the line. However, it is better to space in whenever possible and that was done in this case.

1. The 3-em spaces were kicked out and replaced with 4-ems until there was space enough to get in the "ng" at the end of the line. Note in Figure 17-B that there are still two 3-em spaces in the line — on either side of "by." But the "t b" is an open letter-ascending letter combination, and the "y" is a slanting letter. Both of these should take less space rather than more space between them.

2. Note in Figure 17-C that one of the wider 3-em spaces has been inserted between two ascending straight letters — between the words "full line."

3. Figure 17-D shows the other 3-em space now between "should be." While the spacing in this line does not appear exactly the same between all words, the differences are so slight that the eye does not readily note them.

4. Note that the ligature "fi" was used in composing "filled" in the line shown in Figure 17-D. A *ligature* is two or more connected letters on the same body; a *logotype* is two or more letters (not necessarily connected) on the same body. The five common ligatures are fi, ff, fl, ffi, ffl. Their use is necessary to avoid break-

Fig. 17-D. Space Between Words Should "Look" Equal
"Tied" Letters (Ligatures) Found in Some Italic Fonts

ing the kern at the top of the "f," because in most well-designed types the kern comes in contact with the dot of the "i" and the top of the "l." The kern may break off when a proof is pulled if ligatures are not used.

Ct St tt as is us Sp fr

"Tied" letters (ligatures) found in some Italic fonts

Unit 18

How to Put a Line On Its Feet

Sometimes in setting type, and especially when justifying the line, we find that a letter or space will go part way into the line and then seem to wedge. If this happens, the type line is probably off its feet. Note in Figure 18-A that while the type is against the top of the knee, it slants, and at the bottom the type does not fit against the knee.

To put it back on its feet:

1. Remove the last character in the line. If the last character happens to be a thin one, then take out the first character in the line.

2. With your thumb, push the type squarely against the end of the stick, as shown in Figure 18-B. Work across the line, straightening a few characters at a time.

3. Place the character you removed against the end of the line and push the entire line back against the knee; then push the end character down into place. (See Figure 18-C.)

4. When the type is badly off its feet, it may be necessary to repeat the straightening procedure before the end character will slip into place.

When it is a space that is wedging rather than the last character, simply remove the end character and insert the space. Then, put the line on its feet as previously explained and replace the character. Removing an end character or a quad in a line is a "trick of the trade" frequently resorted to by compositors. When justifying, it is almost impossible to force a thin space into a line without bending or damaging it. After removing the end character, it becomes a simple operation to drop the thin space into place and then replace the thick character.

Fig. 18-A. A Type Line Off Its Feet

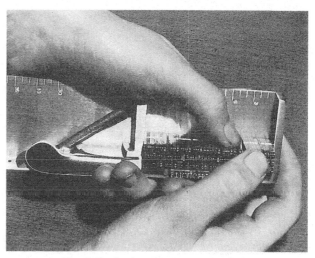

Fig. 18-B. Putting the Type on Its Feet

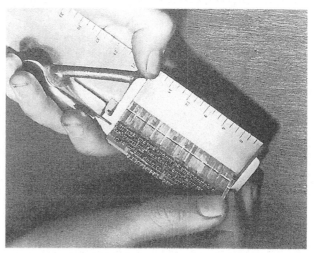

Fig. 18-C. Pushing the Type Against the Knee

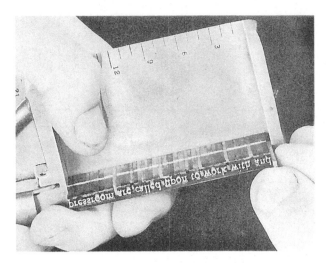

Fig. 19-A. A Line Which Needs to Be "Spaced Out"

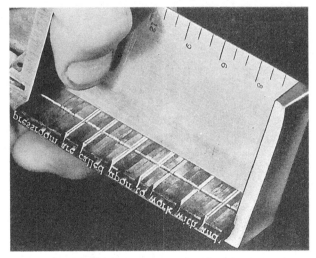

Fig. 19-B. Do Not Exceed an en Quad When "Spacing Out"

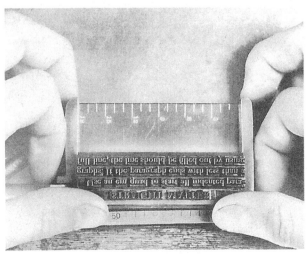

Fig. 20-A. Proper Position for Dumping the Stick

Unit 19

How to Space Out a Line

Figure 19-A shows a line which could not be "spaced in" sufficiently to permit insertion of a syllable of the next word. In such cases spacing out may be resorted to in order to fill the line, provided the space put between the words in a line of normal width type does not exceed an en quad. When more than an en quad is needed to fill out the line, adjustments should be made to previous lines in order to drive over or back enough characters to eliminate the gaps in the line being set.

Two methods can be used to determine the space needed to fill out a short line. One is by trial and error; the other is by arithmetical calculation. An experienced compositor uses the trial and error method, and because of his long familiarity with spacing material is able to justify the line rapidly. A student may spend an hour trying to find a combination which will work. The arithmetical method, in such cases, would be the better method to use. All beginners should calculate several lines, as the practice will help fix the width relationships of the various space combinations.

The line shown in Figure 19-A has 3-em spaces between words, and a 3-em just fills out the remaining space. As there are eight words in the line, there are seven places to put the extra space. $33\frac{1}{3}$ divided by 7 equals $4\frac{2}{3}+$. The space between words plus the extra space needed to fill out is then $33\frac{1}{3}$ plus $4\frac{2}{3}+$ or $38+$ units. But there is no 38 unit space, nor a combination which will make this amount. The nearest sizes are the $33\frac{1}{3}$ unit and the 40 unit combination of two 5-em spaces. Obviously, we will have to put 40 between some words and leave $33\frac{1}{3}$ between the others.

Replacing a 3-em with two 5-em spaces, adds $6\frac{2}{3}$ units to the line; 40 minus $33\frac{1}{3}$ equals $6\frac{2}{3}$. The total space to be added, $33\frac{1}{3}$, divided by $6\frac{2}{3}$ gives 5, which is the number of places the 40-unit combination will have to be used. The other two places will take $33\frac{1}{3}$ units each. Check: 5 x 40 equals 200; 2 x $33\frac{1}{3}$ equals $66\frac{2}{3}$; 200 plus $66\frac{2}{3}$ equals $266\frac{2}{3}$. Eight 3-em spaces (original line) also equal $266\frac{2}{3}$.

Figure 19-B shows the line spaced out with the thinner spaces properly placed next w's.

Unit 20

How to Dump the Stick

The stick should be "dumped" after it is about half full. This avoids the inaccuracies mentioned in Unit 14.

1. Place your galley in position on the bank. (See Unit 22.)

2. Set the stick of type against the lower edge of the galley. Place a slug after the last line of type in the stick.

3. Place the second fingers against the stick, as shown in Figure 20-A, forming an extension of the sides. Let the thumbs rest against the top slug.

4. Place the forefingers against the bottom slug. Hold the lines firmly between the thumbs and forefingers. While the second fingers exert pressure to hold the stick against the galley, push the lines forward along the bottom of the stick, using a slightly rolling motion — but do not lift the lines.

5. As soon as there is room between the head of the stick and the top slug, get a firmer hold on the lines by letting the thumbs go down to the bottom of the stick.

6. Press firmly and slide the lines from the stick to the bottom of the galley, keeping the second fingers in position so that they hold the stick against the galley, and, at the same time, cover the ends of the lines as they come from the stick. (See Figure 20-B.)

7. Do not attempt to lift the composed matter. Slide it along the bottom of the galley until you have it in the position shown in Figure 20-C. It will then be necessary to lift slightly the second finger of the left hand (but not the type) so that the finger will go over the side of the galley. When the ends of the type lines contact the galley, the left hand may be taken away and the lines pushed against the head of the galley, as shown in Figure 20-D.

Note that with the type in this position in the galley, the characters on the open end of the line will not fall down, as the slope of the bank keeps them in place.

8. Never unclamp your stick after your measure is set — you may reset it at the wrong measure. Keep it clamped regardless of whether you are dumping the stick or replacing a line for correction.

Fig. 20-B. Slide the Type from the Stick

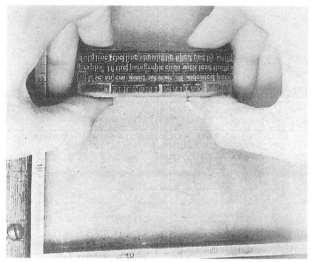
Fig. 20-C. Do Not Lift the Type — Slide It Along the Galley

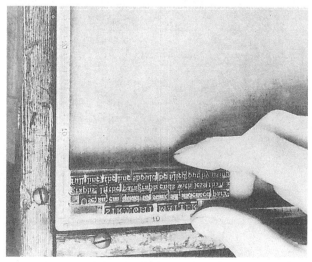
Fig. 20-D. Head of the Type Goes Against the Head of the Galley

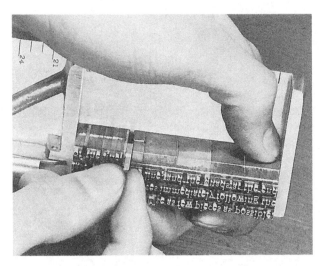

Fig. 21-A. Thinner Spaces Go Next to the Type

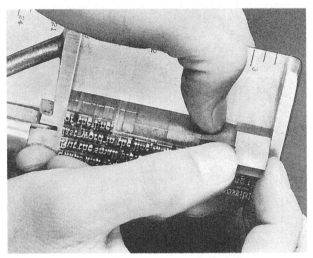

Fig. 21-B. Remove a Quad Before Inserting Thin Characters

Fig. 22-A. Proper Position for Working at Bank

Unit 21

How to Quad Out a Line

When a paragraph ends with less than a full line, the remaining space must be filled out with quads and spaces.

1. Use as few pieces of spacing material as possible. The line in Figure 21-A was filled out by inserting 3-em quads until there was no longer room for another one.

2. The space remaining was not wide enough to take a 2-em quad so an em quad was used. Note that the smaller quads and spaces are put next to the type. Whenever there is a choice, the thinner characters should be buried in the line. The wider characters and quads are less likely to fall over or slip out of place. Should they become misplaced, they are more easily detected.

3. The small opening remaining in the line was filled by inserting an en quad and then trying various spaces until one was found which seemed to be right. The en quad was removed and the thinner space was inserted. Figure 21-A shows that the en quad wedged and would not go in without pressure. It was taken out and again inserted after a 3-em quad was removed from the end of the line.

4. The line was put on its feet (See Unit 18) and the 3-em quad went in without forcing, as shown in Figure 21-B.

Often a line which seems to be too tight will actually be too loose after it has been put on its feet.

Unit 22

How to Work at the Bank

Type cases are usually arranged in cabinets (or stands) in series by families. The cabinets vary widely as to style and arrangement and are constructed of wood or steel. Nearly all of them have a working surface, either flat or slanted, called a *bank*. Figure 22-A shows a slanted work bank atop a wood cabinet which holds forty-eight type cases. A view of the other side of this cabinet is shown in Figure 9-B.

Form the habit of working correctly at the bank. Keep your *alley* (working space between two banks) clean and orderly, with all leads, slugs, spaces, and quads in their proper place.

1. Place your *galley* (the three-sided shallow

tray used for transporting and storing type) on the corner of your bank, as shown in Figure 22-A.

2. Stand facing the head of the galley, with the open end away from you. The head and left side of the galley should be against the railing of the bank so that the galley will not be so likely to slip while you are working with the type on it.

3. The type should be against the head and left side of the galley, with the head of the form near you. (See Figure 23-B.) The type will read correctly from left to right, but it will be upside down. A compositor never reads his type except from left to right and upside down.

4. Type placed in the galley correctly can be easily spread for leading, correcting, or make-up because the slant of the bank keeps the end characters in place.

5. The galley shown in Figures 22-A and 23-B is a brass make-up galley. It has square sides with pica gradations and is carefully made. The make-up galley is for use on the bank (its painted number corresponds with the bank number) and should not be stored. Its cost is about fifteen times that of the steel storage galley. The make-up galley, like all other tools and equipment, should receive careful treatment. It should be kept right side up, should never be turned over for use as an ink slab or writing surface, and should be kept flat against the surface of the bank. All leads, slugs, quads, and other material should be kept from under it, or the bottom will become sprung.

6. Keep your bank clean and orderly. Do not permit it to become cluttered up with material not needed for your work, and keep in order the material you are using.

Unit 23

How to Keep a Form on Its Feet

It is difficult to keep a small form, consisting of only a few lines of type, on its feet while a proof is being pulled. This difficulty can be overcome by putting metal furniture around the form and increasing its size, as shown in Figure 23-A. Note that slugs have been put around the metal furniture. The slugs, being taller than the furniture, make it easier to tie up the form, especially along the edges which come in con-

tact with the side and head of the galley.

Another method of preparing a small form for tying up is shown in Figure 23-B.

1. In this method six or eight extra slugs are put above the type lines and about the same number are put below the last line. These slugs aid in keeping the type lines from tipping forward or backward.

2. A slug is then put along each side of the form. This slug holds the type upright and on its feet sidewise, provided the lines are properly justified.

3. Leads and slugs are added until the length of the form is about two points greater than the length of the slugs along the sides.

Tying up is illustrated in Unit 24.

Fig. 23-A. Build Out a Small Form Before Proofing

Fig. 23-B. Keep Type on Its Feet by Putting Slugs Along Each Side

Fig. 24-A. Tie a Knot about One Inch from End of String

Fig. 24-B. Place Knot at Open Corner of Form

Fig. 24-C. Cross Over Behind the Knot First Time Around

Unit 24

How to Tie Up a Type Form

Figures 24-A to 24-F show a form being tied up without slugs by a method which is sometimes used. This is accomplished by wrapping string along the sides of the type form. Compositors can tie a form in this manner and keep type on its feet. However, the student should put slugs along the sides of the form, as explained in Unit 23, before starting to tie it. (See Figure 23-B.)

The slugs on the sides of a long form, as shown in Figure 24-F (33 picas), will tend to buckle outward after the tying up is completed. To overcome this, insert a 24-point or 30-point em quad between the string and the slug, about halfway down each side. This will tighten the string, and the truss effect will keep the slugs snugly against the ends of the type.

The string used in tying a form should be of good quality — strong, but not too bulky.

1. Place the head of the form against the head of the galley with one side of the form resting against the lower edge of the galley. The galley should be resting firmly against the lower right corner of the working bank. (See Figure 24-A.)

2. Take a piece of string long enough to go around the form five or six times. As shown in Figure 24-A, tie a knot about an inch from one end.

3. Take hold of this inch piece with your left hand and place the knot at the end of the slug at the open corner of the form. (See Figure 24-B.) With the right hand, wrap the string clockwise around the form by drawing it first along the upper side of the form, then down across the head.

4. Continue across the lower side and up along the slug at the foot of the form. Keep the string drawn taut. When you reach the knot at the open corner, the first time around, cross over the string right behind the knot, as shown in Figure 24-C.

5. The second time around, let the string pass above the knot. The loose end of the string is thus caught and held in position by the second and subsequent laps of the string, and the knot aids in keeping it from slipping. Continue wrapping for five or six turns around the form,

keeping the string drawn tight. After the last turn passes the open corner, hold the string in place with the left hand.

6. With a make-up rule in the right hand, push a loop between the string and the form. See Figure 24-D.

7. Catch the loop below the windings and draw it tightly against the corner as demonstrated in Figure 24-E.

8. Figure 24-F shows how to cut off the excess string with the sharp edge of your make-up rule, but be careful not to score the bottom of the galley while doing the cutting. A short end of the string should be left protruding so that the loop can be drawn out easily when the page is being untied. The loop and the protruding end of the string should be kept small so that there is no chance for the string to get under the type in the form.

9. With a make-up rule, push the string down until it is in the center of the slugs.

Unit 25

How to Take Good Proofs

After the type is composed and made up into a form, a printed impression is taken. This print, which is called a *proof,* shows the content and condition of the form. The process of making this print is called *pulling a proof.* Care must be used in pulling proofs so that a clean, sharp print of the entire form will result. A sloppy, messy proof will not permit the person reading the proof (called a *proofreader)* to find typographical errors and damaged type.

It has become standard practice in the better printing plants to try to have the forms as nearly perfect as possible (both as to content and condition of the printing surface) before sending them to the pressroom to be printed. Good proofs are needed to accomplish this.

There has also been a demand for perfect proofs from another source. Offset lithographers and gravure printers do not print from type in these processes. Instead, they prepare plates from reproduction proofs. Such proofs must show every detail of the type, no matter how fine the line.

To meet these demands for better proofs, manufacturers have developed a great many different kinds of proof presses designed to give

Fig. 24-D. Use Make-up Rule to Push Loop between String and Form

Fig. 24-E. Catch Loop and Pull It Tightly against Corner

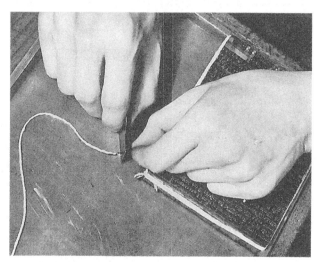

Fig. 24-F. Cut Off Excess String — Leave Short End

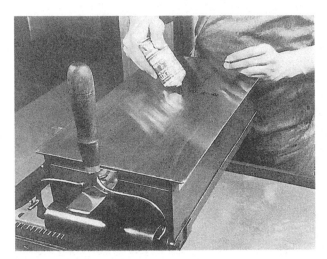

Fig. 26-A. Put a Few Spots of Ink on the Plate

Fig. 26-B. Roll Out the Ink with the Brayer

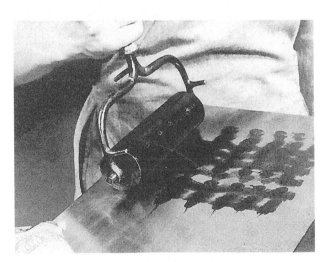

Fig. 26-C. Do Not Cover Entire Surface of Large Ink Plate

good proofs quickly and easily. Some of these presses are quite elaborate and are practical only for the large plants, as they cost thousands of dollars.

Probably the best type of proof press for pulling proofs of type quickly and easily is the precision built cylinder proof press, equipped with automatic inking and grippers, and with a hard packing on the cylinder. The automatic inking device contacts the form with just the right pressure and lays on an even film of ink. The grippers hold the sheet of paper in place as the cylinder is rolled over the form and thus prevent it from slipping and slurring the print. Precision manufacture permits the cylinder to be packed with hard packing, so that a sharp print results from an exactly type high form.

When a soft packing is used on a proof press, the type sinks into the paper and packing and gives a distorted print as some of the beard prints along with the face of the type. Also, the worn and damaged letters will print when the soft packing is used.

Expensive equipment is not necessary, however, to take good proofs. A careful operator can take satisfactory proofs on most any press. Just four things are necessary to take quality proofs. (Each is explained and illustrated in Units 26 to 34.)

1. Ink the form carefully, using clean, fresh ink and a brayer which is in good condition.

2. Place the paper in contact with the form in a manner which prevents slurring.

3. Use a packing of the correct kind and thickness.

4. Strip the proof from the form without slurring it.

Unit 26

How to Ink the Proof Press

The roller device used for inking a form for proofing is called a *brayer*. A tacky (sticky) job or bond ink should be used for proofing.

1. Put a few small spots of ink across the plate, as shown in Figure 26-A. Too much ink will give a smeary proof. Start with a little ink and use more if needed. Be sure to replace the cap on the ink tube, as a skin will form over the ink when exposed to air.

2. Take the brayer in your right hand, as

shown in Figure 26-B. Roll it back and forth across the ink plate, using a gentle pressure. Lift the brayer at the end of each stroke, letting the roller spin. This will quicken the spreading (called distribution) of the ink on the plate. Failure to lift the roller will cause the same points on the brayer and the plate to continue to come into contact with each other, and the ink will not spread evenly.

3. Do not attempt to cover with ink the entire surface of a large plate. Roll the brayer back and forth and then across from side to side, as in Figure 26-C, until you have an ink area each dimension of which is a little more than the width of the brayer.

4. Rest the brayer on the ink plate, as shown in Figure 26-D. The lug at each side and the handle form a three-point support which keeps the roller from resting on the plate. Printers' composition rollers become flattened and useless when left in contact with any surface.

Unit 27
How to Position and Ink the Form

1. Check the press bed. Remove the galley substitute plate. The galley substitute plate is the same thickness as the galley and is used only when a proof is to be taken of a form not on a galley. Use of both the substitute plate and the galley at the same time will cause the form and the press packing to be crushed. Figure 27-A shows the galley substitute plate being removed from a Challenge proof press.

2. See that the bed of the proof press is clean and that it is free from any loose leads, slugs, type, string, or other material which might get under the galley.

3. When you are sure that the press bed is clear, place your galley near the center.

4. Run your hand over the form (Figure 27-B), to see that no type or other material is above the surface of the form. Make sure that the ends of the string are not under the form; that the form is firm against the head and one side of the galley; and that all the type is on its feet.

5. Pick up the ink brayer and run it back and forth across the ink a few times. Hold it as shown in Figure 27-C — this position prevents the lugs from striking the form. Ink the form

Fig. 26-D. Rest Brayer on Three-point Support with Roller Clearing Plate

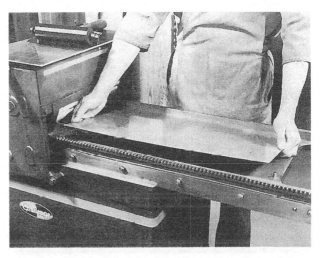

Fig. 27-A. Remove Galley Substitute Plate before Placing Galley on Press

Fig. 27-B. Before Proofing — See that the Type is On its Feet

by rolling the brayer across it from the open corner to the closed corner. Then roll it across the form from the open edge to the closed edge. Never roll the brayer toward the open edges as there is less support there and the type is likely to be pushed off its feet.

6. Use a very light, even pressure when you are inking the form. Hold up the brayer so that there is just enough contact between the form and the brayer to cause the roller to turn as it is carried across the form. Be especially careful at the edges of the form. Too great an inking pressure at the starting edge will cause the ink to pile up and print blacker, while on the finishing edge it will wipe off the ink and give a streaky print.

Fig. 27-C. Ink Lightly — Rolling toward the Solid Corner

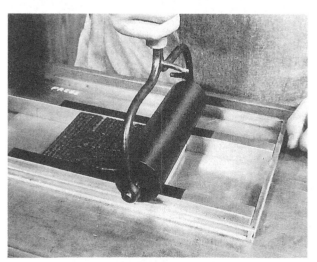

Fig. 28-A. Bearers Eliminate Most Inking Troubles

Unit 28

How to Eliminate Inking Troubles

The difficulty encountered in inking the edges of a form can be eliminated by using type high bearers alongside the form while it is being inked. The bearers support the roller as it comes into contact with the form and again as it leaves the form. The bearers can be removed before the proof is pulled, or they can be left in the galley and the print they make can be trimmed from the proof.

The bearers shown in Figure 28-A are two bars of steel accurately machined down to type high. Any type high (.918 inch) material will serve for bearers. Old engravings or electrotypes are very satisfactory, providing the base is in good condition and the cuts are the proper height.

Unit 29

How to Pull the Proof

It is impossible to give in this manual detailed instructions for the operation of the many makes and models of machines available for use in printing plants or school shops. The fundamentals given here should be supplemented by specific instruction regarding machines in your shop. **Do not attempt to use any machine until your instructor has demonstrated its operation, pointed out precautions you must take, and given you permission to use the particular piece of equipment. Failure to obtain proper instruction and permission may result in personal injury to yourself or classmates, or damage to the machine.**

If an accident does occur, report it at once to your instructor. He can then arrange for treatment of any injuries, and for repair of the equipment. Never attempt to fix damaged equipment except under the supervision of your instructor. Otherwise, the "fixing" may do more damage than did the original accident.

Do not attempt to cover up damage or breakage for which you are responsible. Even though you are censured for your carelessness, your instructor will respect your honesty.

1. After inking the form, again make sure the type is on its feet. Careless inking may have pushed some of the type off its feet.

2. Figure 29-A shows how to lay a sheet of

proof paper on the form preparatory to taking the proof on a press not equipped with grippers. Hold the paper at the two ends and let it dip slightly at the center. Position it by sight so that it centers over the form. Then, carefully bring it in contact with the type, releasing the ends gently as soon as the center touches the form. Slurs result from any moving of the sheet after it touches the inked form.

3. Roll the cylinder over once. If the cylinder does not roll easily, do not force it. Back it off and find out what is wrong — you may have the galley substitute plate on the bed; rags or paper may be in the gears or between the bed and cylinder bearers; or something may be under the galley. Clear the obstruction and then roll your proof. The paper and form are coming from under the cylinder in Figure 29-B.

4. Strip the proof from your form by lifting one corner (Figure 29-C) and pulling with a slow, steady pressure.

5. Examine your proof. One sheet, only, should be used in taking each proof. Do not lay two or three sheets on in an effort to remedy defects in the proof. Show the proof to your instructor — he will tell you how to remedy your trouble. The addition of even one extra sheet in pulling a proof on a precision proof press will produce excessive wear on the type.

Unit 30

How to Use a Proof Press With Grippers

Proof presses, equipped with grippers for holding the sheet while the proof is being taken, usually have a deadline scribed in the press bed or on the bearers. The grippers will smash a form placed past this deadline.

1. Have your instructor show you the deadline on the press so you may place the form in its proper position.

2. The side guide on the feed board must be set in proper relation to the form so the sheet will have the correct margins.

3. The sheet is then placed against the side and front guides and the proof taken.

4. Other operations involved in taking a proof are the same as those on a proof press not equipped with grippers.

Fig. 29-A. Center Paper Over Form and Lay it Down Carefully

Fig. 29-B. Do Not Force Cylinder — It Should Roll Easily

Fig. 29-C. Strip Proof from Form with Slow Steady Pull

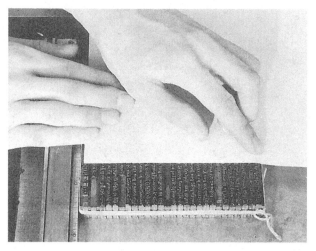

Fig. 31-A. Crease Sheet at Bottom of Last Type Line

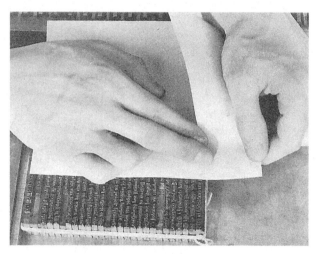

Fig. 31-B. Divide Overhanging Part of the Sheet in Half

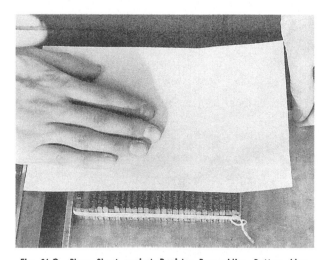

Fig. 31-C. Place Sheet against Register Bar — Align Bottom Line with Pinch Mark

Unit 31

How to Use a Register Bar

Many proof presses, not equipped with grippers, make use of a register bar to get correct margins and to register two-color forms or work and twist rule forms. The illustrations accompanying this unit show a register bar in use on one of the Vandercook gripperless models.

1. Lay the sheet over the form with the top edge in line with the top of the first line of type. Crease the sheet along the bottom of the last line, as in Figure 31-A. The part of the sheet projecting past the form is the combined top and bottom margins.

2. Divide this projecting part by soft-folding it in half and pinch-marking the edge at the middle point, as shown in Figure 31-B.

3. Lay the sheet in position against the top of the register bar and move the galley until the bottom line of the form is in line with the pinch mark. (Figure 31-C.) Keep the head of the form toward the bar.

4. Fill in the space between the bar and the galley with furniture, leads, and slugs. Close register adjustments can be made by using the set screws (one is just visible near the left corner of the sheet in Figure 31-C) and auxiliary bar furnished with the device.

5. Lay the side edge of the sheet in line with the edge of the form. Crease the sheet over the other edge of the form. The part projecting is the combined side margins.

6. Find the width of one margin by soft-folding and pinch-marking the midpoint.

7. Figure 31-D shows how to position the galley sidewise. Place the sheet against the side stop pin and keep the bottom sheet edge parallel with a line of the type. Move the galley until the edge of the form lines with the pinch-mark. Block in the space between the galley and the side of the press.

8. Ink the form. Then push the galley firmly against the furniture at the side and top.

9. Hold up the tail of the sheet and place the head against the top of the register bar. Slide the sheet against the stop pin and hold the sheet firmly. (Figure 31-E.)

10. Let the tail of the sheet down gently. Lift your fingers from the head of the sheet, being careful not to cause the sheet to move once it

has contacted the form. Roll the proof. Strip it, as illustrated in Figure 29-C.

Unit 32

How to Eliminate Proof Slurs

It is quite difficult to get proofs with no trace of slur on a gripperless proof press, as the sheet usually moves, either when being laid on or stripped from the form. Occasionally you may wish to take one or two extra good proofs on such a press.

Proofs of near "press proof" quality can be taken in the following manner from forms in which all parts are type high and in good condition:

1. Position the form in the center of the press, lengthwise, with the blank side of the galley against the side of the press.

2. Ink the form carefully, using bearers. See Unit 28.

3. Loop together two strings of rubber bands. Place them around the cylinder, using paper clips to fasten together the ends. Adjust the paper clips so that they are at the open area of the cylinder.

4. Position the bands so that they are about one-half inch from each edge of the form. The bands must clear the form or they will cause it to be smashed.

5. Insert, under the rubber bands, a sheet of the stock to be printed. Keep it parallel with the cylinder bearers and centered over the form. Avoid creasing it. Smooth it down against the cylinder and then recheck clearance of the bands.

6. Turn the press slowly. Watch the form for clearance of bands, and to see that it will strike the paper. Do not attempt to shift the paper (unless you have positioned it incorrectly sidewise) but move the form along the press bed until it is in position to print on the sheet.

7. Roll your impression and leave the sheet in position. (Figure 32-A.) Put on the packing two pencil marks along the side of the sheet and one at the head, as guides for your next sheet.

8. Shift the form to correct any error in position. Ink, insert new sheet under the bands, check the bands for clearance, and take another impression.

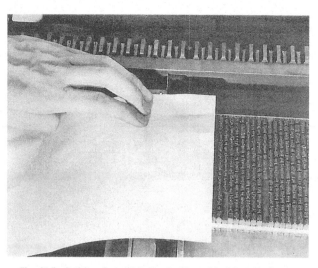

Fig. 31-D. Position Form Sidewise in Line with Other Pinch Mark

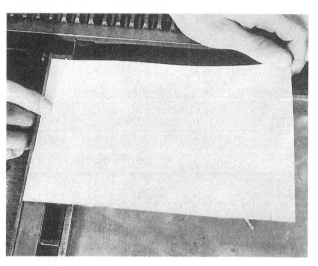

Fig. 31-E. Register Sheet Against Head of Bar and Pin

Fig. 32-A. Eliminate Proof Slurs by Holding Sheet to Cylinder

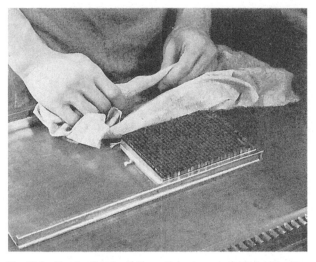

Fig. 33-A. Examine Rag for Buttons, Pins, etc. — Avoid Damaging Type

Fig. 33-B. Dampen Rag with Small Amount of Type Cleaner

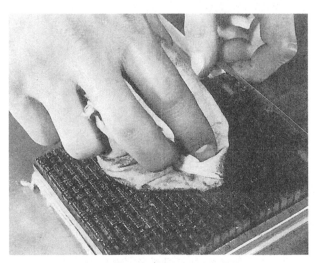

Fig. 33-C. Wash Type by Wiping Toward Solid Corner

Unit 33

How to Wash the Form and Press

Immediately after pulling the proof, the form should be washed to remove the ink remaining on the type. (See Figure 33-A.)

1. Take a small rag and examine it to be sure it is free from buttons, snaps, pins, or other material that would scratch the type.

2. Wad it up to fit your hand and then dampen the exposed surface of the rag with a little type cleaner. (See Figure 33-B.)

3. Wash the form by wiping the dampened rag across it — wiping toward the closed corner of the form, as shown in Figure 33-C. Shake out the rag and dry the form by wiping with a dry portion of the rag.

4. Do not flood the form with type cleaner, as it will wash the ink down into the type form. See that the ink is removed from the top of the quads and spacing material in the blanked-out areas of the form.

5. Wipe the ink spots and surplus cleaner from the proof press bed and the galley.

A type brush may be used to scrub out the counters of the type, but the form should first be gone over with the rag. Then use only a little solvent on the brush.

Two types of brushes are commonly used in cleaning forms. One has fibre bristles and is used for type. The other has copper wire bristles enclosed in a row of fibre bristles — it is a plate brush. Never use it without the permission of your instructor. A plate brush will scratch the type and may ruin a plate when used incorrectly.

There are a number of good type cleaners on the market, but all are quite expensive. Benzene or naphtha are satisfactory solvents for cleaning type, but must not be used to wash the brayer or spilled on painted surfaces. Cleaners should be kept in closed cans to prevent evaporation, as they are highly volatile. Gasoline (unleaded) can be used for cleaning the type, but it often leaves an oily deposit on the surface. The oil prevents proper inking.

Kerosene should never be used for cleaning the type (it is an oil) but is excellent for cleaning the brayer. Find out from your instructor what solvents are available, and the use to which each is to be put.

Unit 34

How to Keep Type On Its Feet

If type is not on its feet when a proof is pulled, it probably will be damaged. A part of each piece of type which is off its feet will be higher than the rest of the form and will therefore tend to be smashed by the extra pressure it receives as the proof is pulled. The reason these parts are higher is shown in Figure 34-A. Each piece of type has, roughly, the shape of a rectangular box. If it is tipped sidewise, backward, or forward, part of it is sure to be higher than the rest of the form.

Use extra care when proofing scripts, shaded and fine line types, as the delicate lines can stand no excess pressure.

Figure 34-B shows a proof taken from a form in which part of the type was off its feet. Note only the right hand part of the letters in the third line are printing. The type in this line is leaning to the left, thus making the right side of each letter higher than the rest of the form. If the back of the proof were examined, it would show that the parts which are printing are punching into the sheet, while the parts which are not printing show no impression.

In Figure 34-C, note that only the top part of the lines are printing. This indicates that the lines are leaning forward, thus throwing the type off its feet. This causes the top part of the characters to be higher than type high and the bottoms to be lower than type high. The back of the proof would show this to be true, with the impression of the tops of the characters punching the paper, while the bottoms would show no impression.

The most common causes of type getting off its feet are: (1) improper justification, (2) improper tie-up of the form, (3) improper inking of the form. Poor justification results in loose lines in which the type gets off its feet due to lack of side pressure. A form tied too loosely or with the string too near the top of the form may cause the type to get off its feet. Bearing down too hard on the brayer while inking the form or rolling toward the open sides of the form may roll the type off its feet. The remedy for these faults is obvious — be careful to do your work correctly and these troubles will be avoided.

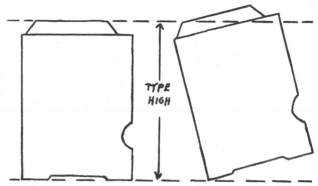

Fig. 34-A. Why Type is Smashed When Proofed while Off its Feet

Part of each piece of type which is off its feet will be higher than the rest of the form and will be smashed

Fig. 34-B. The Third Line Was Off its Feet When Proof was Taken

lines are leaning forward. thus throwing the type off its feet. This causes the top part of the characters to be higher than type high, and the bottoms to be lower than type high. The back of the proof would show this to be true. with the impression of the tops of the characters punching the paper, while the bottoms would show no impression.

Some common causes of type getting off its feet are: (1) improper justification. (2) improper tie-up of the form. (3) improper inking of the form. Poor

Fig. 34-C. A Proof Taken with the Lines Leaning Forward

THE PRACTICE OF TYPOGRAPHY, if it be followed faithfully, is hard work-full of detail, full pet-
ty restrictions, full of drudgery, and not greatly
rewarded as Men now count rewards. There are
times when we need to bring to it, all the history
and art and feeling that we can, to make it bear-
able.
    But in the light of history, and of art, and
of knowledge and of mans achievement, it is as
interesting a work as exists—a broad and human-
izing employment which can indeed be followed
merely as a trade, but which if perfected into an
art, or even broadened into a profession, will per-
petually open new horizons to our eyes and new
opportunties to our hands.—D. B. Updike

Fig. 35-A. Proof with Errors Marked

THE PRACTICE OF TYPOGRAPHY, if it be followed
faithfully, is hard work—full of detail, full of pet-
ty restrictions, full of drudgery, and not greatly
rewarded as men now count rewards. There are
times when we need to bring to it all the history
and art and feeling that we can, to make it bear-
able. But in the light of history, and of art, and
of knowledge and of man's achievement, it is as
interesting a work as exists—a broad and human-
izing employment which can indeed be followed
merely as a trade, but which if perfected into an
art, or even broadened into a profession, will per-
petually open new horizons to our eyes and new
opportunties to our hands.—D. B. UPDIKE

Fig. 35-B. Proof After Corrections Have Been Made

Unit 35

How to Read and Mark Proof

Practically all medium- and large-size printing plants employ trained proofreaders to read the proof and mark errors and changes. In the smaller plants, the compositors sometimes read their own proofs; but even there, the proprietor or some other person usually gives the proof a reading. With so many people handling proofs, it is necessary that some system of standard marking be used so that the compositor may know exactly what correction or change is to be made. A set of symbols, known as *standard proof marks*, has been devised which greatly simplifies the work of the compositor as well as the proofreader. (See Figure 35-C.) A single symbol often takes the place of several words of explanation.

The first reading of a proof consists, actually, of two readings: (a) scanning for typographical errors, and (b) reading aloud for consistency with copy. The number of additional complete readings given a job of printing depends on the nature of the copy. The first reading is usually all that is made on newspapers. For copy which requires absolute accuracy in reproduction, such as technical books, several readings may be made, each by a different person. The first reading done by the printer's proofreader is called an "office reading." The proofreader is responsible for errors he misses, even though someone else also reads the proof.

Proofs should be taken on paper large enough to leave at least a one and one-half inch margin on either side of the type so that the proof marks may be written clearly.

1. See that the proof you are going to read is a good one with a clear, sharp impression of the entire form.

2. Read the proof for typographical errors. Mechanical defects and errors most likely to be present include:

Wrong fonts	"Doublets"
Broken type	Irregular compounding
Bad spacing	Wrong paragraphing
Inverted letters	Improper capitalization
Letter omissions	Bad punctuation
Transpositions	Faulty grammar
Protruding spaces	Inconsistent spelling
Bad divisions	Crookedness in lines
Misspellings	Bad make-up
"Outs"	Wrong indentions

3. When an error is found, mark it in the body of the proof in such a way as not to make the characters illegible, and then place in the margin the correct proof mark. For an error in the first half of the line, place the proof mark in the left-hand margin immediately in front of the line in which the error occurs. When the error is in the last half of the line, place the proof mark in the right-hand margin immediately after the line in which the error occurs. (See the first line in Figure 35-A.)

4. When there are two or more errors in the same half of a line, separate the proof marks with a diagonal line. Put the proof marks in the order in which the errors occur, working out from the end of the type line to the edge of the paper. Note in the fourth line in Figure 35-A that the proof mark for the first error in the left half of the line is next to the type line; the mark for the second error is in the middle, and the mark to the left is for the third error. (Many proofreaders place the marks in the left margin from left to right in the same order as occurrence of the errors.)

5. Proofs should be marked in ink or with a dark-colored pencil. Soft lead pencil marks become smeared and illegible. Marks made with a hard lead or light colored pencil are not easily seen.

6. The rule in most printing offices is to "follow copy, even if it goes out the window." This means that if there is any doubt about something in the copy, it must be composed exactly as it appears in the copy. However, both the compositor and the proofreader are under obligation to correct obvious errors that the author has missed. Also, it is their duty to "query" to the author any questionable point.

7. If the material to be proofread is long, get a copyholder to aid you in reading against copy. The copyholder reads the copy slowly, aloud, while you watch the proof. As the copyholder reads, he indicates to you such things in the

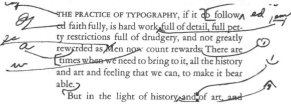

"Kite Strings" are Difficult to Follow, Especially on a "Dirty" Proof

PROOF MARKS

Marginal Mark	Meaning	Mark in Text
a	Insert here	grph
↓	Push down space	push down
✗	Defective letter	famed
℔	Turn over	be∂in
℞	Take out	deleate
⌣⌣⌣	Space evenly	it is as if he
#	Insert space	forthe
⌢	Less space	close up
⌣	Close up entirely	faith ful
⊙	Period	Dr Paul
⋏	Comma	Jan. 1 1940
⊙⊙	Colon	as follows
⟨;⟩	Semicolon	namely
⩔	Apostrophe	its cold
]⊏	Center	] Titles [
=	Hyphen	city wide
≡	Straighten lines	not even
⊐	Move over	Even margins right and left →⊐
⬚	Em quad space	$1.25 $2.95
/-/	One-em dash	A. SIGNATURE
/—²—/	Two-em dash	Wm. Caxton
¶	Make paragraph	area. They
no ¶	No paragraph	bearable. But in keeping
wf	Wrong font letter	wrong font
stet	Let it stand	John Read
tr	Transpose	rewrad
Caps	Capitals	st. louis
s.c.	Small capitals	Goudy
lc	Lower-case letter	President
ital	Italic	indeed
rom	Roman	(indeed)
(?)	Verify	(two) billion
sp. out	Spell out	(17)
bf	Bold face	must
ld	Insert lead	various industrial meetings and then

Fig. 35-C. Standard Proof Marks

copy as paragraphing, capitalization, and punctuation, and spells out letter by letter proper names and unusual words. Your job as proofreader is to indicate, with the proper proof mark, errors which the compositor has made, as well as broken letters, wrong font letters, or other changes necessary to give a correct job. A dictionary should be kept handy for checking the spelling of a word about which you are uncertain and for checking the division of words at the ends of the lines.

If the material to be read is short, you can perform the duties of both the copyholder and the proofreader, checking word by word the proof against the copy.

8. In the upper right-hand corner of the proof, write "First Proof" and sign your initials and the date. If there is a copyholder, put his initials under yours. After the corrections have been made in the form, a new proof should be pulled. It becomes the "First Revise" and is checked with the first proof to see that all errors have been corrected. It should be marked "First Revise," initialed, and dated by the proofreader doing the checking. After errors on the First Revise have been corrected, a Second Revise should be pulled, checked, initialed, and dated. Sometimes as many as five or six revises may be necessary before the form is correct.

Unit 36

How to Untie a Form

Grasp between the thumb and forefinger the end of the string left protruding when the form was tied up. Hold the form down with the left hand and pull out the loop. Unwind the string, counter clockwise, keeping the form against the edge of the galley.

Rewind the string around the spread fingers of the left hand. Stretch the looped string taut between three fingers of each hand with palms up. Give the right hand a half twist forming a figure eight. With the middle finger of the left hand catch one set of strands of the right loop, see Fig. 36-A, and pull them through the left loop as this loop slides down and forms a slip knot. (To untie knot, grasp sides of the loop and pull.)

Unit 37

How to Make Corrections

"Make all corrections in the stick" is a general rule. There are, however, a few corrections (those which do not affect the justification) that can be made in the galley without returning the line to the stick. Some of these are: changing of damaged characters, transpositions, and replacing of a character with another of exactly the same width.

An "n" is to replace a "u" according to the proof shown in Figure 37-A. As these two characters appear to be about the same width, an "n" and "u" from the case should be placed side by side on the bottom of the galley and checked by the method shown in Figures 41-H and 41-K.

When it has been determined that they are the same width:

1. Remove the string from the form and push the type against the head of the galley.

2. Place your forefingers against the ends of the line to be corrected. Put them down as low as possible. Exert an even pressure and lift slowly the entire line until it is about half exposed. (See Figure 37-A.)

3. Push the line against the edge of the galley and hold it there. Remove the left hand from the end of the line.

4. Take hold of the "u" with the left thumb and forefinger. (See Figure 37-B.) Release the pressure of your right hand and hold the "u" as the line goes down in place.

5. Lift out the "u" and put it in the case.

6. Separate the "a" and "d" by tilting the "d" to the right about a pica, using a bottom edge of the "n" held at an angle in the right hand.

7. At the same time, exert pressure on the bottom of the form by pushing with the left hand. This will hold the "d" in the tilted position.

8. Insert the "n" and put the line on its feet.

Difficulty is sometimes encountered in inserting the new character when the letter being changed is at the end of the word, the space being too short to be pushed over. This difficulty can be overcome by first inserting the new character and then lifting the line and removing the incorrect one.

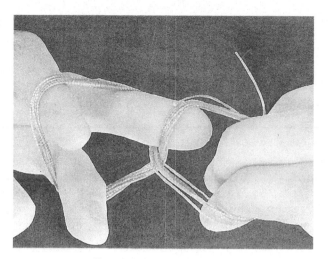

Fig. 36-A. How to Tie String

Fig. 37-A. To Lift a Line — Push In on Both Ends and Raise Carefully

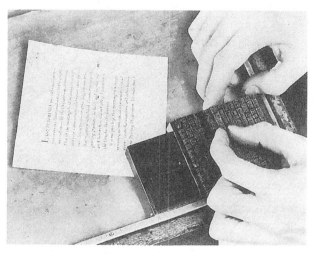

Fig. 37-B. Hold Character to be Removed and Release Line

Fig. 38-A. Make Corrections in Order — Top to Bottom

Fig. 38-B. Open Form by Pushing Gently with the Thumbs

Fig. 38-C. Always Place a Slug at Open End of a Type Group

Unit 38

How to Make Corrections Affecting Justification

Corrections which affect the justification of a line must be made by replacing the line in the stick, making the correction, re-justifying the line, and then replacing the line in the form. The line must be returned to the stick to make such corrections as replacing a character with another character which is not exactly the same width and for adding or deleting a character or space.

The same stick used in setting the job should be used when making corrections. The corrected lines will then be the same length as those in the form. A sliding knee stick can be substituted if the stick originally used is not available. When a sliding knee stick is used to make corrections, the measure should be set by placing in the stick a line from the form and setting the knee up against it.

1. Place the galley and form in proper position on the bank, as shown in Figure 38-A. Place the marked proof near the galley.

2. Untie the form and save the string. The string shown in Figure 38-A has been carelessly looped and is likely to become tangled.

Figure 36-A shows a method of winding that permits saving the string for future use.

3. Make corrections in the order that they appear on the proof, working from the top to the bottom. Find the first correction marked. The first line to be corrected on the proof, shown in Figure 38-A, requires deletion of the "u" and changing of the "ff" to the "ff" ligature. Both of these corrections affect the justification of the line and the line will have to be returned to the stick for correction and re-justification.

4. Figure 38-B shows how to prepare the line for removal to the stick. Place the thumbs and first fingers against the ends of the line. Exert a firm pressure and push the column of type down the galley a pica or two. Put two slugs above the line.

5. Tip the line back and put a slug below it. Push the line to be corrected against the top group of type and insert a slug above the top line of the lower type group. (See Figure 38-C.)

Spread the two groups apart by pushing the lower group down the galley about ten picas.

6. Always keep a slug at the open end of a type group. Then, if a line falls over, it is an easy matter to stand it up again.

7. Set your stick at the proper measure and rest it firmly against the edge of the galley, or the edge of the bank.

8. Take hold of the line to be corrected by grasping it between the thumb and forefinger of the right hand with the second finger pushing in on the end of the line. In the same way, grasp the other end of the line and then slide it out to the open section of the galley, as shown in Figure 38-D.

9. The line may be lifted for carrying over the edge of the galley by squeezing firmly with the thumbs and forefingers and pushing in on the ends as you quickly lift and turn it to the position shown in Figure 38-E.

Avoid lifting type whenever possible. Often there is room at the bottom edge of the galley for the stick, making it possible to slide the line along the bottom of the galley instead of lifting it.

10. Place the line in the stick by quickly turning it feet down against the bank immediately in front of the stick, and then "walking" it into place at the head with a gentle backward and forward motion. (See Figure 38-F.) Remove an end character if difficulty is encountered in getting the line back in place, but do not unclamp the knee.

11. Pick up the stick and remove the slug from below the line. Make the correction and carefully re-justify the line. Replace the slug and remove the line from the stick to its former place on the galley, using the "dumping" method explained in Unit 20.

12. Slide the lower group of type up against the top section. Remove the extra slugs by putting your first finger against the slug end at the open side and pushing up and to the left until you can grasp and remove the slug with the other hand. Slide the form together, to take up the space the slugs occupied. Always keep the top of the form tight against the head of the galley.

13. Find the next correction on the proof and proceed as before. Continue until all corrections are made — then pull a revised proof.

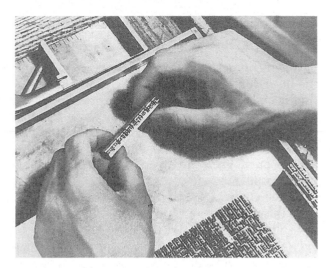

Fig. 38-D. Slide Line to Open Part of Galley Before Lifting

Fig. 38-E. Squeeze Line Firmly — Then Lift and Turn Line Quickly

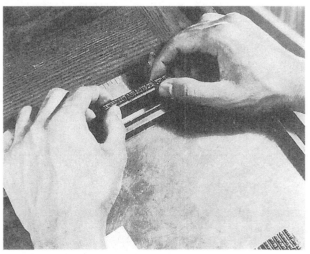

Fig. 38-F. "Walk" Line into Stick

Unit 39

How to Over-Run Type

When composed type must be reset to permit the insertion or elimination of words, the operation is called *over-running* or *re-running*.

1. Place the type in the galley with the foot of the composed matter at the head of the galley. This will place the beginning of the matter at the open end and open side of the galley. (Figure 39-A.)

2. Set your stick at the proper measure.

3. Insert slugs and spread the type.

4. Transfer to the stick from the line to be over-run as many characters as you can pick up easily. Continue along the line until you

Fig. 39-A. Type to be Re-run has Foot at Head of Galley

Fig. 39-B. Partial Lines Will Remain Upright Until Needed

reach the point at which the correction is to be made. In Figure 39-A, the entire line has been lifted to the stick, preparatory to removing the word "some" from the line.

5. Make the correction and then take from the galley enough type to finish the line. (Figure 39-B.)

6. Justify the line and continue by setting from the galley to the stick.

Note that by placing the form in the galley with the head towards the foot of the galley, when all of the line is not transferred to the stick, the part standing in the galley will remain upright. (Figure 39-B.)

When an effort is made to re-run matter with the type on the galley in the usual manner, the slant of the bank will cause the type to fall over as soon as any front characters in the line are removed.

Unit 40

How to Recognize Type by Its Feet

The machine upon which the type is cast determines the formation of the feet. Foundry type usually has a groove, but the groove is not always in exactly the same place.

Figure 40-A, left, shows a piece of newly cast foundry type with the wedge at the bottom; center, the wedge has been broken off, leaving an uneven bottom; right, the uneven broken portion has been planed off, leaving the groove and feet on the foundry type.

European type made on the Didot point system is higher-to-paper than American type, and the feet must be milled off to bring the height down to the American standard of .918 of an inch. In Figure 40-B, the center piece of type is from a European foundry and has a milled bottom in place of feet. The one on the right is American foundry type, and the left piece is Monotype. Notice the appearance of the bottom of the Monotype character. It has no feet — the bottom is flat as cast.

The M at the left in Figure 40-C is from a Caslon *Titling* (all capitals) font cast by an English foundry. It shows one method of cutting down the weight of large sizes of type — by leaving a hollow arch in the body. The feet are quite distinctive, as there are two pairs. The smaller sizes of English foundry type have feet similar to those on American type.

The M at the right in Figure 40-C was cast on the Monotype giant caster, a machine which makes type in sizes up to and including 72 point. This M has the flat foot of Monotype cast type, but like other products of the cored mold giant caster has two hollow areas in the body which greatly reduce the weight.

The M in the center in Figure 40-C is from a French foundry, is cast on the Didot point system, and has the French characteristic of having the nick on the back side.

Unit 41

How to Check Type for Distribution

The returning of type from composed matter to the proper boxes in the case is called *distribution*. The form to be distributed should be placed in the galley with the top of the form to the head of the galley, and the galley in working position on the bank. The form should be clean, but if ink has been left on the face, the type must be cleaned thoroughly before it is distributed.

Locate the proper case in which you are to distribute the type. Do not depend on memory, but use a five-way check on two pieces of type to determine the correct case. Remove the string from the form. Take from your type on the galley a capital H or some other wide letter. From the case which you think is the correct one, pick a cap letter the same as the one from your form. Place the two together and determine:

(1) Is the size the same?
(2) Is the face the same?
(3) Are the nicks the same?
(4) Are the feet the same?
(5) Are the characters the same width?

Replace the cap character in the case and the other character in the form. Now take a lower-case letter from the form and make the same five tests with a similar character from the case. The second check with a lower case letter lessens the chance of error due to picking up a wrong font letter for the first check. Any one of the checks is not enough, but if two pieces of type check on all five points, it is fairly certain you have the right case.

Fig. 40-A. Foundry Type with Jet, with Jet Broken Off, and with Ragged Edge Planed

Fig. 40-B. Feet of Monotype, Foreign Foundry (Planed), and A. T. F. Foundry Type

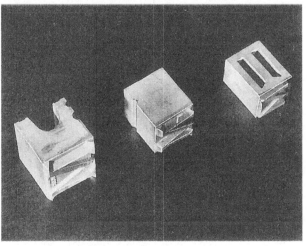

Fig. 40-C. English Foundry Type, French Foundry Type, and Monotype-Cored Mold Type

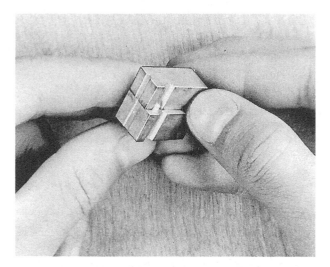

Fig. 41-A. Check 1 — Point Sizes Are Not the Same

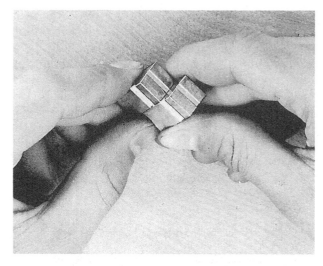

Fig. 41-D. Check 1 — Point Sizes Match

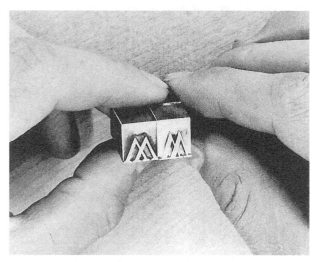

Fig. 41B. Check 2 — Faces Are Not the Same

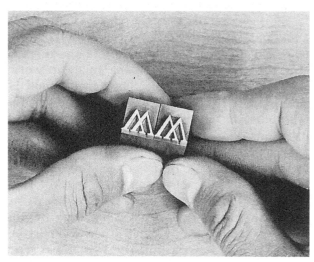

Fig. 41-E. Check 2 — Face Is the Same

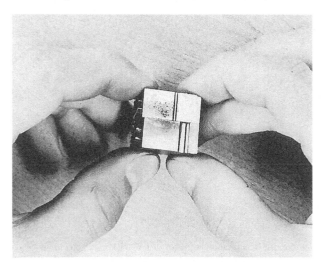

Fig. 41-C. Check 3 — Nicks Are Not the Same

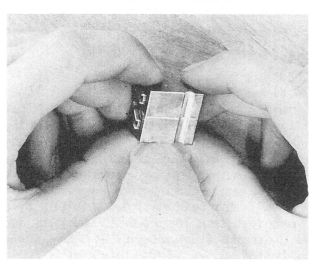

Fig. 41-F. Check 3 — Nicks Match

1. Checking size is easy. (See Figures 41-A and 41-D.) Only the very careless person makes a mistake on this check.

2. Checking the face is difficult, however. The faces of many types closely resemble each other, and we must depend on other checks to make sure the types are the same. In Figure 41-B, the character held in the right hand, a Bodoni "W" from the case, does not check with the "W" taken from a form. The Cloister "W" in Figure 41-E matches.

3. In making the third check, it may be found that the nicks are the same and yet the type face is very different. Many types cast on the Monotype machine have the same kind of nick, regardless of the face. Likewise, many different faces of foundry type have the same nick. Figure 41-C shows two nicks which do not match. The narrow nick is on a Monotype character while the wider one is on a piece of foundry type. Foundry nicks are not always wider.

4. Checking the feet sometimes shows up differences in the type. (Read Unit 40.) Figure 41-G shows a Monotype character in the left hand with a foundry character at the right.

5. The test for width must be made even more carefully than the other tests, as the difference in width is sometimes very slight. To make this check, place the two pieces of type on a flat surface and feel for differences in width, as shown in Figures 41-H and 41-J.

Always check at least two characters.

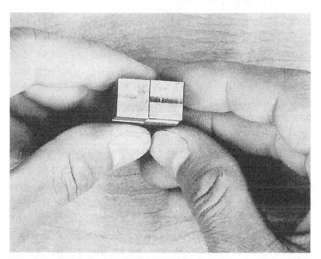

Fig. 41-G. Check 4 — Feet Differ — One Is Monotype, One Foundry

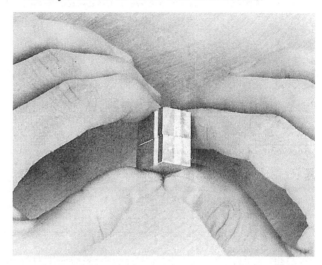

Fig. 41-I. Check 4 — Feet Match, Both are Foundry Type

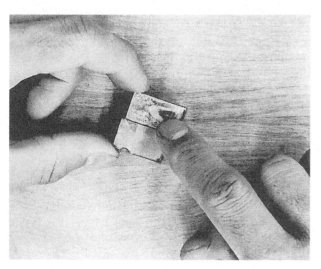

Fig. 41-H. Check 5 — Width is Slightly Different

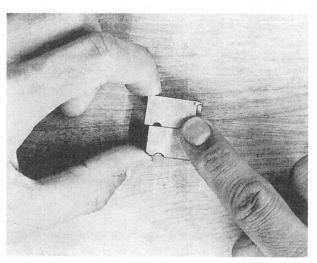

Fig. 41-J. Check 5 — Width Is the Same

Fig. 42-A. Quickly Lift and Turn Lines with Face Toward You

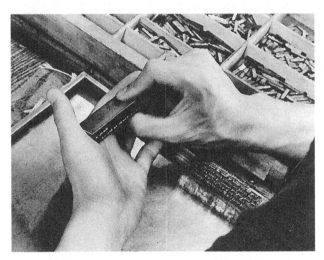

Fig. 42-B. Hold Horizontally with Right Hand — Place Against Left Thumb

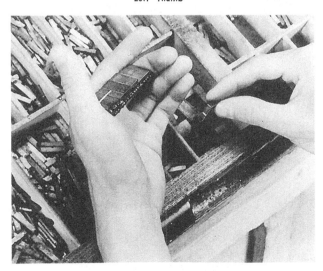

Fig. 42-C. Note Nick is Up — Distribute Quads in the Case

Unit 42

How to Distribute Type

1. After the proper case has been located and the five-way check made of two characters, take two slugs of the same measure as the composed type and place one above and one below the last line of the type group. It is best to handle one, or two, lines at a time when you are learning to distribute; later, you can pick up a "lift" of several lines, the number depending on the point size of the type.

2. Slide the last line away from the others in the form by putting the thumbs behind and the first fingers in front of each end of the line. The end of the line should remain against the edge of the galley.

3. Press firmly with the thumbs and first fingers and place the second fingers against the ends. The edge of the galley will prevent the second finger on the left hand from getting low enough to exert pressure on the type. With this finger gently push the line away from the galley edge until the finger can slide down to the bottom of the galley. You are now ready to lift the line.

4. Press firmly against the ends with the second fingers, and against the slugs with the thumbs and first fingers. Quickly lift and turn the line to a horizontal position so that the face is toward you. (Figure 42-A.)

5. Hold the line level with the right hand, and release your left hand.

6. Place the line between the thumb and second finger of the left hand. (Figure 42-B.) The first finger backs up the line and helps you steady it. It must be held level or the type will slide off. Remove the top slug.

7. If you have picked up the line correctly, the nicks will be showing. With the thumb and first finger of the right hand, lift the last word from the line. Read it, and spell it out as you place each of the characters, one at a time, in its proper box. Do not throw the letters into the boxes or drop them from a distance, as either of these methods of distribution damages the type. The proper method is to carry the types as close to their boxes as possible.

8. Figure 42-C shows 3-em quads from the end of the paragraph being returned to the case. The spaces are left on the galley.

When distributing, a slight rolling motion of the thumb and finger separates the types, and a very slight spreading of the thumb and finger permits dropping one type at a time. (Figure 42-D.) Note that the type is dropped but a very short distance to avoid damaging the face.

9. Continue distributing the other words in the line, working from the end of the line to the beginning.

10. Leave the spaces and return them to the bottom of the galley, as shown in Figure 42-E.

11. After all the type of one size has been distributed, the spaces can be quickly and accurately sorted as to thickness and placed in their proper boxes. Figure 42-F shows how to sort the spaces. Any difference in thickness can be quickly detected.

12. To determine the size of the spaces in each of the sorted groups, take three from the group you think are 3-em spaces. Place them side by side. The combined width of the three should match the body size of a fourth space turned at right angles to them. The sizes in the other groups can be determined in the same way. (Figure 42-G.)

13. Put away all leads and slugs. Sort miscellaneous lengths by placing them on a galley, parallel to and against the head. Lift one side of the galley and shake them down against one edge. Pick out the longest lengths and regroup them at the foot. Continue by picking out successively shorter lengths. Then separate leads and slugs and put them away.

Fig. 42-E. Put Spaces on Galley — Sort them Later

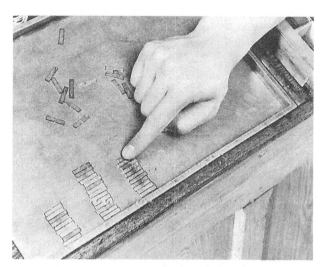

Fig. 42-F. Sort Spaces After Type is Distributed

Fig. 42-D. Pick up a Word at a Time — Drop Type Gently to Case

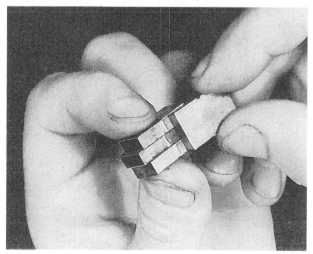

Fig. 42-G. Determine Size of Spaces by Matching as Above

Fig. 43-A. With Form Unlocked, Plane Gently with Midget Planer

Fig. 43-B. Dampen Proof Paper with a Wet Sponge or Rag

Fig. 43-C. Strike Proof Planer Firmly with Handle of Mallet

Unit 43

How to Take a Planer Proof

It is sometimes necessary to take a proof of a form which is too large to go on the proof press, or of a form locked in a chase. A felt-covered planer, called a *proof planer*, is used. (Figure 43-B.) Note that it is lying with the felt side up so as not to pick up dust or metal particles from the *imposing table*. Never use the proof planer to plane down a form — use it only for beating the proof.

A better result is usually obtained if the stone proof is pulled on dampened paper. The dampened sheet will lie snugly against the form and will take the ink better than a dry sheet.

It is difficult to keep a dry sheet from moving during the course of pulling the proof. Special *dry proofing paper* should be used for pulling dry proofs. The glazed side should contact the form.

To take a wet paper proof of a form locked in a chase:

1. Unlock quoins and push them together snugly with your fingers.

2. Plane the form with a midget planer, tapping the planer lightly with a quoin key, as shown in Figure 43-A. Run your hand over the surface of the form to make sure no type is protruding.

3. Ink the form.

4. With a wet sponge or wet rag, dampen one side of the sheet upon which you are to pull the proof. (Figure 43-B.) The sheet, probably, will absorb the water unevenly. When the last wet spot disappears from the surface (the wet spots will shine while the other parts of the sheet will have a dull appearance), pull the proof immediately on the side which was not dampened.

5. Hold the sheet by two opposite corners and let the center sag toward the form until it contacts it. Then lower the rest of the sheet down on to the form, being careful not to move the paper, or ink slurs will result.

6. Place the felt side of the planer against the sheet approximately in the center of a page. With your left hand, hold the planer firmly in position and strike it a sharp blow (not too hard) with the handle of a mallet or hammer held in the right hand, as shown in Figure

43-C. One blow is enough — a second blow usually causes the planer to move, slurring the proof.

7. With a slightly rolling motion (Figure 43-D), lift the planer with the left hand and set it down on an adjoining area of the form, letting it overlap slightly the section you have just beaten. Strike the planer again with the mallet handle, and then move the planer to another part of the form. (Figure 43-E.)

8. Continue until you have covered the entire form. When you reach the edges, allow the planer to overlap the edge only about an inch. Otherwise, it will tip when struck with the mallet and your proof will be spoiled.

9. Remove the sheet from the form by lifting one end or a corner (Figure 43-F), and stripping it off with a slow, steady pull.

10. If the resulting proof is slurred or double-printed, it shows that you have moved the paper after contacting it with the form. This may have happened when you placed the planer on the form, when it was struck with the mallet, or when the planer was lifted to be moved.

11. After the proof is taken, relock the form before you leave the stone. Otherwise, someone may attempt to lift the chase, thinking it is locked, and a pied form will result.

Heavy papers and hard-finish papers often become quite wavy when dampened. The wavy sheet will not lie flat against the form, but will spring up and down as the proof is taken, causing a slurring print. To overcome this, immerse the entire sheet in water for about a minute. Remove the wet sheet, place it between two dry sheets, then quickly and gently rub your hand over the top sheet until it contacts all parts of the wet sheet. Remove the dampened sheet and blow gently on any spots where the water glistens on the surface. Place the sheet on the form as soon as the wet spots disappear and pull the proof immediately. A sheet which is either too wet or too dry will not take the ink properly.

A beaten proof seldom approaches the quality of a proof taken on a proof press but it should be perfectly legible. When the dampened sheet dries, it is likely to be curled and wavy, and probably will have shrunk considerably — sometimes as much as a quarter inch — and therefore cannot be used to check register.

Fig. 43-D. Lift Planer with Rolling Motion — Avoid Moving Paper

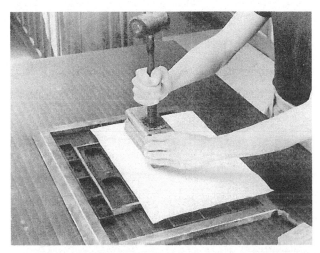

Fig. 43-E. Let Planer Overlap Slightly Area Just Proofed

Fig. 43-F. Strip Proof from Form, Being Careful to Avoid Slurring

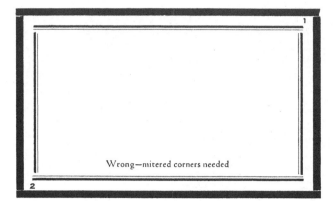

Fig. 44-A. Butted Corners Are Seldom Satisfactory

Fig. 44-B. Rouse Slug and Rule Cutter Set at 26 Picas

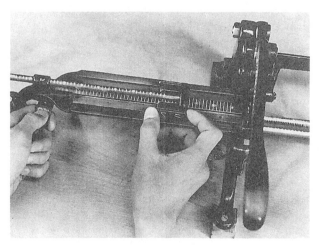

Fig. 44-C. Push Down Winged Thumb Piece to Change Left Guide

Unit 44

How to Use the Slug Cutter

The lead and rule (slug) cutter, shown in Figure 44-B, is widely used for shearing leads, slugs, strip rules, and strip cardboards. Thin brass strip material may also be sheared on this machine.

Corner No. 1 in the outer rule panel of Figure 44-A shows the rough cut which usually results when material is sheared on the cutter. Corner No. 2 of the same panel has had the ends of the rules smoothed on the mitering machine after the rule was "rough cut" on the lead and rule cutter. (Operation of the hand miterer is explained in Unit 46.)

Suppose we want to cut Monotype strip rule to make a contrast rule panel, 17 x 10 picas, as shown in No. 2 of Figure 44-A. As the corners must be mitered, we have to cut the rule 17½ x 10½ picas.

1. Figure 44-B shows the left hand gauge of the cutter set at 26 picas. The gradations are in picas but the round rod is notched at 6-point intervals, making it possible to set the gauge at half-pica measures. The gauge is released by pushing down on the thumb piece marked "Push Down."

2. Figure 44-C shows how to change the measure. Hold the thumb piece down with the left hand, and slide the gauge along until it is at the 17½-pica position (halfway between 17 and 18). Release the thumb piece and push gently against the guide to make sure the notch is engaged.

3. Move the right-hand gauge out of the way, as shown in Figure 44-D. Hold out the knurled nut (marked "Pull") with the left hand and slide out the gauge with the other hand. Turn the auxiliary holder "A" into position.

4. Place the strip rule against the gauge as shown in Figure 44-E. Note, the rule face is outward so that it will not be damaged by contact with the bed of the cutter. Either the front or rear bed can be used, but the front one is more convenient.

5. Hold the rule against the gauge and shear it by pushing down the handle with the right hand. (Figure 44-F.)

6. Cut a second piece of rule with the gauge set at 17½. Then, reset the gauge at 10½ and

cut the other two pieces needed for the panel. Replace the left-over rule strip in its proper place and you will then be ready to miter the four pieces of rule.

The right-hand gauge is generally used when several pieces are to be cut the same measure. The left-hand gauge may be removed by moving it all the way to the right and lifting it out. The strip material may then be fed against the right-hand guide by pushing the material over with the left hand, while the right hand stays in position on the cutter handle.

The right-hand gauge is also removable, but it should be removed only when necessary. Both gauges should be replaced before you leave the cutter.

Lengths up to 100 picas can be cut on the slug cutter by removing the left-hand gauge and inserting it in the outside position. The scale for setting the cutter at measures above 55 picas will be found on the round rod instead of on the bed plate.

Quantity cutting of leads, slugs, and slug machine composition is done in most composing rooms on composing room saws. At least one saw is found in the composition departments of all except the very small plants. Material cut on these machines is not only sawed, but is smooth-trimmed during the same operation, to pica gauges adjustable to half-point gradations. Stereotypes and wood-mounted electrotypes can also be sawed; and on many models, similar to the one below, rules and borders may be mitered. On the larger models, adjustable height of saw or table permits other operations.

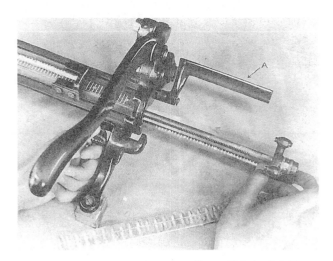

Fig. 44-D. Pull Out Knurled Nut to Change Right-hand Guide

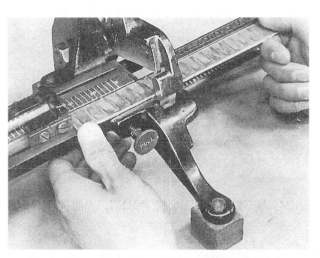

Fig. 44-E. Keep Face of Rule Away from Bed of Cutter

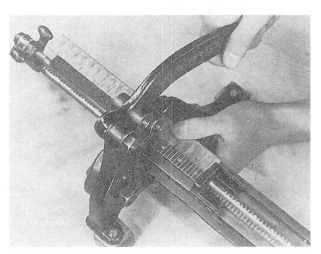

Fig. 44-F. Hold Rule in Place as You Push Down on Handle

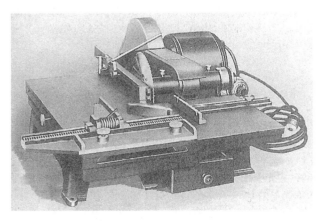

Miller Bench Model Saw Trimmer

Fig. 45-A. Micrometer Gauge Set at 14 Points
(1 Pica + 2 Points)

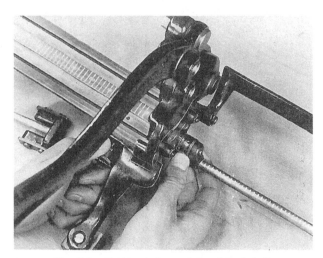

Fig. 45-B. Right-hand Gauge Being Set at 1 Pica

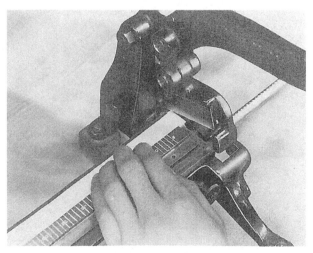

Fig. 45-C. Thin Material is more Easily Cut on Back Bed

Unit 45

How to Use the Micrometer Gauge on Cutter

The micrometer point adjustment on the right-hand gauge must be set correctly when that gauge is used. The micrometer feature is very useful, as it permits cutting card and paper strips, as well as leads, to point sizes.

To cut 12-point cardboard spaces:

1. Remove the left-hand gauge by sliding it to the right and lifting it out when the rod is free of its retainer.

2. Pull out on knurled nut marked "Pull," and move the right-hand gauge to the "1" mark on the rod. Figure 45-A shows the gauge at "1" pica on the rod, but the micrometer is at 2 points. The gauge is therefore at 1 pica plus 2 points, or 14 points.

3. Figure 45-B shows the correct setting for cutting 12 points. The micrometer is at "0" while the other gauge is at "1." The setting of both the micrometer and the rod should be checked. It is possible to start the micrometer on the wrong thread, causing it to be 3 points off on its reading.

4. Figure 45-C shows the cardboard strip being fed against the guide. The handle should be operated with the right hand. Note the back part of the cutter is used for thin material.

5. Check for size the first piece cut by matching it with a 12-point space.

6. Insert a small sheet of paper under the cutter to catch the card spaces as they fall. This aids in picking up the spaces.

The cutter shown in the illustrations is mounted on blocks of wood (spools are sometimes used) to give more clearance between the cutter bed and the cabinet top.

Unit 46

How to Use the Hand-Mitering Machine

Hand mitering machines are manufactured by several different concerns. Basically most of the machines are similar and consist of three main parts — the *bed,* the *work holder,* and the *knife holder.* Figure 46-A shows the Rouse hand miterer, a model popular with many printers.

The numbers marked along the outer edge of the bed (Figure 46-A) show the position for the work holder when cutting designs of that number of sides. When cutting triangles or pentagons, the 3 or 5 setting will give the correct angle only if each of the designs has sides all of which are equal in length.

Notches in the outer edge of the bed of the machine are engaged by a spring projection on the work holder, thus keeping the holder at the exact angle desired.

Note in Figure 46-B the work holder is held against the bed by means of a bolt (see the nut just above "&" in the name) and a spring. One loop of the spring and the knurled nut holding it are visible under the bed — near the end of the left forefinger. Some mitering machines have a thumb screw, instead of the spring, for securing the holder to the bed. Examine the mitering machine in your shop to find out which device is used on it.

To change position of the work holder on a spring-equipped machine, disengage the projection from the notch in the bed by pulling out on the little rod, using the left forefinger, as shown in Figure 46-B. Hold the rod out and move the holder with the right hand until the position wanted is reached. Release the rod and test — by trying to move the holder with the right hand — to see that the projection has engaged the notch.

Before trying to move the holder on a machine equipped with a thumb screw, loosen the screw one full turn — but do not loosen it more than one turn or the holder may jump its track. After the holder is positioned, the thumb screw must be tightened with thumb and finger pressure. Never use a wrench on a thumb screw.

A great many of the rule designs we see have perfectly joined corners, but most of them have been printed from electrotypes. The electrotyper, while making his wax mold, has joined the corners for the printer.

A trick used by some compositors to get better rule joints is to insert a narrow strip of cardboard under the work holder near the knife. (Figure 46-C.) On spring-equipped miterers, the work holder can be lifted enough to insert the cardboard by pushing down on the parts extending past the curved edge of the bed. When the rule is placed face up on the

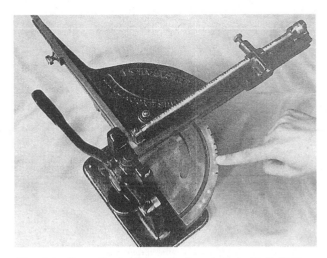

Fig. 46-A. Rouse Hand Miterer; Numbers Indicate Work Holder Position

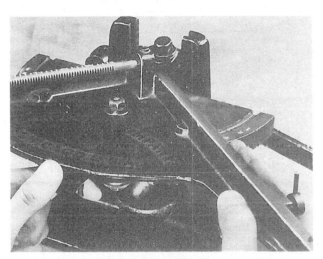

Fig. 46-B. Changing Work Holder Position on a Spring Equipped Machine

Fig. 46-C. Cardboard Strip Causes Rule Face to Be Cut Slightly Longer — Gives Better Joints

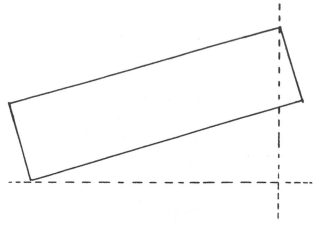

Fig. 46-D. Miterer Takes More From Bottom When Rule
Is Raised with Cardboard

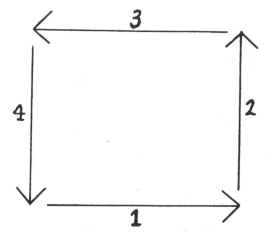

Fig. 47-A. The Four Motions Used in Mitering

Fig. 47-B. Set Sliding Gauge so that About Three Points Will Be
Mitered Off Rule

mitering machine, the cardboard will cause the bottom of the rule to be cut slightly shorter than the top. This is illustrated by the diagram in Figure 46-D. The slightly extra length on the face edge should give a better joint.

Present day printers try to avoid designs which make use of rule borders with joining corners. Even when the utmost care is used in mitering, lock-up, and make-ready, it is still very difficult to get perfect joints at the corners of the rule. Poorly joined corners detract from the appearance of any printing job, and if rules are used, the corners should be made to join.

Unit 47

How to Miter a Rectangle

To miter a rectangular contrast rule panel with an outside measure of 17 x 10 picas (the ticket shown under Unit 49 has such a border), proceed as follows:

1. Cut, on the lead and rule cutter, two pieces of strip rule, 17½ picas, and two pieces, 10½ picas, in length.

2. Loosen the thumb screw which fastens the work holder to the bed. Move the work holder, as shown in Figure 46-B, until each of its sides is in line with the figure 4 on the bed. Figure 47-B shows the work holder in the new position.

3. Insert a narrow cardboard under the end of the work holder, as shown in Figure 46-C. Tighten the thumb screw.

4. Place one of the 17½ pica pieces of rule against the side of the rule holder nearest you. The face of the rule should be up, with the hairline side nearest the knife. Set the gauge (Figure 47-B) so that about three points can be mitered off the end of the rule.

5. Figure 47-A diagrams the four motions used in mitering. The position at the finish of Motion No. 1 is shown in Figure 47-C. The knife holder is at the bottom and is being held against the right hand side of the slide by the pressure on the handle.

6. Figure 47-D shows the position at the finish of Motion No. 2. The knife holder has reached the top of its stroke. The holder is kept against the right hand side of the slide during the second motion so that the knife will clear the rule on the up stroke of the holder.

7. At the end of Motion No. 3, as shown in

Figure 47-E, the work holder is still at the top, but the face of the holder is now against the end of the rule. The knife is above the rule ready to start its cut.

8. Figure 47-F shows the knife making a shave during Motion No. 4. This motion should be made with a slow, steady stroke, all the while keeping the holder firmly against the end of the rule. The knife should shave about a half point at each stroke when correctly adjusted.

9. Continue mitering, using the 1, 2, 3, 4 motions until the knife no longer shaves because of contact of the knife holder against the left side of the slide.

10. Miter the second piece of 17½ pica rule, using the same gauge setting.

11. Figure 47-G shows the gauge on the other side of the rule holder being set to miter the other end of the two rules. The thumb screw has been loosened, the plunger depressed with the first finger, and the gauge moved to the 17-pica position. The micrometer gauge at the end of the graduated rod must be set at "0." (Figure 46-A.)

12. Lock the gauge with the thumb screw. Place one of the rules against the work holder with its mitered end against the gauge. Hold it in position, as shown in Figure 47-H, and miter the other end, using the 1, 2, 3, 4 motions. Miter the other rule.

13. Reset the gauge and miter the two shorter rules to 10 picas.

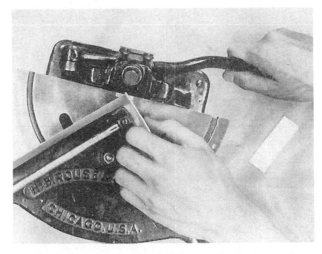

Fig. 47-C. Position at End of Motion 1 — Handle Down and to the Right

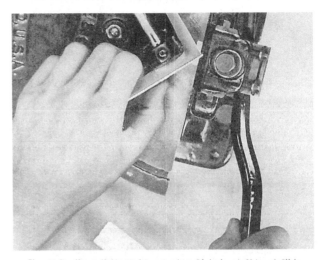

Fig. 47-D. Keep Knife Holder Against Right-hand Side of Slide During Motion 2

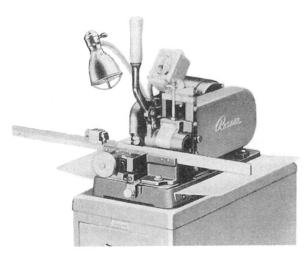

Rouse Vertical Miterer

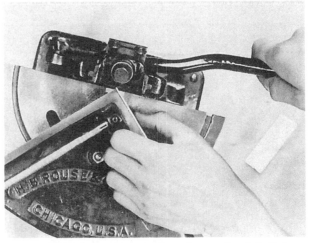

Fig. 47-E. Motion 3 Brings Knife Holder Against Rule End with Knife Above Rule

Fig. 47-F. Knife Makes its Shave During Motion 4

Fig. 47-G. Setting the Gauge to 17 Picas Preparatory to Mitering
Second End of Rule

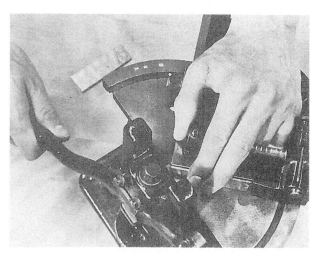

Fig. 47-H. Mitering the Second End of Rule

Unit 48

How to Miter Other Designs

To miter regular polygons of 5, 6, 8, 10 or 12 equal sides, set the near side of the rule holder at the number which corresponds to the number of sides in the figure to be mitered. Cut the rules on the slug cutter, making them one-half pica longer than the side. Place the strip of cardboard in position; set the gauge so that about three points will be mitered off the end of the rule and miter one end of each of the rules, making sure that the face is up and the shoulder of the rule is turned the proper way. Move the rule holder over to the far edge so that the number showing is the same as the one used in mitering the first end of the rule. Set the gauge at the exact measure wanted. See that the cardboard is in position; and, then, miter the remaining end of each of the rules. For example:

To miter a regular pentagon (five-sided figure with all sides equal), place the rule holder so that the near edge leaves the figure 5 in view. This will give a 54° angle. Miter one end of each of the five rules, then move the holder into position so that the figure 5 on the far side of the bed is left showing. Miter the other ends of the five rules. This angle will also be 54°. When the rules are placed into position, the two 54° angles will give the 108° angle of the pentagon.

The following table shows the rule holder setting for the most common designs:

Type of Polygon	Work Holder Setting	Resulting Angle
	0 (unmarked)	15°
	1	18°
	2	22½°
Triangle (equilateral)	3	30°
	3½	36°
Square or rectangle	4	45°
Pentagon	5	54°
Hexagon	6	60°
Octagon	8	67½°
Decagon	10	72°
Duodecagon	12	75°

The positions 0, 1, 2, and 3½ are useful in cutting such figures as five-pointed stars, diamonds, and triangles of unequal sides.

Citmas Club Dinner

EIGHTY-FIVE CENTS

MONDAY EVENING : MAY SECOND

FIVE-THIRTY : COMMONS ANNEX

Unit 49

How to Set a Job With a Border

An order for a quantity of printed matter is usually called a *job*. To set a job with a border, such as the ticket shown here:

1. Determine the outside measure of the border. Get the proper border and bring it to your bank. The rules shown in Figure 49-A are Monotype strip material and were cut and mitered as explained in Units 44 and 47.

2. Compose the type in narrowest measure possible and place it on the galley.

3. Place the left side and the top of the border in position, as shown in Figure 49-A. Place a six-point slug next to the side border. Always try to have at least one slug between the border and the ends of the type lines. The slug is absolutely necessary for borders made up of units or for strip borders with ribs, such as Linotype, Intertype, and Ludlow slugs.

4. Place the type in position and space it out as shown in Figure 49-B. Do not place the bottom and right hand border in position until the type has been leaded out.

5. Figure 49-C shows the type spaced out and with the bottom border in position. A slug has been inserted along the right side. The final operation before tying up the form is the placing of the right hand border.

6. Borders made up of units should have a six-point slug placed around each side to keep the units in position when the form is tied up.

In the form shown, the type measure is 15, the 6-point slug and 6-point border along each side add 2 picas, making the outside width of the border 17 picas.

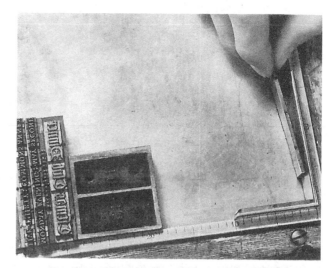

Fig. 49-A. Place Left Side and Top Rules in Position

Fig. 49-B. Place Type in Position and Space it Out

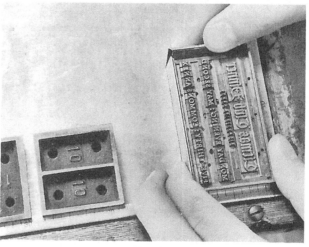

Fig. 49-C. Placing of Bottom and Right-Side Rules
Completes Make-up

Fig. 50-A. Slide the Form from the Galley to the Stone
— Avoid Lifting Type

Fig. 50-B. Place Furniture in Position on Two Sides
of the Lock-up

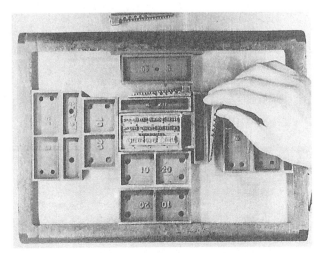

Fig. 50-C. The Inside Quoins Should Point Toward the Solid Sides

Unit 50

How to Position a Form for Lock-Up

For many years, the preparation of type forms for the press was carried out on imposing tables having a flat, smooth stone surface. Imposing tables are still called *stones* although the working surface now is usually metal, instead of the sandstone formerly used. Likewise, imposition and lock-up are called *stonework,* and *stoneman* is the name given to the man performing these operations.

Lock-up is the operation of fastening the type in a cast iron (or steel) chase so that the chase and its type form may be inserted in the press for printing.

Four factors must be considered and a decision made as to which ones are to influence the positioning of a form in the chase for lock-up:

(a) Ease of feeding the paper stock into the press. Whenever possible, the sheet should fall to the left of, and above center, on the platen, with the long dimension of the sheet parallel to the long dimension of the platen.

(b) Inspection of the printed piece by the press feeder, without interruption of his feeding operation. The sheet should come from the press in proper position for reading. The feeder can then watch for "pull-outs," poor inking, and other common troubles.

(c) Maintaining register. The head of the form should fall at a guide edge on the press — at either the bottom or left side on hand-fed presses. The bottom guide edge, having two gauges, is preferred for the head, as the form then always will be parallel with the top edge of the sheet.

When the head is positioned at the side guide, any variation in the angle between the two guide edges of the paper (caused by out-of-square cutting, etc.) will keep the form from printing parallel with the head of the sheet.

(d) Printing of heavy forms. Large heavy forms should fall slightly below center on the platen, as the impressional strength of the press is greatest at that point.

After the foregoing factors have been considered, proceed with the lock-up as follows:

1. See that the surface of the imposing table is clean.

2. Slide the type form from the galley to the

stone. (Figure 50-A.) It is best to remove a large form from the galley to the stone by holding the form steady and quickly pulling the galley from under it.

3. With the head of the form toward you, place the chase around the form. Do not remove the string. A form of small or medium size should be placed a little above center, vertically, and slightly left of center, sidewise.

4. Fill in the space between the head of the form and the edge of the chase with *furniture* (wood or metal blocks) slightly wider than the form (see Figure 50-B). Next, fill in the area from the left side of the form to the chase, allowing the furniture to overlap, slightly, that which has been put in on the other side.

5. Each of the remaining sides of the form should have placed against it a four- or five-pica piece of furniture, again using lengths that are only slightly longer than the width and depth of the form. Leave about a four-pica space at each side for the *quoins* and fill in the remaining space with furniture. (See Unit 53.)

6. Note in Figure 50-C that an extra piece of furniture, 3 x 10 picas in size, has been put in at the right side of the form. This is permissible when the width or length of the form happens to be such that a narrow, standard length will square up the lock-up. Usually, however, the "chaser" method of furniture positioning, explained in Unit 53, is preferred.

7. Place the inside quoins (ones next to the form) in position — pointed toward the solid sides of the lock-up. (See Figure 50-C.) The solid sides are the two sides in which quoins are not used with the furniture.

8. Put the outside quoins in place, and remove the string from the form. Insert six-point *reglets* between the sides of each pair of quoins and the furniture adjacent to them, as shown in Figure 50-D. When wood furniture is being used, the inexpensive reglets protect the more expensive larger pieces from damage by the quoins. The reglets aid in preventing slippage of the quoins in an all-metal lock-up.

Figure 50-E shows cards being inserted in the form to guard against slippage of metal furniture due to lack of friction.

Figure 50-F shows the quoins being tightened with the fingers, preparatory to planing. Unit 51 explains planing and locking.

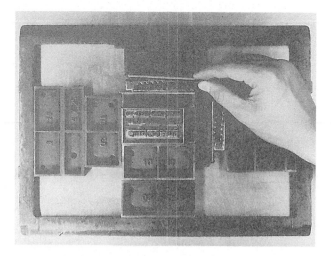
Fig. 50-D. Put a Reglet on Each Side of Each Pair of Quoins

Fig. 50-E. Insert Cards Between the Pieces of Metal Furniture to Prevent Slippage

Fig. 50-F. Do Not Plane a Locked Form. Push the Quoins Together with your Fingers and then Use the Planer

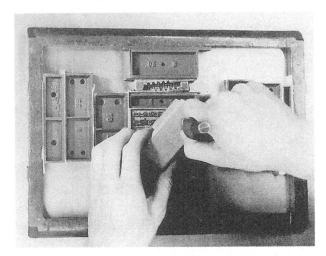

Fig. 51-A. Plane the Form Lightly, Using a Midget Planer and the Quoin Key

Fig. 51-B. Tighten Slightly Each Set of Quoins and then Sound for Spring. Lock Just Tight Enough to Lift

Fig. 51-C. Raise the Chase Only High Enough to Get the Quoin Key Under It — Then Test for Lift

Unit 51

How to Plane and Lock a Form

1. After the form has been positioned in the chase with the furniture and quoins in place, run your hand over its surface to see that all the type is down in position.

2. Plane the unlocked form lightly, using the quoin key for tapping the midget planer. (Figure 51-A.) Do not use a mallet — the mallet and the large planer have no place in job press lock-up. They should be reserved for the plant which considers the condition of the face of the type of secondary importance.

3. Tighten the quoins slightly with the quoin key, as shown in Figure 51-B, and again plane the form. Listen to the sound given off when the form is planed. In this way you can determine whether or not the type is remaining down against the imposing table surface. A hollow sound indicates that the form has sprung. The spring must be eliminated before the form is sent to press. See Unit 54. A proper make-ready is impossible with a form that does not lie flat against the bed of the press.

4. Lock the form a little tighter and sound it again. Continue until the form is locked just tight enough to lift. Avoid locking too tight — you may spring, or even break, the chase.

5. Test it for lift by raising the chase just high enough to slide the quoin key under the edge of the chase. (Figure 51-C.) Any parts loose enough to fall of their own weight will still remain in the form, providing the chase has not been lifted too high.

6. Press down on the furniture to see that it is secure. Then, press down on the form surface with the fingers to find any loose type. (Figure 51-C.) Poor justification, improper leading out, and binds due to long leads and slugs, or improperly placed furniture, may be responsible for any loose parts. The locking tightly of one set of quoins before the other set is tightened slightly may also prevent the type from lifting.

7. Pull the quoin key from under the chase. The parts of the form which went down under a slight pressure, as well as the parts which were loose, will come back into position.

8. Unlock the form, correct the faults, and then plane and relock properly.

Unit 52

How to Lock Up a Rule Border

Special care must be taken in locking up a form with a rule border, so that the corners will join perfectly.

1. The form should be placed in a chase in the usual manner, and the quoins tightened and the type tested for lift.

2. Loosen the quoins and bring them together lightly with the fingers.

3. Push together the two rules at the solid corner of the lock-up, as shown in Figure 52-A.

4. Then join the rules at the top right-hand corner of the border. (Figure 52-B.)

5. Figure 52-C shows the next step — joining of the lower left hand corner of the border.

6. Next, tighten the quoins lightly and plane the form. Then, tighten the quoins so that the form will lift.

When three corners of the form are put into position as explained, the fourth corner usually will join when the form is locked, providing the lines have been properly justified and the rules mitered to the correct length. After the form has been planed and locked, examine the corner joints. They should fit tightly — if they do not, the form should be re-justified, or the rules recut so that the joint will be perfect.

The lower left corner, shown in Figure 52-D, is satisfactorily joined, but the upper left corner shows a gap at the joint.

An electrotyper's finishing rubber can be used to advantage in joining mitered corners. Figure 52-D shows the lower right-hand corner being rubbed. Note in this figure that the upper right-hand corner has already been rubbed and joins perfectly. When using the finishing rubber, it should be held flat against the form and rubbed gently over the surface of the rule near the corner. Only a few rotary strokes are necessary. The form will be worn away rapidly if the rubbing is continued, as the finishing rubber is an abrasive. Light rubbing of the corners tends to level off the two pieces of rule and fill in the slight crevice at the joints.

It would be useless to rub the upper left corner, shown in Figure 52-D, as this corner is not joined. This form should have been re-locked and all corners made to meet satisfactorily before starting to rub the corners.

Fig. 52-A. Rule Corners Are Difficult to Join — Start by Joining the Two Rules at the Solid Corner

Fig. 52-B. Hold the Top Rule in Position and Join the Right Upper Corner of the Border

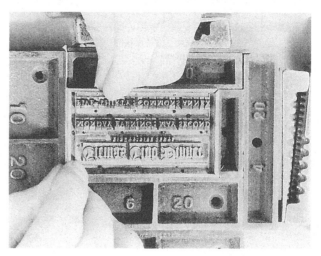

Fig. 52-C. Third Step is to Join the Bottom Rule with the Left-hand Piece

Fig. 52-D. Rubbing Corners with an Electrotyper's Finishing Rubber Often Improves the Joint

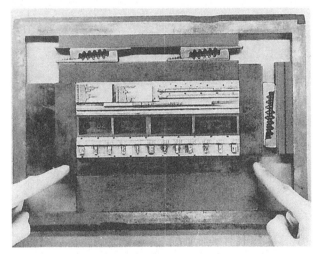

Fig. 53-A. The "Chaser" Method of Positioning the Furniture is Less Likely to Produce Binds

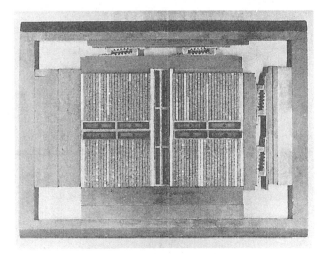

Fig. 53-B. The "Squared-up" Lock-up is Satisfactory Provided Binds are Guarded Against

Unit 53

How to Position the Furniture

The squared up method of lock-up, as applied to a small form, was explained in Unit 50. This method often results in "binds" due to the locking of furniture against furniture instead of properly putting the pressure against the form.

Most stonemen, therefore, prefer the "chaser" (overlapping) method of positioning the furniture, as with this method binds are seldom encountered. (Figure 53-A.) Note that each piece of furniture adjacent to the form is slightly longer than the form and overlaps the next successive piece of furniture. When pressure is applied to the quoins, the furniture is free to slip by the corners.

To guard against binds, put widths of furniture next to the form, which will leave a gap of about a pica between the end of one piece and the edge of the next piece. In Figure 53-A, the fingers are pointing at two such gaps.

Standard widths of furniture, either wood or metal, are usually 2, 3, 4, 5, 6, 8, and 10 picas. The job furniture case provides for lengths of 10, 15, 20, 25, 30, 40, 50, and 60 picas. Reglet — wooden furniture 6, 12, and 18 points in thickness — is available in lengths up to three feet.

Avoid using the pyramid lock-up, as well as the method of filling the entire chase with furniture, when locking a small form. Both are insecure and may allow the form to fall out while on press.

The furniture between the form and the quoins (preferably) should not be less than four picas nor more than six picas in width. This gives the shortest possible span and helps eliminate spring in the form.

Furniture used in other parts of the form should be the widest available. Do not use warped or twisted furniture at any time.

Use as many pairs of quoins as you have room for, but do not allow the ends to bind against adjacent quoins or furniture or they will likely work loose.

Figure 53-B shows four pages of linotype material locked with the squared up method. It would be almost impossible to lock up this form as shown without getting binds and spring. However, a few simple precautions, explained in Unit 54, would make it press-worthy.

Unit 54

How to Eliminate Spring in Forms

Because it springs up from the bed of the press after each impression, a springy type form results in slurs, work-ups, and wear on type and cuts. Make-ready on such forms is often worthless, as the constant up-and-down movement in the form frequently causes a spot which was high at the start of the run to become low. A low spot may start punching because the form has come up at that point.

Common causes of spring in a form are: too tight a lock-up, binds, excess pressure on certain areas because of inaccurate material or poor make-up, cuts out of square, and warped furniture.

If, in sounding for spring during lock-up, it is discovered that the type is not resting firmly on the imposing table, the form should be unlocked and the cause of the spring determined and corrected. Possible sources of binds should be removed.

Figure 53-B shows a form likely to have binds. The addition of a lead at the bottom of each page, and the insertion of a lead between the furniture and the side of the two top pages, as shown in Figure 54-A, gave enough squeeze allowance to eliminate binding of the lock-up furniture on the metal furniture separating the pages.

In Figure 54-B, a cardboard is being inserted to test for clearance between the metal furniture. If the card can be inserted with the form locked, it is obvious there is no bind.

One of the most practical methods known for the elimination of spring is the insertion of sinkers (¼ inch strips of light-weight cover paper) around the form. Figure 54-C shows a sinker being pushed down with a make-ready rule. The other sinkers are in position, ready to be inserted between the furniture and the form. They should be pushed all the way down, and care should be taken to see that the corners do not bunch or overlap.

The addition of the strips may cause the edges of the chase to spring up when the form is relocked. This is not a fault as long as the form stays down. The springing up of the chase will make sure the form is kept in contact with the bed when the chase is clamped in the press.

Fig. 54-A. Binding Can Often be Eliminated by Insertion of an Extra Lead for Squeeze

Fig. 54-B. Various Units of the Furniture Should Have at Least a Cardboard Clearance

Fig. 54-C. "Sinkers" Should Be Placed Around All Forms to Guard Against Spring

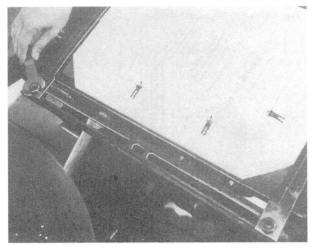

Fig. 56-A. Move the Grippers to the Outer Ends of the Gripper Bar and Fasten Them in that Position

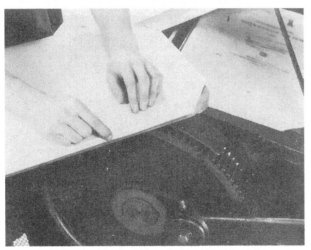

Fig. 56-B. Crease Each Sheet So that it Will Hug the Bottom Edge of the Platen

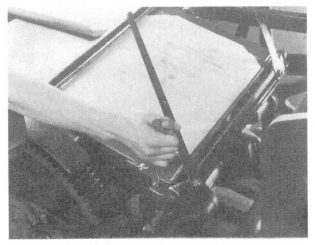

Fig. 56-C. Use a Bail Wrench, or a Screw Driver, to Pry Up the Tympan Bails

Unit 55

How to Avoid Accidents

The units which follow deal with the operation of the platen press, a machine — and all machines, no matter how well guarded with safety devices, are dangerous when operated by thoughtless or careless persons. When working at a press, unnecessary discussion, arguments, "horse-play," speeding up of the press, and reaching into the moving press to retrieve sheets, adjust the guides or grippers, to oil, ink up, etc., should all be avoided in the interest of safety. Follow carefully the precautions suggested in this and other units. Remember: **"Accident is more than just a word when it happens to you."**

Unit 56

How to Put On the Packing

The thickness of the packing used depends upon the size of the form to be printed and the thickness of the stock upon which you are to print. Play safe and start with a thin packing. Too thick a packing will smash the form.

Most pressmen consider as proper packing for an average platen press form: a pressboard, four sheets of 50 pound super, and an oiled manila tympan top (draw) sheet. All sheets are fastened under the bottom bale. The make-ready spot sheets are attached to the supers. The impression screws on the press must be set for such a packing, and sheets may be added for heavier forms. For lighter forms the pressboard may be replaced with one or more oiled tympan sheets.

Such a packing is known as a *hard packing* and is preferred by most good pressmen, as it gives a clean sharp print with minimum wear on the form.

The steps in *dressing the platen* are:

1. Consult your instructor as to the thickness of the packing to be used.

2. Turn the press by hand until the rollers are at the bottom of their stroke.

3. Loosen the grippers (using a wrench which exactly fits the gripper nuts) and move them until they are against the pin stops at the outer edges of the gripper bar. (Figure 56-A.) Tighten the nuts so that the grippers will stay

put and not work over and smash the form.

4. Cut a sheet of oiled tympan and four sheets of super, four or five inches wider than the sheet you are to print and long enough to reach from bail to bail. Clip the corners. Clipping the corners aids in keeping the sheets flat. Always use as narrow a packing as possible, as it lies flatter and also saves on material.

5. Lay the sheets one at a time on the delivery board, letting the edge of the sheet overhang the sharp edge of the board about a half inch. Hold the sheet in place. Run your fingers along the edge and crease the sheet, as shown in Figure 56-B.

6. Pry up the tympan bails with a screw driver (or use a bail wrench if you have one) and remove the old packing. (Figure 56-C.) Do not go away from the press while the bails are unclamped; someone may start the press and serious damage may be done.

7. Put the creased edges of the sheets together, with the oiled manila sheet on top. Place the creased edge of the combined packing along the lower edge of the platen. The crease should be exactly along the edge and the folded portion should extend below the platen. Hold the packing firmly and clamp the lower bail in place. (Figure 56-D.)

8. Test, by pulling the sheets taut, as shown in Figure 56-E, to see that the bail is holding the sheets securely. Consult your instructor if the sheets slip when you pull on the loose end. He may instruct you to paste them to the edge of the platen, under the bail.

9. Insert the pressboard and a loose sheet of super under the clamped sheets. Leave out the pressboard when printing a light form, such as an envelope corner card consisting of a few lines of type.

10. Place the loose ends of the packing sheets under the top bail, draw the sheets smooth and taut and clamp the bail into position. The packing should lie flat without wrinkles. Tear off any excess paper extending beyond the bail. (Figure 56-F.)

11. If there are wrinkles or bulges, they are probably due to improper clamping of the bail. Lift the bail, smooth out the sheets, and clamp the bail down again.

The next operation is to "ink up" the press. (See Unit 57.)

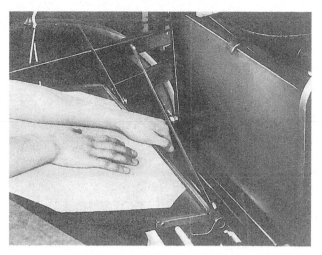

Fig. 56-D. Hold the Creased Edge of the Packing in Line with the Lower Edge of the Platen and Clamp the Bail

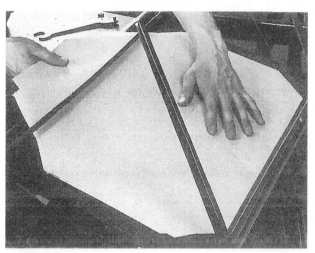

Fig. 56-E. Pull the Loose End to Make Sure the Bail is Holding the Packing Firmly

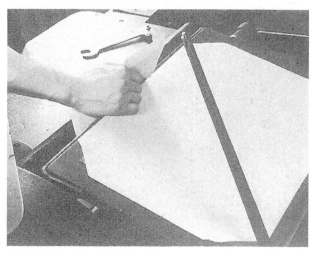

Fig. 56-F. Tear Off the Excess After the Packing has been Stretched

Fig. 57-A. Keep the Ink Surface Level — Do Not Dig Down Into the Can of Ink — Take Only from the Surface

Fig. 57-B. With the Press Motionless, Spread a Small Amount of Ink on the Left Side of the Disk

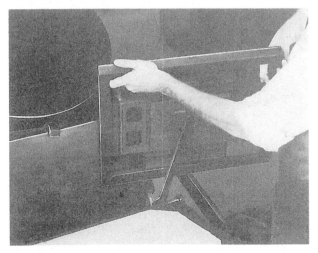

Fig. 58-A. Rest the Chase on the Side Arm While You Get Yourself Balanced for Lifting the Form into the Press

Unit 57

How to Ink Up a Platen Press

Carelessness in taking ink from the container is responsible for wasting a great deal of ink in both school shops and commercial printing plants. Ink oxidizes rapidly when exposed to air — the larger the surface exposed, the more rapid the oxidation. Buying ink in pound cans proves economical, providing the surface is kept covered and the users do not dig down into the can and leave pockets of air which quickly scum over and ruin the remaining ink.

Tubes are preferred by many when the quantity of ink needed at any one time is small. The small surface exposed practically eliminates loss from oxidation — unless through careless handling the tube is split. One manufacturer recommends that ink be taken from the tube in the following manner: "With one hand over the bottom of the tube and the other around the top of the tube, squeeze the tube, exerting equal pressure from both hands. The hand around the bottom of the tube removes any possibility of it bursting at that point." Read Unit 69, then select an ink.

Whenever possible, the press should be inked before the form is placed in position. Otherwise, lumps of ink may be deposited on the form and fill up the type. When this happens, the form must then be washed out with a brush, using a quick-drying solvent. Care must be taken not to allow the solvent to drip on the rollers. Protect the rollers by holding a rag below the brush as you scrub the form.

1. With the power off and the press motionless, wipe any dust or lint from the ink plate, using a dry rag which is itself free from dust and lint, as well as oil.

2. Turn the fly wheel by hand until the rollers are in position where they, too, can be wiped. Wipe them, but do not rub too hard.

3. Open the can of ink and remove the paper covering. With the ink knife, remove any "skin" and oxidized ink lumps from the surface.

4. When the top of the ink is free from skin and lumps, take a little ink from the can with your ink knife. Do not dig down into the can; keep the ink surface level. (Figure 57-A.)

5. With the press motionless, put a small amount of ink on the left side of the ink disk.

Spread it with the ink knife. (Figure 57-B.) Always start with a very small amount of ink — more can be added later if needed. Putting on too much ink in the beginning will make it necessary to wash up the press and start over.

6. Check the tympan bails. See that they are down in place. Turn the press over once by hand.

7. Turn on the motor and let the press run at slow speed until the ink has been distributed on the plate and rollers.

With the platen dressed and the press inked, you are ready to put the chase in the press. (See Unit 58.)

Unit 58

How to Put a Chase in the Press

1. With the impression lever in the "off" position, turn the fly wheel by hand until the roller carriage is at the lowest point of its stroke.

2. Wipe off the press bed.

3. Test the form for lift and spring, especially if it has been locked for any length of time or if it is locked with wood furniture. Wipe off the back of the form.

4. Pick up the chase in such a manner that the front of the form is facing you and the quoins are at the top and on the right side.

5. Carry the form to the right hand side of the press. Rest the bottom edge of the chase on the side arm until you get yourself firmly balanced. (Figure 58-A.)

6. Lift the chase from the side arm, then gently and carefully insert the bottom edge behind the two lugs at the bottom of the press bed. (Figure 58-B.) Be careful not to strike the face of the form against the grippers or other parts of the press. Also be careful not to damage the rollers by dragging the chase across their surface.

7. Hold the chase with the left hand and lift the top chase clamp lever (under the ink disk) with the right hand. Push the chase back against the bed and let the spring clamp engage the top of the chase. (Figure 58-C.)

8. Check to see that the chase is behind the bottom lugs and is firmly clamped at the top.

9. Stand in front of the press and sight the grippers with relation to the form. (Figure 58-D.) If they will clear the form, you are ready to position the guides. (See Unit 59.)

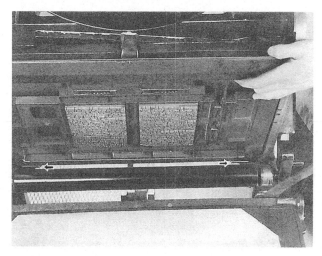

Fig. 58-B. Be Sure the Chase is Behind Both Lugs at the Lower Edge of the Pressbed

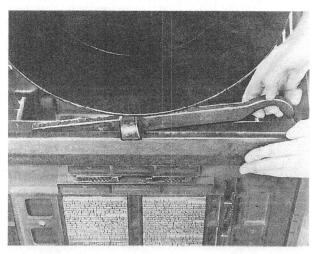

Fig. 58-C. Clamp the Chase Firmly with the Top Chase Clamp

Fig. 58-D. Sight the Grippers for Form Clearance Before Taking an Impression

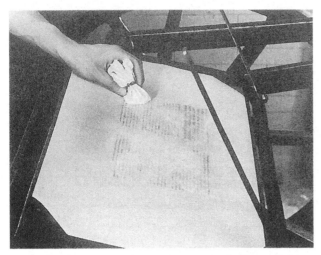

Fig. 59-A. Wash the Ink from the Packing

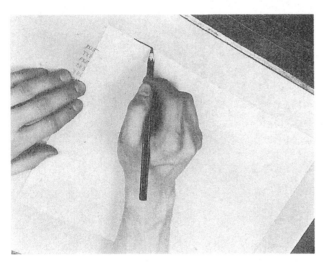

Fig. 59-B. Mark Position of Left Bottom Guide on the Tympan

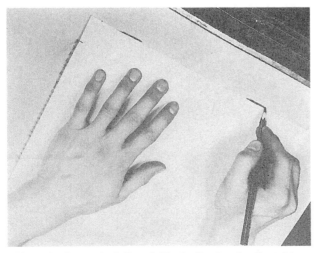

Fig. 59-C. Square the Bottom Guides by Keeping the Sheet Edge Parallel with the Edge of the Impression

Unit 59

How to Position the Guides

Make certain that you have the proper thickness of packing for the form you are to print and that the grippers clear the form.

1. With the impression (throw off) lever on, take an impression by turning the flywheel slowly by hand. In the event that you have the press over-packed, you should be able to "feel" the excess pressure and back up the press before the form is damaged. The flywheels on most platen presses turn away from you, but you should check with your instructor regarding the wheel on the press on which you are working.

2. Wipe the ink from the top sheet. Use a clean rag dampened with a little type cleaner. Then, dust a little talcum powder over the washed area and wipe off the excess with a clean rag. (Be sure your teacher approves the use of talc.) (Figure 59-A.)

3. To position the guides for a form that is to center on the sheet, take a sheet of super that is the same size as the stock on which you are to print the job.

4. Place the top edge of the sheet at the top of the printed impression, with the sheet covering about half the print. Make a pencil mark in line with the bottom line of the form. The part of the sheet projecting past the printed area is the combined width of the top and bottom margins.

5. Divide this combined margin width by soft folding it in half and pinch-marking the edge at the center point.

6. Place the pinch mark in line with the bottom of the last printed line and make a pencil mark on the tympan at the top edge near the left side of the sheet.

In Figure 59-B a pencil mark is in line with the top of the first type line because a head margin of 6½ picas is wanted.

7. With the top edge of the sheet in line with the pencil mark on the tympan, move the sheet until its side is parallel with the side edge of the form. (Figure 59-C.) Then, make another pencil mark at the top edge, but near the right hand side.

8. Indicate on the sheet with a pencil mark the width of the form. Fold and pinch mark

the side margin. Place the pinch mark at the edge of the printed impression, with the top edge of the sheet parallel to a type line. Make a pencil mark on the tympan at the left-hand edge of the sheet and about two inches up from the other marks, as shown in Figure 59-D. This is the position of the side guide.

9. Hold the sheet in the same position and mark the location for the bottom guides by putting two vertical marks at the top edges of the sheet and in from each side, about one-sixth the width of the sheet.

10. Attach the gauge pins to the tympan in the positions marked. For forms with narrow margins, place the guides so that the tongues will not strike any of the type in the form.

11. Place a sheet of super against the guides and pull an impression. Check the margins and make whatever adjustments are needed in the position of the guides.

12. Pull another impression and, when the margins are correct, have your instructor give you an O. K. for position.

13. Fasten the guides into position by tapping them *lightly* with a press wrench so that the points will engage the draw sheet and prevent the pins from slipping. (Figure 59-E.) The points also prevent the sheets from going under the guides. Avoid damaging pins — tap lightly.

14. When printing long runs, close register work, or heavy card stock, fasten the guides in place with sealing wax as an extra precaution to prevent them from moving.

15. Place one of your printed sheets in position against the guides. Then, loosen the grippers and move them into position. They hold the paper flat against the packing and prevent slurring while the sheet is being printed, and immediately after while it is being stripped from the form. The grippers should be set over the paper margins but must clear the form and the guides.

Pull the grippers down by hand and check their clearance — they should clear the printed area on the sheet by about a pica. Often, the left-hand gripper cannot be positioned over the paper margin. When this is the case, strings can be used in the open areas to aid in holding down the sheet. See Figure 59-F, which shows the grippers, auxiliary grippers, and strings in position.

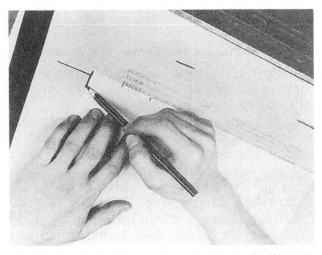

Fig. 59-D. Use the Pinch Mark to Locate Position for the Side Guide

Fig. 59-E. Tap the Gauge Pins Very Lightly to Engage their Points in the Packing to Prevent Slippage

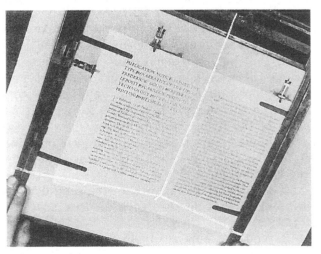

Fig. 59-F. Grippers Must be Set to Clear the Form and Guides

Unit 60

How to Prepare the Platen — A Summary

1. Move grippers to outer edge of the platen. Tighten the gripper nuts so that the grippers will stay clear of the form.

2. Dress the platen. Consult your instructor as to the amount of packing to be used. The amount will vary with the nature of the form and the impression setting of the particular press upon which you are working. Be sure to start with a thin packing. (See Unit 56.)

3. Ink the press with an ink suitable for the paper you are to use. (See Units 57 and 69.) Use very little ink, just enough to get an impression.

4. Wipe the bottom of the form and place the chase in the press with the quoins up and to the right. (Unit 58.) A lock-up O. K. should be secured before the form is sent to press.

5. Sight grippers to see that they clear the form, and bearers, if bearers are being used.

6. Pull an impression on the tympan draw sheet.

7. Wipe ink from the draw sheet with a clean rag dampened with gasoline. Rub the printed area on the draw sheet briskly with a clean rag while the gasoline is evaporating.

8. Position the sheet by placing the bottom gauges (guides) about one-sixth the length of the sheet from the ends, and the side gauges about one-third the width of the sheet from the lower left corner. Adjust gauges so the margins are correct width and straight with edge of the sheet. (See Unit 59.)

9. Check gauges, and especially the gauge tongues, to see that they clear the form.

10. Pull an impression on a sheet the same size as the stock you are to use for the job and get a "position O. K." from your instructor. Examine the back of this sheet to see that no parts of the form are punching.

11. Move grippers into position over margins of the sheet. Grippers must clear the type form and the gauges.

12. Attach strings or other stripping devices to the grippers. Be sure such devices clear the form.

13. You are now ready to proceed with the make-ready.

Unit 61

How to Make-Ready

Make-ready is the process of adjusting the pressure on the various parts of a form so that the entire form will print properly. Make-ready is necessary on a platen press mainly because of two factors: (1) type, rules, and cuts are often of varying heights and present an uneven surface to the platen; and (2) the construction of the platen press is such that even though a perfectly level form is being printed, more pressure is exerted on the edges of the form and, consequently, the edges receive a heavy impression, while the center, lacking pressure, prints light. A job is made-ready by taking an impression of the form on a sheet of super, "marking out" the weak areas, adding pressure to these marked-out areas by pasting on tissue patches (spotting up), and registering this "spot up" sheet in the packing.

Hard packing (see Unit 56) requires more care in the make-ready than does a soft packing of newsprint or machine finish stock. With the hard packing, the impression must be even over the entire form to get a good print. The time required to do a good job of make-ready is well spent, as the hard packing gives a clean, sharp print with minimum wear on the form.

Make-ready with a soft packing often consists of merely "adding another sheet" until the weakest point in the form prints. This slipshod method results in not only printing the face of the type but part of the beard as well. A few hundred impressions, using this "matrix" packing with its excess pressure, rounds off the type and rules, and wears the cuts. While it is true that with this method the job can be "started to run" more quickly, constant resort to soft packing make-ready soon results in a shop with nothing but worn out type and material. Obviously, such a shop cannot produce a quality piece of printing.

Unit 62

How to Mark Out a Type Form

Do not start make-ready until you have a position O. K. from your instructor. Otherwise the make-ready may have to be done over if the form is relocked or the gauges moved.

Forms of types, rules, and line cuts are "marked out" on the back of the sheet. Note that the entire process of make-ready is directed toward getting proper pressure on the various parts of the form, and for this reason practically all the work is done on the back of the sheet, where variations are easily seen.

Marking out should always be done on the same kind and weight of paper, regardless of the stock on which the job is to be printed. Fifty pound super is good for marking out, as it is a fairly thin, hard sheet that will not absorb the impression. Soft or thick sheets do not allow the impression to show through to the back of the sheet. Coated paper is not good for make-ready as it quickly takes on an indented "matrix" effect that does not make for a sharp, clean printing of the form.

1. Pull a trial impression on a sheet of super. Be sure the sheet is up to the guides.

2. Examine the impression, showing on the back of the sheet you have just printed, by holding it at an angle toward the light, as shown in Figure 62-A. (If there is offset from ink on the packing, wipe off the packing with gasoline, dry, and pull a new impression.) An irregular impression with individual characters or lines punching in a form of this kind indicates poor planing and lock-up, and possibly a springy form. The bottom of the form should be examined; dirt or imbedded particles removed; the form unlocked, planed, and relocked.

In cases where the packing is damaged by punching characters, or in some other way, new packing should be put on the press and a new position O. K. secured.

An impression which shows one side of the form uniformly heavy and the other side uniformly light probably indicates the platen is not parallel to the press bed. Show the sheet to your instructor — possibly he will want to adjust the platen.

A medium-sized or large form of type, which is of uniform height and condition, should show a stronger impression at the corners and edges and a gradual weakening impression toward the center. The marking out sheet for such a form should have the impression on the corners about right for printing. If the impression is too heavy, remove a sheet from the packing; if it is too light, add a sheet to the packing. Then,

Fig. 62-A. Hold the Sheet at an Angle to the Light to Study the Impression Showing on the Back

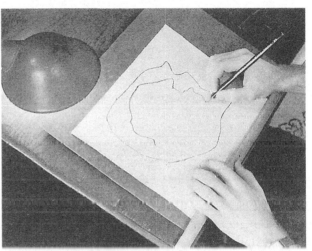

Fig. 62-B. Outline the Weak Areas of the Impression with Continuous Lines — Outlines Must Not Cross Each Other

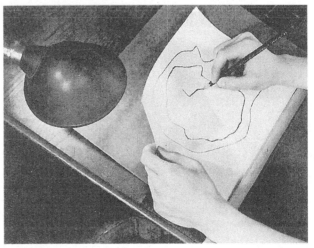

Fig. 62-C. Look Through the Sheet to Make Sure that Absence of Impression is not Due to Open Spaces in the Form

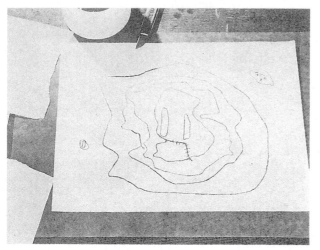

Fig. 63-A. Place Marked Out Sheet Face Down on a Piece of Press Board for Spotting Up

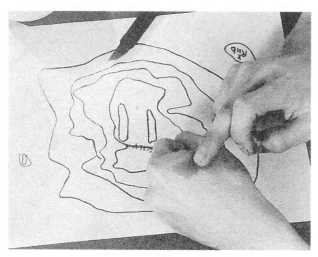

Fig. 63-B. Tap out a little Paste on your Second Finger

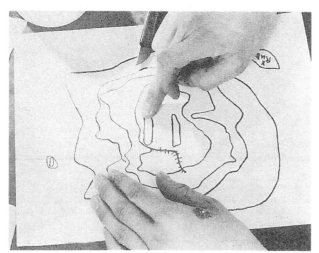

Fig. 63-C. Tap a very Little Paste on the Smallest of the Outlines

pull another print on super. When the corners have correct impression, proceed with the marking out.

With the sheet face down on a smooth surface, such as a pressboard or drawing board, hold it at an angle toward the light so that you can see the variations in the impression showing on the back. Use a soft lead pencil, and carefully outline the areas which show a weak impression. Your outlines should have continuous lines which completely enclose the weak areas. (Figure 62-B.)

Do not guess at where the impression slopes off. Twist the sheet or change the angle to the light until you are certain where the pencil lines should go. Outline the largest areas first and then the smaller ones. The lines of any two outlines must not cross each other.

Look through the sheet toward the light frequently (Figure 62-C), to see that the absence of impression is not due to margins or open spaces in the form. Note, also, in Figure 62-C that the outlines which overlap the edge of the type do not go completely to the outer edge of the sheet, but stop just past the type.

When marking out is completed, you are ready to "spot up" the sheet.

Unit 63

How to "Spot Up" a Sheet

While "spotting up" is a less difficult operation than marking out, it does require considerable experience before a craftsman-like job can be done. Therefore, before starting to spot up an actual job, it would be well to mark out, on a sheet of super, a few outlines of various sizes, and then practice spotting them up until you get the knack of putting on the right amount of paste and cutting the tissue.

1. Place the marked out sheet face down on a smooth surface, such as a sheet of pressboard. Have a make-ready knife and some make-ready tissue at hand, as shown in Figure 63-A.

2. Put a small dab of make-ready (sphinx) paste on your left hand and replace cover on paste container.

3. Tap out on your second finger a very thin film of paste, free from lumps. (Figure 63-B.)

4. Tap the paste on the smallest of your outlined spots (Figure 63-C), keeping the paste inside the outline. Only a very, very little paste

is needed — just enough to hold the tissue in position. If the moisture in the paste causes the sheet to swell and wrinkle, you are using far too much paste. The lumpy, inaccurate make-ready resulting from excess paste is often worse than no make-ready at all. The extra thickness may smash the type when an impression is pulled if the excess paste is allowed to dry before the sheet is put into the packing.

5. Smooth down a piece of make-ready tissue over the paste, covering the outline. Whenever possible, fit the edge of the tissue along one edge of the outline — this saves cutting away the tissue along that line. (Figure 63-D.)

6. The pencil marks should show through the tissue. Cut through the tissue with a sharp make-ready knife. Follow the pencil outline *exactly* and use just enough pressure to cut the tissue, but not the super. (Figure 63-E.) Hold the patch in place and lift off the excess tissue.

You must work rapidly when spotting up. Paste occasionally gets outside the outline, especially on the small spots, and the excess tissue must be lifted off before the paste sets. Otherwise, the surface of the super is pulled away with the tissue and the make-ready sheet is ruined.

7. Continue spotting up until all the outlines have been covered. In spotting the larger outlines, do not cover the entire surface of the outlined area with paste. Tap on only four or five very small spots of paste along the edges and corners of the outline — just enough to hold the patch in place.

8. Moisten your finger slightly with your tongue and rub any areas marked for that operation. (Figure 63-F.) Rub lightly, being careful to avoid tearing the sheet.

9. When all spotting up has been completed, the sheet is ready for insertion in the packing.

Unit 64

How to Insert a Spot-Up Sheet

1. Place the make-ready sheet against the guides. Hold it in position and stab through the sheet and the draw sheet. Make your stab mark at the right in the shape of a $\wedge$ with the point away from you as you stand in front of the press. (Figure 64-A.) The other stab mark should be of this shape $\ulcorner$ with the point toward the side guide. Stabs made in this

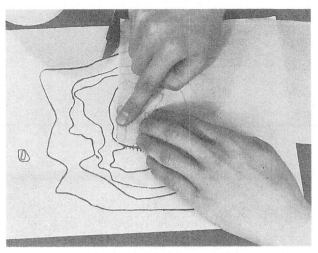

Fig. 63-D. Smooth Down a Piece of Make-ready Tissue over the Paste — Cover the Outline

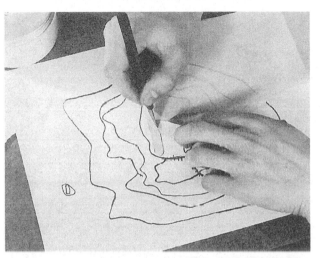

Fig. 63-E. Follow the Pencil Outline Exactly with Your Make-ready Knife and Cut Through the Tissue but Not the Super

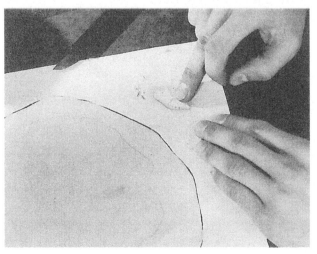

Fig. 63-F. Moisten Finger and Rub Down High Spots but be Careful Not to Tear the Super

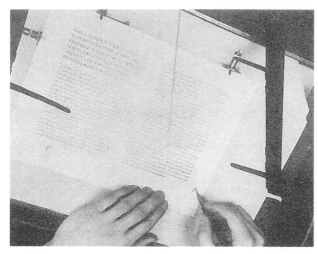

Fig. 64-A. Stab the Spot Sheet So It can be Registered to a Sheet in the Packing

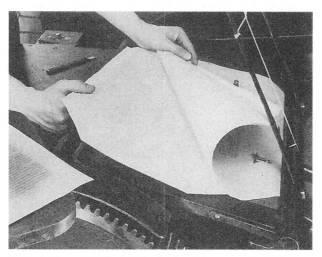

Fig. 64-B. Remove a Sheet from the Packing to Compensate for the Thickness of the Spot Sheet being put in

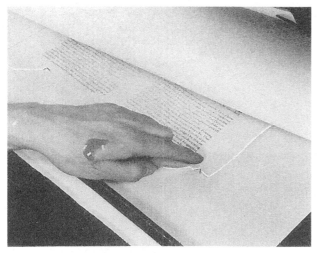

Fig. 64-C. Register the Stab Marks on the Spot Sheet to the Stab Marks in the Packing and Paste Down the Make-ready Sheet

way will not interfere with a sheet being fed to the guides.

2. Lift the upper tympan bail. (Never lift the lower bail after position O. K. is received.) Remove from the packing a sheet of the same thickness as the make-ready sheet you are to insert. (Figure 64-B.)

3. Cut away the loose point of each stab on your make-ready sheet. Place the sheet in register over the stab marks in the bottom sheet of super which is clamped under the lower bail. Hold the make-ready sheet in place and lift one upper corner. Put a little paste on the under side, and then smooth the corner into place. (Figure 64-C.) Paste the other corner down in the same way.

4. Check the register marks to see that the make-ready sheet did not slip during pasting.

5. Transfer the pressboard in the packing from below the supers to above your spot sheet.

6. Smooth tympan into place; draw it taut; and clamp it under the top bail.

7. Take a print on super and examine the back for evenness of impression. There will be little need for further make-ready, providing a good job of marking out and spotting up was done on the first sheet. If the impression is still uneven on the back, mark out, spot up, and insert another make-ready sheet in the packing. Fasten it to another of the supers clamped under the lower bail, or to the previous make-ready sheet. (Always remove a sheet of equal thickness from the packing for each make-ready sheet that is inserted.)

8. When the impression on the back shows evenly and without too much punch, examine the face of the sheet. There may be one or two individual characters which need additional pressure to print well. They may be spotted with tissue directly on the face of one of the make-ready sheets already in the packing.

9. You will be ready to pull a print on the stock to be used on the job after you make necessary adjustments in the packing to take care of difference in the thickness of the job's stock and the thickness of the super you have been using during make-ready.

After the adjustment of the packing is completed, you have only to get the right *color* (right amount of ink, whether black or colored) and the job should be "ready to run."

Unit 65

How to Use Quads for Guides

Quads are sometimes used for guides. Eight- or ten-point, two-em quads are satisfactory for this use and should be placed in position with the narrow edge contacting the paper.

1. After the pencil marks have been put on the top sheet, put a little paste on one side of the quad.

2. Put the paste side down against the top sheet, press it firmly and slide it from left to right, about an eighth of an inch. Then wiggle it into position, maintaining a firm pressure. This sliding and wiggling causes the excess paste to come out from under the quad. (Figure 65-A.)

3. Put the other two quads into position, and pull your impression for checking the margins. Slight position adjustments can be made by wiggling the quad. When setting quads for guides, you must work rapidly, for the paste will dry, making impossible further adjustments.

4. After the proper position has been secured, the quads should be reinforced with gummed paper. (Figure 65-B.)

5. To prevent the sheets from going under the quads, a small ∧ should be cut in the packing in front of each of the quads being used as bottom guides. The point of the ∧ should be about a lead away from the guide edge of the quad, and should be bent slightly upward, as shown in Figure 65-B.

6. A ⌐ slit should be used at the side guide quad, as shown in Figure 65-C, as a ∧ slit at the side would probably interfere with feeding the sheets to the guides.

7. Fenders, cut from pressboard, should be inserted in slits alongside and about eight points back from the guide edge of each quad. (Figure 65-C.) The purpose of the fenders is to prevent the sheets from going over the quad guides; to keep the sheets flat against the packing; and to help strip the sheet after printing. Put a little make-ready paste on the upper side of the part of the fender that goes under the tympan. After they are pasted in, bend them slightly upward, but do not break them.

8. Check the position and length of the fenders to see that they clear the type form.

Fig. 65-A. Wiggle the Quad into Position while Exerting Pressure on it to Squeeze Out Excess Paste

Fig. 65-B. Reinforce Quad Guides with Gummed Paper, and Cut a " " in Front of Each

Fig. 65-C. Insert Pressboard Fenders to Keep the Sheet from Going Over the Guides

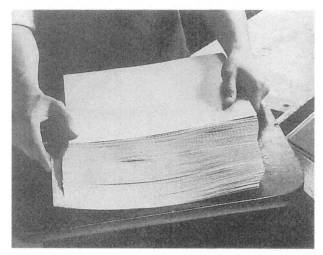

Fig. 66-A. Fan Out the Pile of Stock

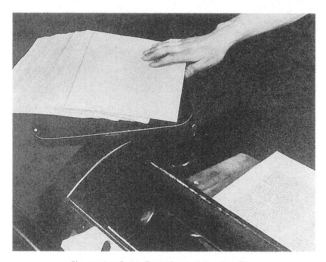

Fig. 66-B. Drag Top Sheet from the Pile

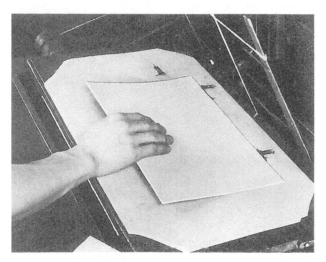

Fig. 66-C. Contact Bottom Guides First

Unit 66

How to Feed the Platen Press

The skill and coordination necessary for the feeding of a platen press can be acquired in a short time provided the student applies himself diligently and forms only correct habits.

The beginner should practice for several minutes at a motionless press before he attempts to feed the press under power. No form is needed for practice feeding, but the rollers should be given a coat of oil to prevent friction with the disk. A lightweight card stock, such as an index bristol of a size near 6 x 4 inches, is easy to feed and should be used during the first practice session.

1. Put a sandpaper finger stall on your left middle finger.

2. Position the guides and fasten them.

3. "Fan out" the pile of card stock, as shown in Figure 66-A, lifting with the fingers and forcing the top part of the pile forward with the thumbs. Put no more than two inches of stock on the feedboard at one time.

4. Place the fanned-out pile of stock on the feedboard in the position shown in Figure 66-B.

5. Stand in front of the press and pick up the top sheet by dragging it from the pile. (See Figure 66-B.) Allow the thumb to go under the sheet.

6. Feed the sheet to the bottom guides on the open platen. At the time of contact, the sheet should be about a half inch from the side guide and the hand should be traveling to the left and slightly downward. (See Figure 66-C.) The thumb should be withdrawn from under the sheet just after this contact has been made.

7. Allow the fingers to drag with just enough pressure to cause the sheet to move, and follow through with the feeding motion, as demonstrated in Figure 66-D. After the side guide has stopped the sheet, but not the left and downward motion of your hand, lift your fingers and bring your hand out of the press and back to the stock pile in a sweeping curve.

8. Grasp the next sheet and hold it ready for feeding, with the fingers resting on the feedboard. (When the press is operating, there is a short interval during which the platen is closed. Operation 9 occurs just after the platen again opens.)

9. Remove the "printed" sheet by dragging it over the edge of the platen, with the sandpaper covered finger resting on an unprinted area. (See Figure 66-E.) Grasp the sheet between the finger and the thumb and remove it to the pile on the delivery board.

10. Feed the next sheet to the guides as soon as the printed sheet is out of the way.

11. Jog the delivered sheet (see Figure 66-F) while Operation 10 is being completed.

12. Repeat the feeding routine until you have mastered the technique of picking up one sheet at a time and feeding it to the guides with one sweeping motion which brings your hand out of the press.

13. Run the press at its slowest speed and feed the entire pile through several times. Coordinate your feeding with the motion of the press. Never interrupt the sweep of your feeding motion when you fail to get a sheet to the guides. Making a second attempt to register the sheet not only breaks up your timing but is likely to cause your hand to be caught in the closing press. Instead, throw off the impression lever with your left hand, and put the sheet up to the guides on the next revolution.

When you are able to feed with not more than one miss in fifty impressions, you are ready to increase slightly the running speed. After you have progressed in the feeding of card stock to a speed of about 800 per hour, change to a lighter weight stock, such as a 20 pound bond.

The pressfeeder is responsible for maintaining the quality of the presswork on a job of printing. In addition to the responsibility of seeing that every sheet is squarely up to the guides, he must be constantly on the alert to catch any flaws which develop while the job is running. The guides must be watched to see that they do not slip; a constant check must be kept on the grippers to see that they do not work loose; "pull outs" and defective printing of letters must be watched for by stopping at intervals and looking over the entire job, or by frequent examination of the printed sheets as they are being delivered; and "color" must be kept uniform. Sheets should be checked at frequent intervals with a "color" sample which the instructor has OK'd. Too little ink gives a gray print, too much results in smudge and offset.

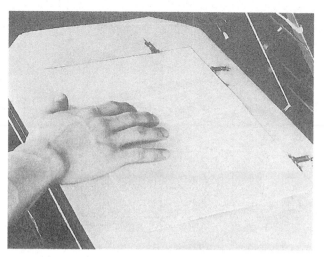

Fig. 66-D. Drag Sheet to the Left and Slightly Downward

Fig. 66-E. Keep Fingers Off Freshly Printed Ink

Fig. 66-F. Jog Sheets as They Come From Press, Except When Jogging Might Cause Offset

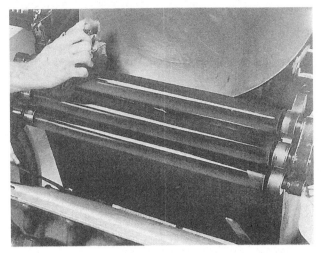

Fig. 67-A. Turn the Fly Wheel Slowly by Hand While Washing the Rollers with a Kerosene-soaked Rag

Fig. 67-B. Dry the Rollers by Rubbing the Surface Gently with a Dry Rag

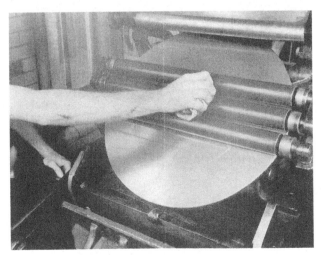

Fig. 67-C. Turn the Rollers Up Across the Disk and Wipe any Spots Previously Missed

Unit 67

How to Wash the Platen Press

1. Wash the ink disk, using gasoline or kerosene, but do not dry it.

2. Turn the flywheel until the rollers start on the disk, then, turning slowly, wash the rollers. (Figure 67-A.) Back the rollers off the disk and wipe the disk dry.

3. Run the rollers up until the top roller is about 1/4-inch away from the disk. Wipe it dry, rubbing gently lengthwise as you turn the flywheel slowly. Too much energy in rubbing will take the surface from the roller and ruin it for further use. Dry the second roller as it comes into the same position; likewise, dry the third roller. (Figure 67-B.)

4. Turn the rollers up across the disk. Wipe any spots that you have missed. (Figure 67-C.) Turn the flywheel by hand until the rollers are at their lowest point. Wipe off kerosene or ink that may have gotten on the pressbed.

5. When the press is idle with no form on it, the roller carriage should be left so that the rollers center over the pressbed, to relieve tension on the roller springs. Rollers must never be left standing on the ink disc or on the type form for any length of time or they will become flattened. See Units 103 and 104 for descriptions of presses used by early printers and those used in modern printing.

Unit 68

How to Care for Rollers

The rollers on the platen press and the brayer on the proof press are manufactured from glue, glycerine, and a small quantity of other special materials. Glue and glycerine both have an affinity for water, and the rollers should never be brought into contact with water. If any water gets on them, it will cause the rollers to swell and blister. The rollers, also, must be protected from excessive heat. If left standing near a radiator in the winter or left in the bright sunshine during the summer, the rollers will melt. (Synthetic rubber and all-season rollers, both of which are relatively unaffected by temperature changes, are available but have not as yet replaced the composition roller for quality printing.)

Rollers are made with special compositions,

depending upon the season in which the roller is to be used. Winter rollers are made softer than summer rollers. A drop in temperature of a few degrees will cause a summer roller to become so hard that it cannot be used. A roller in good condition will have a shiny surface and will feel slightly sticky (tacky) to the touch. Ink should not be allowed to dry on a roller. When in use, the roller should be washed daily — more often, if the ink starts to dry — with kerosene or some similar oily solvent. The more volatile solvents, such as high-test gasoline and benzene, may cause the surface of the roller to crack because of the rapid evaporation. When the roller is washed, it should be rubbed gently with a rag moistened with kerosene. Special care should be taken to remove the ink near the ends. The entire roller should then be gone over with a dry rag. If rubbed too briskly, the shiny appearance will disappear. This indicates that you are rubbing away the surface of the roller and damaging it.

After the roller is cleaned, it should be covered with a thin coating of machine oil — both on the surface of the roller and at the two ends. The oil forms a protective coating and keeps the moisture in the atmosphere from uniting with the glue and glycerine compound in the roller. When rollers are left exposed in humid weather, they absorb moisture so that they become water-logged and will not take the ink. Rollers, properly cared for, will last for a great length of time, but rollers which are neglected will lose their tack very quickly.

The brayer on the proof press has a three-point support which lifts the roller from the plate when the brayer is set down properly. If allowed to remain in contact with the plate, the roller will flatten out, and when left in this position long enough, it will become so out of round that it will be worthless.

Likewise, the rollers on the platen press must not be left in contact with the form or the ink plate, or they, also, will be ruined. When the rollers are removed from the press for any reason, they should be placed on end in such a manner that they will not fall to the floor and bend the steel cores. Also, they should be so placed that the roller composition will not be damaged through contact with any surface, or through exposure to heat.

When the rollers are to be stored, they should be coated with machine oil and placed upright in a cabinet or rack. Care should be taken that the storage cabinet is not near an outside wall, or near a radiator or steam pipe.

Unit 69

How to Suit Ink to Paper

The choice of the correct ink for the paper on which you are going to print will eliminate a great many of the ink troubles commonly encountered in presswork. A general rule is to have the ink as stiff and tacky as possible. Ink is too tacky when it "picks" (pulls the surface from the paper).

Hard papers, such as rag bonds and ledgers, require a heavy-bodied bond or cover ink to get a clean sharp print. (See Units 113-116.)

Softer bond inks are suitable for most of the deckle edge and higher grade book papers made today as most of these papers are now being hard-sized for offset printing.

Book inks are suitable for the general run of machine finish and supercalendered papers, except that when a halftone is being printed, halftone inks are preferable as they are more finely ground.

Book or halftone inks are used on coated papers as tacky inks would pick the surface.

Job inks are a mixture of bond and book ink and are suitable for sulphite bonds and semi-hard finish papers.

The problem of mixing and matching colors is best solved by using an ink manufacturer's color kit such as an I.P.I. Match Box. Such a kit shows sufficient colors to take care of most any job, gives the exact quantities of the various inks necessary to mix them, and in addition has examples of good color combinations, as well as considerable information on the manipulation of ink.

Transparent colors should be used for overprinting, whenever possible, as they seem to work better and are less likely to show mottle in solid areas. The darker color should be printed first, (unless the other color is the key form for register) and the transparent color then laid down over it.

When mixing colors without the aid of a formula, start with the lighter color and add very small amounts of the darker color to it.

Unit 70

How an Illustration Prints

Unlike a photographic print, an illustration printed by letterpress cannot have continuous tones, as the inking rollers deposit a film of ink of approximately the same density over the entire surface of the plate. (See Unit 110.)

Figure 70-A is a reproduction of a drawing in which the artist achieved tones by varying the width and direction of the lines. The letterpress plate used for printing this drawing is a line engraving, also called a zinc etching, a line plate, or a line cut. In Figure 70-B,

Fig. 70-A. Line Engraving — Shading Through Varying Lines

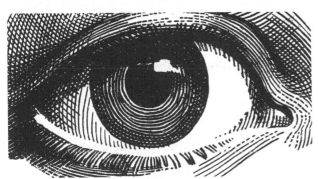

Fig. 70-B. Line Engraving — Shading Through Cross-hatching

cross-hatching, as well as varying the width of lines, was used by the artist in the original drawing to achieve shading.

Reproduction of a continuous tone photograph by the line cut method would give a silhouette effect, with middle tones and highlights printing as either black or white.

Several methods can be used to break up the surface of a line plate so that it will not print as a series of sharply contrasting solid masses of black and white. For example, in the Ben Day Process, screens of various patterns can be applied to line engravings before they are etched, to give the print a special overall "texture" or shading. Examples of illustrations "toned" by this and similar processes can be found in newspaper advertisements.

The most common way of producing gradations in tone, or a range of highlights, middle tones, and deep shadows, is to photograph the original of an illustration through a halftone screen — a clear glass plate, diagonally ruled with black lines which cross at right angles. The intensity of the reflected light passing through the screen determines the size of the dots on the finished plate. Printing plates produced by this method are known as halftone photoengravings.

Figure 70-C is a reproduction of a section of a print from a 120-line screen halftone, enlarged approximately 8½ times to give it a screen value of about 14 lines to the inch. Viewed from a distance of about ten feet, it appears to be a continuous tone print, with dense black areas in the eye and lips and a gradual shading off to white in the cheek and nose. Compare the eye in this print with that shown in the line plate in Figure 70-B.

When viewed from reading distance, the screen pattern in Figure 70-C is evident, and it can be seen that the difference in the tonal value is due to the size of the individual dots. The dots in the highlight area on the cheek are very small and are surrounded with a relatively large area of white. In the darker areas, such as around the eyes, the dots are larger and the white between them is correspondingly smaller. In the very dense areas, as in the eyebrows, the printing surface takes on the appearance of a solid, interspersed with white dots which vary in size.

The 120-line screen is probably the most widely used of the various screens available for halftone work. It has 120 lines per inch on each dimension, thus giving 14,400 dots per square inch on the surface of the printing plate. This is fine enough so that the screen pattern is not readily evident to the naked eye, yet it is not so fine that it cannot be used for printing on such papers as super, and the better grades of machine finish.

133-line, 150-line, and sometimes 175-line screens are used for illustrations requiring finer detail in reproduction. Glossy coated papers (enamels) are needed for use with these fine screens. When printed on rougher papers, many of the fine dots (the 150-line screen has 22,500 dots per square inch) strike in the "valleys" of the paper surface and do not print, thus giving a broken screen reproduction.

Coarse screens are needed to print rough papers, and screens ranging to 50-line are available. A few newspaper plants have successfully printed 85-line screen halftones, but most of the metropolitan dailies use 60-line to 80-line.

There are no solid blacks in a halftone plate, unless the engraver has burnished (rubbed down) the near-solid areas to eliminate the screen. Likewise, there are no areas in the highlights which are without the screen pattern, unless the dots have been etched out, tooled out, or mechanically "dropped out," by the engraver.

Correct printing of a halftone requires that every dot print with its true value as shown on the engraver's proof. A few satisfactory prints can be made from a new halftone with practically no make-ready by simply applying pressure. However, a careful make-ready is required to do a uniformly good job of halftone printing, and to avoid damaging the plate on a run of any considerable length.

Improper make-ready results in numerous troubles. Excessive pressure on highlight dots will cause them to wear and print larger. The highlights then appear "muddy." Wear in the middle tones and shadows causes the plate to become shallow in those areas, with the result that the screen fills up with ink, and detail is lost in the print.

Failure to apply an edge sheet will result in wear to the edges of the plate and will give a "wire edge" print. Also, the punch on the back of the sheet will likely cause offset, by picking up ink from the printed sheet below.

Lack of proper pressure on the middle tones and deep shadows may result in one of the following effects, which will spoil the reproduction: (1) picking of the paper surface; (2) a broken screen; (3) fill-up of the screen and offsetting of the ink, resulting from use of too much ink in an effort to overcome poor make-ready; or (4) fill-up due to failure of the ink to lift properly. Continuing to print under such conditions permits some of the ink to remain after each impression and build up until the screen becomes completely filled.

Fig. 70-C. 120-Screen Halftone Section Enlarged About 8½ Times

Fig. 71-A. Too Much Impression for Marking Out

Fig. 71-B. Impression Correct for Marking Out — Broken Screen is Evident

Fig. 71-C. Halftone Marked Out on Face of Sheet

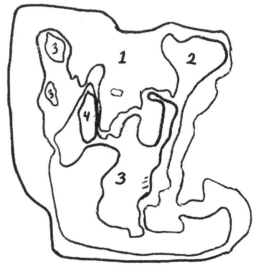

Fig. 71-D. Carbon Marks Transfer to the Back of the Stabbed Super

Fig. 71-E. Outlines of the Patches Show if Make-ready Is Not Buried Under Pressboard

Fig. 71-F. With Pressboard Over the Make-ready — Patches no Longer Evident

Unit 71

How to Make-Ready a Halftone

Make-ready for halftones is divided into two parts. First, a sheet is marked out and spotted up with tissue to even the impression over the entire area, and an edge sheet is applied to relieve pressure on the edges of the halftone to prevent punching and wear. This is called a "flat make-ready." An "overlay" is then inserted in the make-ready to exert extra pressure on the "solids" or black parts of the halftone and to relieve pressure on the "highlights" or light portions of the engraving. Sometimes the overlay also takes the place of the edge sheet.

To make a flat make-ready:

1. Ink the press with a small amount of halftone ink. Use enough ink to get rid of grayness in your print, but not as much as would be used in running the job.

2. Set the guides and get position O. K.

3. Adjust the thickness of the packing until you get a print on coated stock that shows only the highest points of the halftone printing clearly. Figure 71-A shows a trial impression with the packing too heavy. The screen appears broken in only a few places.

Figure 71-B shows an impression which is about right for marking out. Only two areas are printing clearly — the lower right hand corner and a section along the left side. Note the additional broken screen (low) areas in 71-B which do not show in 71-A.

4. Pull impressions on one sheet of coated stock and one sheet of super. As these sheets are to be used for make-ready, they should be carefully placed against the guides before the print is taken. Stab the sheet of super as explained in Unit 64.

5. Halftones must be marked out from the face, as the only impression which shows on the back is along the edges of the halftone. Lay a sheet of carbon paper face up on a smooth surface. Place the stabbed sheet of super, face up, on top of the carbon, and over this register the sheet of coated. Hold the sheets in register with a little paste in two corners, and mark out the halftone on the face of the coated sheet. The marks will be transferred by the carbon to the back of the stabbed super.

The first outline marked out should take in,

if possible, the entire area that shows a broken screen. Continue marking out until all low areas are outlined. Figure 71-C shows the halftone marked out on the face of the coated sheet.

Figure 71-D shows the marks as they appear on the back of the stabbed sheet of super. The numerals in Figure 71-D indicate the number of thicknesses of tissue there will be in that area after spotting up is completed.

6. Lay the coated sheet aside — you have no further use for it. Review Unit 63 and then spot up the back of the stabbed sheet.

7. Remove a sheet of super from the packing and register your make-ready sheet to the bottom sheet of super, held under the lower tympan bail. Place the pressboard on top of your make-ready. The pressboard softens the effect of the edges of the patches. Each patch may show up on the printed sheet (Figure 71-E) if the make-ready sheet is placed in the packing too near the top draw sheet.

The outlines of the patches no longer show in Figure 71-F, which is an impression taken after the spot sheet was properly "buried" deep in the packing and under the pressboard.

8. Pull another print on coated stock and examine it for defects in the printing, such as broken screen or punching highlights. If a few small patches are needed to complete the make-ready, they may be spotted to the face of the make-ready sheet you have just inserted.

Unit 72

How to Sharpen a Make-Ready Knife

Put a few drops of oil on the stone. Hold the knife so that it cannot turn, with your fingers resting on the stone, and your forefinger holding the blade in contact. Push away from you, straight along the stone, five or six times. Keep the blade at the same angle during the entire stroke. Lift the blade on the return stroke and set it down at the same angle each time. Turn the knife over and stone the other side. Remove the "wire edge" by alternately stroking one side and then the other two or three times. Do not allow the knife point to become rounded — keep the cutting edge straight and at an angle to the back of the blade.

Unit 73

How to Make an Edge Sheet

When the halftone is printing correctly over its entire surface (compare your print with the engraver's proof if the proof is available), an edge sheet should be made.

1. Take two impressions on super and stab one of the sheets. The stabbed sheet is for insertion in the packing. The edge sheet is cut out of the other one.

2. Lay the unstabbed sheet on a piece of pressboard resting on a smooth surface. Hold your make-ready knife at an angle so as to cut with a bevel outward, and cut the print from the sheet. Cut about a point inside the edges of

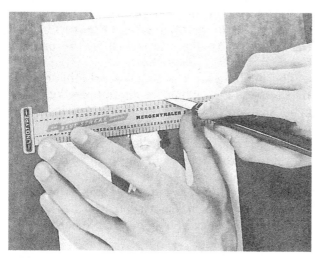

Fig. 73-A. Cut with a Bevel, about One Point Inside the Print When Making Edge Sheet

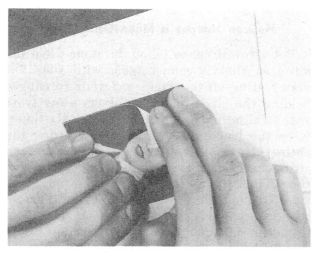

Fig. 73-B. Paste Edge Sheet in Register on the Stabbed Sheet

the print. If the halftone happens to be square or rectangular, the cutting can be done along a straight edge. (Figure 73-A.)

3. Hold the edge sheet in register over the print on the stabbed sheet. Lift one corner, as shown in Figure 73-B, put on a very little paste and rub the corner down in place. Paste down the other corners.

4. Insert the stabbed sheet into the packing, registering it to the stab marks and fastening it to the sheet immediately under the manila draw sheet and above the pressboard.

5. Remove two supers from the packing to compensate for the two thicknesses inserted. Fasten the bail.

6. Take another impression on coated paper. If the edge sheet has been cut and registered properly, the impression on the edges will have been relieved and you will be unable to see any impression on the back of the sheet. A broken screen line along an edge on the face of the print will indicate that you have either failed to register the edge sheet or have cut it too small.

Edge sheets should also be used when making ready tint blocks, large bold type, and other solid areas, such as heavy blacks in line cuts.

Unit 74

How to Make an Overlay

The make-ready described in Unit 71 is called a flat make-ready of a halftone. Quality presswork on most halftones requires the use of an overlay in addition to the flat make-ready already described. The purpose of the flat make-ready is to even the impression. The purpose of the overlay is to exert heavy pressure on the solid areas in the engraving, as solids require more pressure to print correctly; to exert medium pressure on gray tones; and to relieve pressure on the highlights to cause them to print clearly and cleanly and to prevent excessive wear as the job is being run.

Overlays are of three general types: mechanical overlays, of which the chalk overlay is probably the most widely used; hand-cut overlays, using two, three, or four sheets of super; and marked-out overlays. Chalk overlays secure gradation of thickness with an etching solution, hence, the name mechanical. Hand-cut overlays are not very satisfactory for platen presswork, as the difference in thickness is too great and the platen "bears off" on the thick part of the overlay. The marked-out overlay is a combination of hand cutting and spotting, and as the differences in thickness are not great, it can be used with good results on platen presses. The lightly etched chalk overlay is also suitable for platen presswork.

To make a marked-out overlay, proceed as follows:

1. Complete your flat make-ready spot sheet and insert it in the packing. Cut the edge sheet but do not paste it to the stabbed super.

2. Place the stabbed super sheet face up on a sheet of carbon paper and mark out, according to the tone gradations. Do not attempt to outline more than three or four distinct gradations. Figure 74-A has four outlined:

"x" — the highlight area in the hat. It is to be cut out. The whites of the eyes and the curved white line in the scarf are also to be cut out.

"o" — the light gray areas in the face and dress. They are to be left unchanged.

"1"—the background, part of the hair and eyes, the lips, and the gray area of the scarf. These are to be spotted with one folio.

"2" — the dense blacks of the hair, eyes, and the scarf. An extra folio is to be put on these near-solids.

The "o," "1," and "2" were marked on Figure 74-A to aid in the explanation and are not needed as guides in spotting up.

3. Work on the face of the sheet and cut out the highlights. Hold the knife so that it cuts with a bevel. Irregular outlines, like those formed by the highlights showing in the hair in Figure 74-A, should be feathered off (by scratching with the knife blade) rather than cut out sharply in a line.

4. Spot up the back of the marked-out sheet, using French folio — a thin sheet about twice the thickness of make-ready tissue. Figure 74-B shows the outlines which resulted from the marking out, illustrated in Figure 74-A.

Patches, which have part of their outlines in common with a larger patch, should be spotted with folio and cut out only along the single line, as indicated by the dots and arrows at "a" in Figure 74-B. The overlapping folio remain-

ing on the patch will be cut away when the larger patch "b" is spotted and cut out.

5. Paste the edge sheet in register on the face of the spotted-up sheet, and the overlay is complete.

6. Register the overlay sheet to the stab marks in the sheet of super immediately below the draw sheet. The pressboard should be *under* the overlay but *above* the flat make-ready.

7. Take two sheets of super from the packing.

8. Take an impression on coated paper and examine it for breaks in the screen and for faulty register of the overlay. Spot up with tissue any weak spots in the highlights or middle tones. There probably will be a few weak spots resulting from bear off on the thicker parts of the overlay.

Fig. 74-A. Print Marked Out for Four Tone Gradations in the Overlay

Fig. 74-B. Outlines As they Appear on the Back of the Sheet of Super

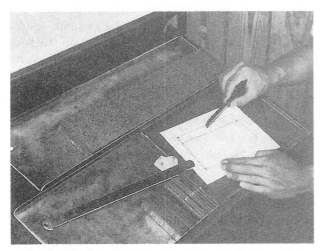

Fig. 75-A. Material Should be Gathered and Placed on Bank
Before Starting Make-up

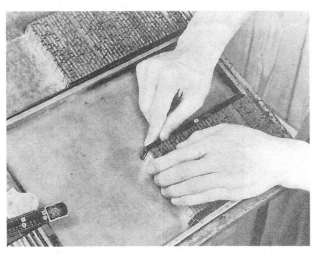

Fig. 75-B. Notched Furniture Makes a Good Page Gauge

Fig. 75-C. Slugs and Leads Should Be Added to Bring Page Even
with the Gauge

Unit 75

How to Make Up Pages

Forms to be printed may consist of uniform materials, or they may include a variety of printing surfaces. Hand-set headings are sometimes intermingled with slugs cast on the Linotype, Intertype, or Ludlow machines and, sometimes, with Monotype cast text. Any of these surfaces, or combinations of surfaces, may also be used with line cuts or halftones. (See Units 105-110.) The general principles in page make-up are the same regardless of the printing surface, and a definite order should always be followed.

1. See that you have an O.K'd galley proof. When make-up is attempted before final O.K., corrections frequently require re-make of several pages.

2. Get a layout with complete specifications: page size, number of lines, running heads, leading, and folios (page numbers) to be used.

3. Collect all of the material you will need for the job and place it on or near your bank before any of the make-up is started. Figure 75-A shows material assembled for use in the make-up of a Linotype set booklet.

4. A page gauge should be used so that all pages will be made up to exactly the same length to insure register. Furthermore, if pages are not all the same length, difficulty will be experienced when locking the form. Notched metal furniture, like that shown in Figure 75-B, makes a good page gauge. If metal furniture is not available, a slug can be used. Be sure to use the same slug for gauging each page, because slugs may vary in length.

To determine the length of the page gauge, a solid page of text should be used — one that has no extra leading, headings, illustrations, or other material to break up its uniformity. Note in Figure 75-B that a section of slugs from the middle of the galley is being used to determine the standard page length.

Not many sizes of type will permit setting a page to exact pica lengths. When the pages do not come out to the exact length of one of the pieces of furniture, slugs or leads may be added to the bottom of the page to bring it out even with the gauge. Eight points is being added to the page shown in Figure 75-C in order to bring it out even with the 42-pica gauge. After each page is gauged, this extra material should be set aside so that it can be used in gauging subsequent pages.

5. The lines of type used for determining the standard page length should be returned to their proper place in the galley. Make-up can then be started with the first page of the text. Title or chapter headings should be positioned and spaced out. Figure 75-D shows the hand-set heading and the first "take" of slugs in place. Sufficient lines of the text should then be added to bring the page to proper length.

6. Figure 75-E shows how to check the length of the page. Exert pressure on the page with your left hand and feel with the forefinger how much the page extends past the gauge. It should be about a point. Spacing above and below the heading should be adjusted to achieve the proper page length.

7. A drop folio is usually put on an opening chapter page. The folio should not be counted in as part of the page, but should be put on after the page has been gauged for length. Figure 75-F shows the drop folio being inserted on the finished page. When there are to be several drop folios in the job, it is well, when determining the page length and the gauge, to include space for the folio. If this is done, however, extra precaution must be taken to see that the space is allowed on each page which does not have a folio. It is very easy to forget about the folio and get an extra line of text where the folio should be.

8. After the page is made up, it should be tied up; a proof pulled; and the type stored. The storage galley number should be marked on the proof when the form is stored away in the galley racks.

It is considered poor make-up to have make-up widows (a short line which falls at the top of the page) in the job. In fine work where the spacing has been done correctly, about the only way a widow can be eliminated is to have the copy edited so that the line will be made at least three-quarters full, or eliminated.

Expedients frequently resorted to in commercial work in order to eliminate a make-up widow are: to increase or decrease the amount of space around the sub-headings; to insert extra leading between paragraphs and, some-

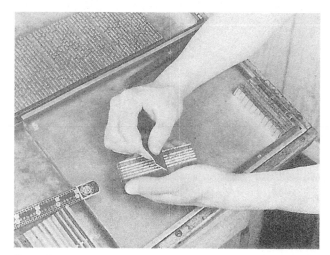

Fig. 75-D. Bottom of Slugs Must Be Scraped Before They Are Put in the Page

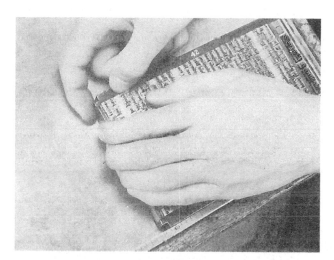

Fig. 75-E. Test Length of Each Page Made Up

Fig. 75-F. Drop Folios Should Be Put on Opening Chapter Pages

Fig. 75-G. Make Sub-heads and Space Around Them Replace a Specified Number of Lines

Fig. 76-A. Slugs from Composing Machines May Be Wider at One End

Fig. 76-B. Page Can Be Squared Up by Inserting Short Lengths of Lead-high Papers

times, even between lines; to wide-space the paragraphs in order to drive over more words to the line; or to use extremely thin spacing to drive back the widow to the preceding line. While these experiments are often used, they are frowned upon by printers who place emphasis on good typography. Troublesome make-up problems can often be solved by obtaining permission to make minor revisions in copy.

Leading and spacing should be uniform throughout the job, except in certain kinds of material, such as catalogs and directories, which naturally divide into separate items and where space between items aids the reader.

Make-up will be simplified when there are sub-heads if the head and spacing around it is made to equal an exact number of lines. For example, if the headings occupy one line and an extra line of spacing is distributed above and below the heading, as in Figure 75-G, the page will still come out to the proper length. However, when an arbitrary amount, say six points above and two points below the heading, is specified and the page is set in 12-point solid, it will be impossible to bring the page out to the proper length without resorting to expedients which will mar the page make-up.

Unit 76

How to Overcome Slug Inaccuracies

Unless slug-casting machines are kept in perfect adjustment, the slugs they deliver are likely to vary somewhat. Therefore, to make up material set on the Linotype or Intertype calls for certain precautions that do not apply to hand-set or Monotype composition.

1. The bottom of the slugs should be scraped with a make-up rule, as shown in Figure 75-D, in order to remove metal chips and fins which may have become imbedded on the bottom of the slug. Special care should be taken near the end of the slug, as a fin often turns back at that point. The make-up rule should be kept fairly sharp, so that it will go under and lift up these thin pieces of metal. If these metal pieces are not removed, they will cause the slugs to be too high and the lines will punch.

2. Type lines from slug machines are sometimes thicker at the top than at the bottom.

This can be detected in make-up by exerting pressure on the bottom of the page. If the slugs are thicker at the top, the type will have a tendency to form an arc and lift up the center of the page from the galley. To correct this condition, cut strips of 60 pound super about a quarter of an inch tall and about half a pica shorter than the width of the page. Drop a few of these "sinkers" in at intervals down the page and see that they go down to the galley. Be careful not to use too many sinkers, as then the fault of the form will be reversed and the bottom will be wider than the top.

3. Sometimes slugs are wider at one end than at the other. Two page gauges of exactly the same length should always be used when making up each page of slug machine composition. By exerting pressure on the end of the page and feeling with the fingers, you can determine if one side of the page is longer than the other. The difference in thickness between one end of the slug and the other is often so slight that it is impossible to detect it on a single slug. When several slugs are put together on a page, however, the error is multiplied and the difference can be seen when the gauges are used. Figure 76-A shows a page which has this fault.

To even up the two sides, lead-high strips of paper about one-fourth the width of the measure should be inserted at intervals down the shorter side of the page. (Figure 76-B.) They should be pushed down to the bottom of the form so that they will not print when the form is put on the press. Care must be used that they do not get turned under the bottom of the slug. Paper, used in correcting these inaccuracies, should never be thicker than about a 60 pound S & SC. Some printers resort to cardboards so that they do not have to put in so many pieces. The trouble with using cardboard is, that it oftens spreads the lines to such an extent that the additional space is noticeable.

4. The standard point is .01384, but for determining the thickness of their slug, the slug machine companies use a point which is .0140. As their point is larger, 25 lines of 12-point type will usually make slightly more than 25 picas. Added to this is the fact that the trimming knives on the machines are frequently not set to the machine point size. It is, therefore, difficult to calculate exactly how long a page of slug composition will be. The difficulty is not serious, however, as the pages can all be made up to exactly the same length if a definite number of leads and slugs are placed at the bottom of each page to bring it out even with the gauge.

Unit 77

How to Determine Margins

Progressive margins are used in book work: the back margin is the smallest; the top, outside, and bottom margins are progressively greater. For a book of approximately 2:3 proportion, such as a 6 x 9 upright:

Make type page length 70 per cent of paper page height and let width be 45 per cent of the paper page height. Type page is then 24 x 38 picas. Divide margins in ratio of 2:3, 3:5, or 5:8. Using 3:5, margins are: back (binding) 4½, top (head) 6, outside 7½, bottom (tail) 10. (See Figure 77-A.)

The diagonal method is convenient for finding proper length of the type page when width is given. Use one of the accepted proportions and find back margin. From the intersection of this margin and the diagonal, draw a line the given width of the page and from its end drop a perpendicular. The intersection with the diagonal is the bottom of the page. See dotted lines in Figure 77-A. Slight shifts can be made to keep the margins progressive, if more lines of type must go on the page.

Narrow margins are often used on trade books and are sometimes allocated by centering the type page and then pushing it "up and in" a pica or more, depending on the amount of space available.

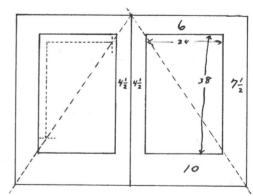

Fig. 77-A. Diagonal Method of Allocating Margins Illustrated by the Dotted Lines

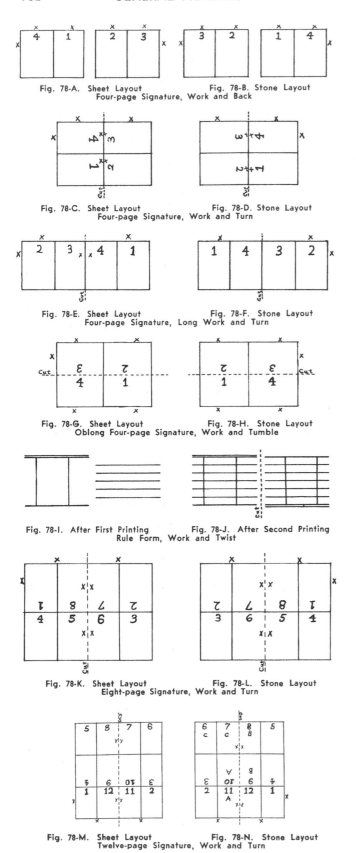

Fig. 78-A. Sheet Layout   Fig. 78-B. Stone Layout
Four-page Signature, Work and Back

Fig. 78-C. Sheet Layout   Fig. 78-D. Stone Layout
Four-page Signature, Work and Turn

Fig. 78-E. Sheet Layout   Fig. 78-F. Stone Layout
Four-page Signature, Long Work and Turn

Fig. 78-G. Sheet Layout   Fig. 78-H. Stone Layout
Oblong Four-page Signature, Work and Tumble

Fig. 78-I. After First Printing   Fig. 78-J. After Second Printing
Rule Form, Work and Twist

Fig. 78-K. Sheet Layout   Fig. 78-L. Stone Layout
Eight-page Signature, Work and Turn

Fig. 78-M. Sheet Layout   Fig. 78-N. Stone Layout
Twelve-page Signature, Work and Turn

How to Impose Forms

Imposition is the placing of the pages in the form so that they will be in proper position and sequence when the sheet is printed and folded. Not all folding machines fold a sheet in the same way. Some impositions are more easily hand folded than are others. To determine the proper imposition, make a sheet layout showing the position of the pages on the printed sheet by folding a blank sheet exactly as the signature is to be folded, and then numbering the pages. A stone layout shows the position of the pages in the form.

A signature is a sheet folded and ready for binding. Two or more signatures, inserted one within the other, are called a section. A signature may be imposed to print as follows:

Work and back (sheetwise), using two forms. One side is "worked," then a new form is put on the press and the printed sheets turned over and "backed" to complete the signature. See Figures 78-A and 78-B, in which "x" indicates press or folding guide edge.

To maintain register, the side guide must be changed to the opposite side of the press (same edge of the paper) on the backup of all forms.

Work and turn, using one form. All pages of the signature are locked in one form. The stock, cut double size, is printed on one side, then "turned" and printed on the other. When cut apart, there are two duplicate signatures. See Figures 78-C, 78-D, 78-E, and 78-F.

Work and tumble, using one form. Similar to the work and turn in that all pages are locked in one form and two duplicate signatures are delivered from the double size stock, this method differs because the sheet is "tumbled." The tail of the sheet is brought against the guides for printing of the second side. For this reason register is difficult and the tumble imposition is therefore avoided whenever possible — when used, the stock must be squared up before printing is started. Figures 78-G and 78-H show a work and tumble imposition.

Work and twist (work and whirl), using one form and printing it twice on one side of the sheet only, is widely used to print rule forms, the advantage being that the rules cross without breaks. See Figures 78-I and 78-J.

The eight page signature shown in Figures 78-K and 78-L, and the other work and turn signatures shown, could be printed work and back by locking and printing separately the right and left halves of the forms.

Books and booklets must be trimmed after binding to even the edges and open the bolts (folds). Allowance for trim — a minimum of one-eighth inch — must be put in the form.

Before starting lock-up, a page chart, shown in Figure 78-Q, should be made. It enables one to visualize the margins and trim, and prevents fumbling and errors at the stone. As a check, the margins, type form width, and trim added together should equal the untrimmed page width. Length is similarly checked.

A lock-up chart, Figure 78-R, is then made, and the width of the gutters (space in the form which gives margins on the printed sheet) is indicated. This information is obtained from the four figures shown in circles on chart.

Note that pages ordinarily lie head to head and back to back, in pairs, called mated pages. The sum of the folios of two mated pages is one more than the number of pages in a booklet.

Procedure for imposing and locking forms:

1. Fold a sheet layout. Mark folios, heads, and folding guides. Marking trim also may help.

2. Make a page chart, putting the information on it in a neat and orderly manner.

3. Make a lock-up chart.

4. Wipe off the surface of the imposing table.

5. For a sheetwise imposition, determine which side is to print first. Place that side of the sheet layout face down on the stone with the double x guide edge toward you.

6. Fold back enough of the layout sheet for you to see one row of the pages on the under side. Mark on the stone, with chalk, the folios and position of the heads on these pages; then continue, row by row, and mark the position of the other pages.

7. For work and turn imposition, draw a chalk line straight in front of you. Place the double x edge on the line and the single x toward you. Mark position of one half as in No. 6. Then pivot the sheet on the line and mark other half.

8. Put pages on stone in positions shown. Put chase around them and put in furniture in accordance with the lock-up chart.

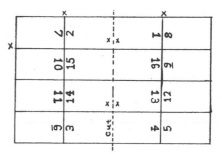

Fig. 78-O. Stone Layout, Sixteen-page Signature, Work and Turn

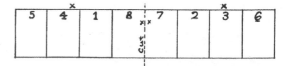

Fig. 78-P. Stone Layout, Eight-page Signature, Work and Turn, Parallel Folds

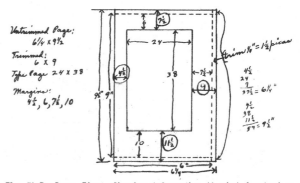

Fig. 78-Q. Page Chart, Showing Information Needed for Lock-up

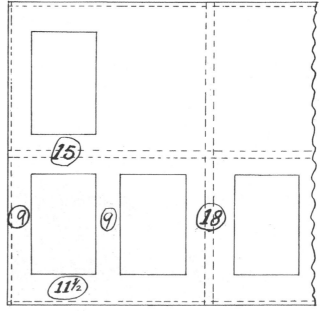

Fig. 78-R. Lock-up Chart, Made Up from Page Chart

Date	Opponent	Game At
Sept. 30	Wittenberg College	Springfield
Oct. 7	Notre Dame	South Bend
Oct. 14	New York University	New York
Oct. 28	Case	Cleveland
Nov. 11	University of Pittsburgh	Pittsburgh
Nov. 18	Holy Cross	Worcester, Mass.
Nov. 30	Temple	Philadelphia

Fig. 79-A. Copy for a Tabular Form Suitable for Multiple Justification

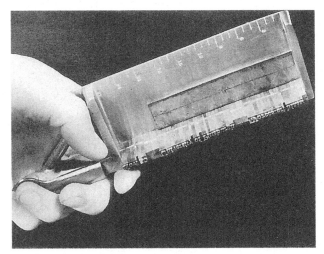

Fig. 79-B. Justification Gauges Should Be Pica Length, Six-point Slugs or Brass Rule

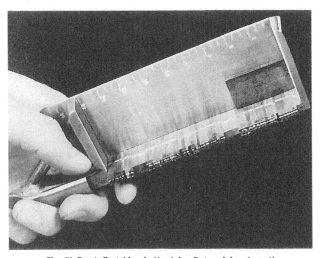

Fig. 79-C. A Test Line is Used for Determining Length of the Gauges

Unit 79

How to Multiple Justify

Figure 79-A shows copy for a football schedule, to be set in tabular form in 12 point Goudy Bold. Multiple justification (individual justification of two or more columns or groups in the same line) should be used in order to get vertical alignment of the columns. Multiple justification is achieved by inserting gauges which permit each column to be set to its measure without changing the stick setting.

The procedure to be followed in setting a tabular form, such as Figure 79-A, is:

1. Study the columns and pick out the widest group of words in each. Picking out the widest group is important. In the "date" column shown, "Sept. 30" has one more character but is not as wide as "Nov. 30." When in doubt as to which is the wider of two groups, set them in type and then compare them.

2. Calculate the approximate measure needed and set the stick. For rough calculation, the average width of a type character or space can be considered as that of an en quad. Allow four characters — two ems — between the columns. Counting across the three widest groups (circled) in the example, it is found there are 55 characters and spaces. A 12 point en quad is 6 points wide. A pica equals 12 points.

Calculating: (55 x 6) ÷ 12 = 27½ picas. Half measures are to be avoided, so the stick should be set at 27 picas.

3. Compose a test line, consisting of the widest group from each column, and then adjust the measure if necessary. Type characters often average as much as 10 per cent less than an en quad. Goudy Bold, however, is a wide type and the calculated measure is satisfactory. (Figure 79-B.) Note that the thinnest possible space, a 5-em, was used between "Nov." and "30."

4. A slug, or a brass rule, six points in thickness, should be used for the justification gauge. Columns should be kept to even pica measures if possible. Figure 79-B shows that the start of the second column falls closest to 21 picas, so a 21 pica slug was chosen for the gauge. Two 5-em spaces, inserted after the two quads, will cause the start of the second column to align. However, it is not necessary to change spacing in the test line as that line is not used.

A slug used as a gauge should have an "x" penciled on its side so that a slug of a different length will not unintentionally be picked up and used.

5. Figure 79-C shows an 8 pica slug being tried as a possible gauge for setting the second column. Its length is satisfactory, as the last column can be shifted sufficiently by taking out space after "Mass." to align the start of the column with the slug.

6. The start of the actual composition of the job is shown in Figure 79-D. The gauge material — consisting of the 21 pica slug, a 2-em quad, and two 5-em spaces — has been put in the stick and "Sept. 30" set. The column is being justified after the period, as alignment at the end as well as at the beginning of the group is desired.

7. The next step is to substitute the shorter gauge in place of the longer one used for the first column, and then compose the type in the second column group. Figure 79-E shows the group set and being justified against the 8 pica slug.

8. Figure 79-F shows the final step in justifying the last column group in the third line. No gauge is required for the last column — the type is set and justified in the space remaining between the preceding column and the end of the stick.

The tabular form, shown here as Figure 79-G, has six columns, but it can be set from most types with a single justification for each line. Figures in most types are cast on an en quad body, and figure columns composed from such types are self-justifying.

Card Gothic, Engravers Roman, and some book types, have figures which are not of uniform width; therefore, they must be set with multiple justification if used for composing a table, such as Figure 79-G.

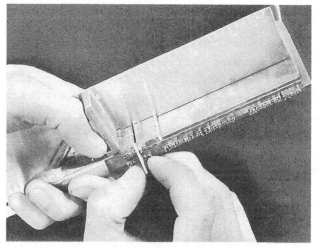

Fig. 79-D. The First Column is Justified with the Long Gauge in Place

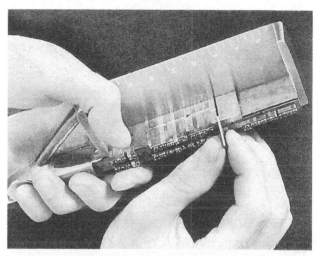

Fig. 79-E. Wrong Justifications will Affect the Alignment of the Columns

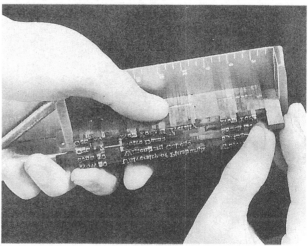

Fig. 79-F. No Gauge is Needed for the Last Column

ALPHABET LENGTHS IN POINTS

	8 pt.	10 pt.	12 pt.	14 pt.	18 pt.
Caslon	102	128	153	161	195
Bodoni	109	127	146	167	214
Kable Light	102	120	137	155	174
Century Expanded	119	142	162	194	228

Fig. 79-G.

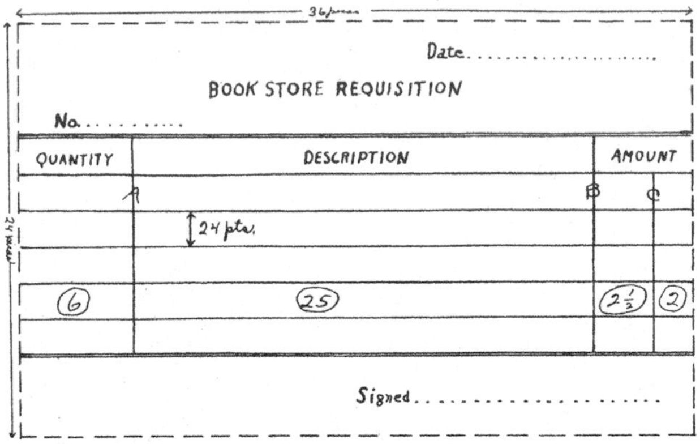
Date.....................
BOOK STORE REQUISITION
No..........
QUANTITY
DESCRIPTION
AMOUNT
A
B
C
24 pts.
6
25
2½
2
Signed.....................

Fig. 80-A. Copy for a Rule Form to Print on a 6 x 4 Inch Sheet

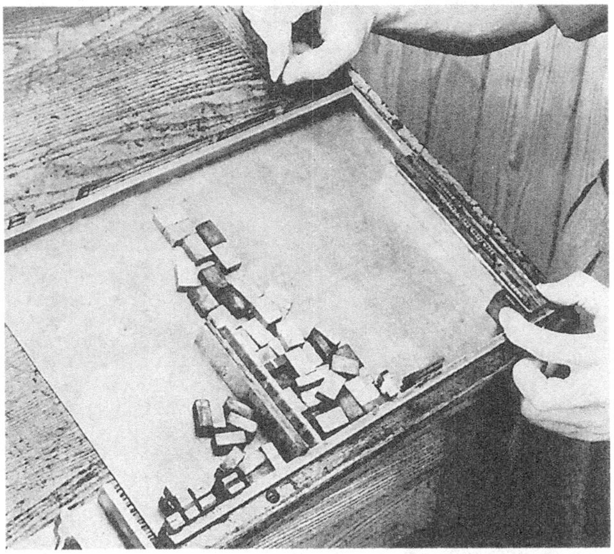

Fig. 80-B. Build Up the Form in the Galley — Never in the Stick

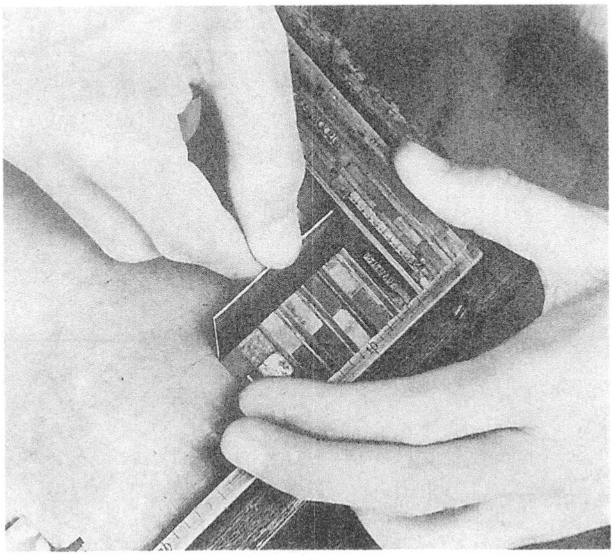

Fig. 80-C. Set Column by Column from Left to Right

Unit 80

How to Set a Rule Form

Figure 80-A shows hand-drawn copy for a rule form to be printed on a sheet 6 x 4 inches in size. This job could be produced from a wax plate furnished by an electrotyper; from a rule form set either on Ludlow, Intertype, Linotype, or Monotype machines; or from a form set by hand, using brass rule or strip (type metal) rule. The hand-set form could be composed in three ways: as two forms, printing one form over the other — requiring two press runs; as a work and twist form; or as one form with the horizontal rules broken at the intersection with the vertical rules. The last mentioned method is the one explained in this unit.

Faces and body sizes available in brass and type metal rules include:

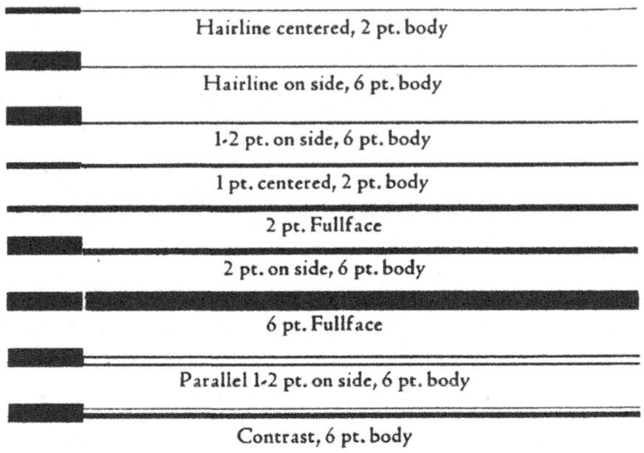
Hairline centered, 2 pt. body
Hairline on side, 6 pt. body
1-2 pt. on side, 6 pt. body
1 pt. centered, 2 pt. body
2 pt. Fullface
2 pt. on side, 6 pt. body
6 pt. Fullface
Parallel 1-2 pt. on side, 6 pt. body
Contrast, 6 pt. body

Faces in a wide variety of weights and combinations are also available on the above and other body sizes, such as 1, 3, 4, 8, 12, 18, and 24 point.

Brass rule is available in labor-saving fonts, with lengths which increase from 1 to 10 picas by half picas, and from 10 to 36 picas by picas. A line, or nick, is scribed near the face edge of most brass rule. Forms should be laid out so that standard lengths can be used with as little piecing together as possible.

Type metal strip rule comes in two-foot lengths (brass rule does, too) and can be cut to the length wanted.

Hairline rule is used for the cross lines on most forms; vertical rules are usually either hairline, one-half point or one point face. Head and foot (cap) rules are usually as dark as or darker than the vertical rules, and often have a double (parallel) face.

To set the job from the copy shown in Figure 80-A, proceed as follows:

1. Measure the overall width of the copy with your line gauge. It measures 18½ picas, approximately half the width wanted. Measure the copy depth — it also is about half size.

2. Make a rough sketch of the form so that you can do your figuring on the sketch and thus not mutilate the original copy.

3. Measure the width of the first column under the box head "Quantity." It measures about three picas, but as the copy is half size, a "6" should be put in this column and circled on your sketch. The "Description" column measures 12½ picas, which becomes 25 on the sketch. The dollar and cents column, under "Amount," are to be put down as 3 and 2, as they measure about 1½ and 1 pica respectively.

4. Total the figures you have put on the sketch: 6 + 25 + 3 + 2 = 36, which is the overall width of the form. No allowance has been made for the space occupied by the three vertical rules. Each is hairline centered on a 2 point body, so the space occupied will be six points or one-half pica. Reduce the space occupied by the dollar column, as it is unlikely that space for more than three figures will be needed on a Book Store Requisition.

5. Measure the vertical rules A, B, and C and put down their length (twice their measurement) on your sketch.

6. Calculate and list the kind and amount of spacing material needed between the horizontal lines in each column. The hairlines are to be 24 points apart; the body of the rule is two points. Therefore, 22 points between rules will give the proper spacing. The spacing must be exact in the various columns if the rules are to align horizontally. If possible, use the same number of pieces of quads or furniture to get the vertical dimension of your spacing. Three pieces have been used to get the 22 points needed in the example. Horizontal spacing material should be the widest available, to avoid handling unnecessary units and to make the form more solid. Small pieces are likely to work up.

7. The space to be filled between rules in the first column is 6 picas by 22 points. Few school plants have any great quantity of 72 point

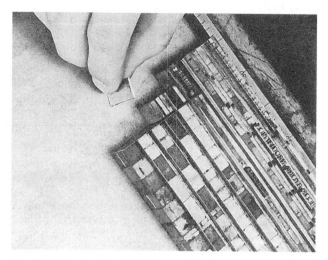

Fig. 80-D. Plugging for Odd Measures Can be Avoided by Using a Micrometer Stick

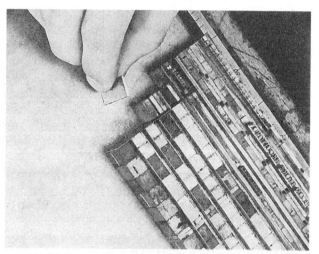

Fig. 80-E. Quads are Better Than Leads and Slugs for Spacing Between Rules — Less Springy

Fig. 80-F. Same Number of Pieces (Three Here) Vertically Between Horizontal Rules Aids Alignment

spacing material. Therefore, use two 36 point en quads side by side, and two 6 pica leads to fill the space.

Eight 36 point en (18 point 2-em) quads, two 18 point 3-em spaces, and two 25 pica leads will fill the space in the second column. The dollar column is 30 points wide; material 30 x 22 points is needed. List the available 30 point quads and spaces, cross off the fractional ones and consider the others one by one until the proper combination is obvious:

em quad	30 x 30 — too large	
en quad	30 x 15 — 22 – 15 = 7; no 7 listed	
3-em space	30 x 10 — 22 – 10 = 12; two 5-ems equal	12 pts.
4-em space	30 x 7½	
5-em space	30 x 6	

It is clear that a 3-em and two 5-em spaces will occupy 30 x 22 points.

8. The last column needs 24 x 22 points of spacing material. List the 24-point quads and spaces and it can easily be seen that two 3-ems and a 4-em space give 22 points.

9. Make a list of the rule needed for the job, indicating the number of pieces, length and face. Cap rules are to be parallel half point face on a six point body to give rigidity.

10. Get the rule from the rule case if you are to use brass rule; cut the rule if you are to use strip material. Monotype strip rule was used in the example.

Gather the quads, leads, slugs and other material and arrange it on your bank in an orderly manner.

11. Set your stick for 36 picas, compose the heading and space it out on the galley. Insert the head rule (parallel ½ on 6, 36 picas).

12. Re-set the stick to 6 picas and compose the box heading "Quantity." Use six point type (seldom larger than eight point) for box heads. Put the head in place, as shown in Figure 80-B. Put a slug and a lead (8 points) above and below the type. Keep leads away from the ends of columns. Why? Insert a rule, and make-up the balance of the column.

Figure 80-C shows the first column made up and the vertical rule is being inserted. Why is the spacing material at the bottom of the column 72 x 24 points?

13. Set the second head, insert it and make-up the column.

14. Center "Amount" on a 4½-pica measure and put it in place. Figure 80-D shows how to put a lead (2 x 18 points) at the end of the heading to space it out to the overall width of the two columns and the rule below.

15. Make up the remaining two columns. Figure 80-E shows the "dollar" column being spaced out with 30 point spaces.

16. Space out the "cents" column. Put on the foot rule. Set the signature line, using two-dot-to-the-em leaders. Insert the line and space it out. Figure 80-F shows the completed form ready for tying up.

Unit 81

How to Classify Types

Type faces can be divided into many different classifications. For our purpose, the serif classification below will serve:

1. Round Serif or Oldstyle

2. Transitional

3. **Flat Serif or Modern**

4. Sans Serif

5. Square Serif

6. *Decorative*

Most of the types which fall in the first five classifications are available in the regular roman and italic forms, and many of them are cast in both roman and italic in such additional forms as bold, extra bold, condensed, extra condensed, and outline.

Oldstyle types of *good design* are considered to be our most legible and artistic form, and are therefore excellent for all text composition. The larger sizes of most of these faces are suitable for display. Excellent oldstyle types are Caslon, Garamond, and Cloister.

Flat serif modern roman is the form of letter most widely used for text at present, although it is said to be less legible and definitely lacks the grace and character present in the better oldstyles. The everyday "workhorse," Century Expanded, in which this book is composed, is one of these types, and similar forms are found in newspapers and magazines the country over. Obviously, these types are not recommended for work which has beauty as a prime requisite. However, many of the defects of their design can be overcome by a typographer with taste.

Flat serif types, such as Bodoni, with sharp contrast between the thick and thin strokes, are good types for display and short portions of text. Although they are also used rather widely as a text letter in magazines, and frequently in books, types of less contrast would often be a better choice.

While most of the transitional types have some of the crisp, business-like character of the moderns because of the incorporation of thin lines and angular serifs in some of the letters, they are usually more closely related in design to the oldstyles. The better types of this group, such as Bulmer and Baskerville, because of their high legibility and good design, are suitable for all around use.

Sans serif and square serif types are monotone letters and because of their lack of contrast are considered less legible than oldstyle and modern. Their use as text letter should be limited to advertisements and short booklets. They can be used for job and display work, but require careful handling. "Decorative" includes all types not listed in the preceding five classifications. Decorative types are best used occasionally and then only for a word or two. Some types which fall in this classification are:

Script, **Black-letter,** *Script*

Lines of all capitals of Black Letter (and Script) are illegible and should not be used. Black Letter is variously called Text, Wedding Text, and Old English, but its true name is Gothic. However, American designers have given the name Gothic to sans serif types, which in Europe are known as Grotesque.

The fitting of disconnected scripts, and display lines of roman and italic, caps or lowercase, can be improved by careful letterspacing. When there is sufficient white space around the line, interspacing (spreading) will often make the line more effective. Interspacing of lines of extra condensed display types is essential if they are to be legible. Connected scripts should never be interspaced or letterspaced.

Swash letters, which are elaborated italics, are intended for occasional use at the beginning or end of a line or word.

Unit 82

How to Identify Types

It is a hopeless task to attempt to learn to identify all types on sight, because there are thousands of different type faces. However, the ability to recognize types most commonly used can and should be attained. Things to look for are: *a.* serif formation; *b.* contrast between the thick and thin parts of the letters; *c.* the general appearance of the type in mass; and *d.* peculiarities of particular characters.

Round serif (oldstyle) types have two common characteristics: *a.* gradual change from the thick to the thin strokes, and *b.* round (bracketed) serifs.

Most flat serif (modern) types, in contradistinction to the oldstyle, have: *a.* an abrupt change from the heavy stroke to the extremely thin line usually present in these types; *b.* flat serifs which join the stems at right angles; and *c.* a curly-tailed "R."

Oldstyle Figures 1234567890 SMALL CAPITALS

Modern Figures 1234567890 CAPITALS

Shown here are identifying characters of four common type faces. T, r, and g will show serif formation and contrast, and in addition are likely to have slight differences in design. To these add three letters which differ most in design from those in other fonts, and you will have six letters, easily remembered, which will usually give the key to identification. Specimens of a wide variety of type faces are shown on pages 118-121.

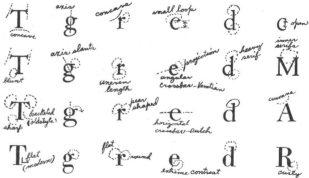

Fig. 82-A. Identifying Characteristics of Garamond, Cloister, Caslon, Bodoni

THE OPENING
WEDNESDAY
APRIL 3, 1940
ADA'S
BEAUTY SHOPPE
SPECIALIZNG IN
ALL BRANCHES OF BEAUTY CULTURE
FORMERLY PETER PAN BEAUTY SHOPPE
251 ATWOOD STREET, TWO BLOCKS BELOW
FORBES ST., PITTSBURGH, PENNA.
ADA ATKINSON, Prop.   SChenley 8560

Fig. 83-A.   Commercial Setting of Beauty Shop Announcement

ADA ATKINSON ANNOUNCES

THE OPENING APRIL THIRD OF

ADA'S BEAUTY SHOPPE

AT 251 ATWOOD STREET: TWO BLOCKS SOUTH OF FORBES

SCHENLEY 8560

Fig. 83-B.   Student Re-setting of Above Announcement

Unit 83

How to Use Display

A finished piece of display typography is, in reality, a picture. Therefore, the rules which govern the arrangement of the display elements in printing are essentially the same as those which are used as guides in determining the points of emphasis in the composition of a good photograph.

A writer on photography defines composition as "the means taken to insure that the subject is given the importance that it deserves and not lost or overpowered by its surroundings; and that the picture, as a whole, is pleasing or carries out the feeling that was intended."

He also says, "Of as great importance as any device of composition is simplification — the use of plain, unobtrusive backgrounds and foregrounds, and the elimination of competing subjects: miscellaneous doors, windows, clapboards, and common objects of all sorts which make the principal subject actually hard to find in the picture."

Try to find the principal subject in the mailing card shown as Figure 83-A. It took real ingenuity and considerable time to put together this typographic concoction of three illustrations and nine kinds and sizes of type. The result is, to say the least, not pleasing, nor does it carry out the feeling intended. The principle of simplification has been applied to the student re-setting shown as Figure 83-B. Only one type face (in two sizes) has been used, and unimportant copy has been eliminated.

Every piece of printing, whether it be a simple business form, an advertisement, or a fine book or brochure, has a specific job to do. The printed piece must be designed to do that job. Many printers excuse their crude typography with the statement, "It is good enough for the purpose," apparently feeling that the function is achieved so long as the words of the copy are printed on the sheet. They are risking an unpleasant reaction on the part of the reader by ignoring man's inherent love for the beautiful.

To a certain extent, the use of display is a matter of taste or preference on the part of the person designing or composing a printed piece. Several typographers, given the task of designing a job involving display, would prob-ably each present a different rendition. However, careful examination of their work would show that certain principles have been followed.

The pervading principles of typography involve orderliness, simplicity, logical arrangement, pleasing appearance, and appropriateness for the purpose intended. These principles must be applied with sincere consideration of the reader's interests, desires, and habits. The typographer seeks a harmonious relationship among the type faces used, a sense of balance between display and text types, and appropriate placement of the composition elements on the page in relation to white space.

In most instances, the purposes in using display types and introducing variety into a typographic arrangement are to attract the reader's attention, arouse his interest, and make it easy for him to read and decipher quickly the message conveyed by the printed job. Usually the typographic arrangements involving display are related to the purpose of convincing the reader of the importance of the message being conveyed and, frequently, inducing a desired action on his part. In achieving this latter purpose, a typographic design may make a contribution, but the primary responsibility rests with the text itself.

The possibilities of display are almost limitless because it may be achieved by variations in type arrangement, contrast in weight of the type face, contrast in shape, and variation in size, all of which may be supplemented by the use of symbols, illustrations, and color. Display lines may be set in type of the same family as that used in the main body of the printed piece, type of another family, or special display types which harmonize.

Students using this book will do well to devote their practice efforts to the simpler forms of achieving contrast, harmony, and balance, leaving novelty and "trick" typography to those more experienced in their application. In this connection, one should recognize that much of the effort that is expended commercially in seeking to achieve novelty in the use of display and typographic layout is not only wasted but, to a certain extent, the result is offensive to the reader. A good slogan to remember in preparing and executing a typographic layout is "type was made to be read."

Unit 84

How to Set Display

1. Analyze the copy carefully and pick out the most important feature, and possibly one or two other points that will aid in presenting the subject of the copy.

2. Decide on which device or devices you will attempt to use to attract attention.

3. Make several "thumbnail" (small) sketches, arranging the main body of the copy as a background for the display elements.

4. "Blow up" the most likely sketch to full size and copyfit to check the arrangement.

5. The display elements should be the key to the arrangement — set them first.

6. Set text without justification; re-arrange it to eliminate word breaks, etc.; then justify and make changes if necessary.

In setting display, it is extremely important to consider carefully the purpose to be achieved and to take into account the tastes, desires, and reading habits of the persons to whom the job is being directed.

Good typography may be said to be "transparent" because the designer has done his job so logically and so well that the reader concentrates solely on the message and is unaware of any typographic devices which have been used. A simple, orderly, and logical arrangement of the type, with careful attention to details, will often create the pleasant atmosphere necessary for the proper consideration of a printed message.

The exact opposite of transparent typography is illustrated by the program shown as Figure 84-A. Not being satisfied with an absurd arrangement of type, the designer further disregarded the purpose of the program by printing it on sheets of colored poster paper, 12 by 18 inches in size. Presumably the printed piece was supposed to contribute a weird effect because of the nature of the play, but that effect was amply taken care of in the dialogue and the stage settings.

The program should have served as a convenient means of making the audience acquainted with the information about the play which the producers were trying to convey. Instead, great inconvenience and commotion resulted when members of the audience attempted to turn the large, crackly sheets of paper to the many angles necessary in attempting to decipher the text scattered about the page in groups of poorly printed, large and small sizes of bold face type.

A further insult to the reader's intelligence was committed through the use of "cockroach" typography, including the elimination of all capitals from proper names in listing the cast of characters.

The illustrations of typography shown in Figures 83-A and 84-A, when compared with illustrations 83-B and 85-A, emphasize the most important principle of typography:

Display should be used for a purpose, but the purpose should be to win the cooperation of the reader, rather than alienate him.

Consult Units 89 and 91 for special instructions on copyfitting and preparing layouts.

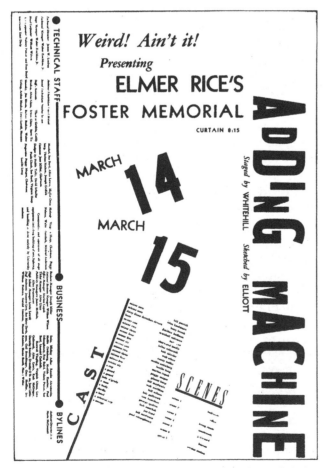

Fig. 84-A. A Program — With Purpose Completely Ignored

Unit 85

How to Display Advertising

One hundred fifty years ago, people eagerly sought and read every line of the small newspapers which were being established throughout the country. The advertiser, like the editor, was certain his offering would be read and re-read, because in most of the homes the only other reading matter available was the Bible. Today, printing must compete for time and attention with television, the radio, the movies, the automobile, and hundreds of other recreational activities. The average person has time to read but little (estimated to be less than five per cent) of the great quantity of newspapers, magazines, books, advertisements, and other printing which comes before him.

To get and hold the attention of the reader, the newspaper, through the use of headings and sub-headings, must offer a sample of the news stories. The headline stops the reader, the sub-heads give him additional pertinent information, and if he is interested and wishes a more detailed account, he may read the small type of the complete story. Likewise, the advertisers, through display, must offer the prospective reader a sampling that will attract his attention and then enable him to determine if the subordinate material is likely to be of interest.

Advertising printing, unlike such printing as program covers, title pages, etc., usually must compete with other units for attention. In an effort to get more forceful display — punch — many typographers resort to the use of bold face types and types of unusual form. Others use appropriate conventional types set in a manner which commands attention.

One or more of the following devices is often used for attracting attention to an advertisement: white space, large type in the heading, contrast with surroundings, illustration, pleasing appearance, color, decoration, unusual letter forms, and unique layout.

Figure 85-A makes use of a combination of an illustration, white space, and unusual type form to attract attention, while Figure 87-A, to achieve the same purpose, has a combination of white space and large type which gives it a pleasing appearance and contrasts it with the adjacent advertisements.

While the first aim of display typography is to attract attention, of equal importance is the function of presenting the copy so that it may be easily grasped by the reader. This second function is usually accomplished by careful selection of the features to be emphasized, in order that the displayed elements will tell the story, even though the subordinate text is not read. Figure 85-A is an excellent example of choice of pertinent points for display. What is being advertised, the maker, the price, and where to get the product are all quickly evident. It is well to keep in mind that the eye can take in only three or four elements at one glance. Note that in Figure 85-A the display is in two groups, the top group having three elements, and the lower group two.

Fig. 85-A. Pertinent Points Displayed

Unit 86

How to Make Conventional

Type Arrangements

It would be well for the beginner in typography to remember the saying, "There is nothing new under the sun," and to master the conventional way of arranging type. Book pages are arranged today essentially the same as Jenson and the other early masters arranged their pages nearly 500 years ago. Display typography started with the first title page, about 1500, and has evolved gradually to its present form. Thousands of different arrangements have been tried and most of them have been discarded. The patterns which have survived, and they are few, have done so probably because they are more pleasing.

There are certain general principles and rules which can be pointed out to the beginner, and they should be thoroughly learned. But knowledge of the rules is not enough. He must also have, or acquire, taste — the ability to discern and appreciate the pleasing, the refined, and the proper.

The conventionally arranged title pages shown as Figures 86-A, B, C, and D, were designed by contemporary typographers of recognized ability. Study of these specimens will show that the designers, either consciously or unconsciously, were guided by certain principles in arranging the type. Some of these principles are discussed in the following paragraphs.

Contour. The outline of the type mass should present an orderly, pleasing pattern. Shapes found to look especially well are those which suggest, but do not follow rigidly, the contour of the inverted pyramid and the oval. Figure 86-A is a natural arrangement in a shape suggesting the inverted pyramid with a short line above. Figure 86-C is a similar arrangement, but here the inverted pyramid is more regular in outline. Figure 86-B has the top group arranged in an oval shape. Squared-up rectangular contours, such as 86-D, are attractive because of their orderly appearance, but they are difficult to achieve. It is seldom that the copy is so worded that it will lend itself to proper division and emphasis and still come out to even line lengths.

Unity. The type should be massed around one or two main points. Avoid spotty effects which occur when the type is scattered over the page, when spacing between words is greater than leading between lines, and when leading between lines is greater than the margin surrounding the composition. Figures 86-A and 86-D are definitely unified into one group, while Figure 86-B consists of two units.

Harmony of Shape. The shape of the type group and the page upon which it is printed should harmonize. Note that all four of the examples shown are upright pages (taller than they are wide), and that the type groups are of the same general shape. Note particularly that the oval group in Figure 86-B is more in harmony because of the addition of the flag ornament to give it length. In Figure 86-D the space inside the page border has been divided into two sections — the large upper panel giving information regarding the volume, while the small panel below the hairline rule is reserved for the publisher's imprint. Note that the rectangle formed by the imprint line harmonizes in shape with the panel enclosing it.

Harmony of Tone. The most pleasing effect usually occurs when there is harmony of tone between the various types, borders, ornaments and illustrations. Figure 86-C is the best example of tone harmony in the four pages shown, the large lines contrasting but slightly with the remainder of the composition. Type becomes blacker as it becomes larger in size (the change is more pronounced in some types than it is in

A History of
The Printed Book
BEING THE THIRD NUMBER OF
THE DOLPHIN
Edited by Lawrence C. Wroth
*Librarian of the John Carter Brown Library
Providence Rhode Island*

NEW YORK
The Limited Editions Club
1938

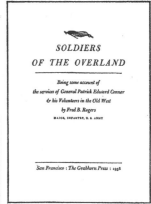

*SOLDIERS
OF THE OVERLAND*

*Being some account of
the services of General Patrick Edward Connor
& his Volunteers in the Old West
by Fred B. Rogers*
MAJOR, INFANTRY, U. S. ARMY

San Francisco : The Grabhorn Press : 1938

Fig. 86-A. Title Page
by Carl Rollins

Fig. 86-B. Title Page
by Edward and Robert Grabhorn

others), hence to keep harmony of tone it is sometimes necessary to use a different and lighter typeface for the display lines.

In the full-size originals of Figures 86-A and 86-D, the illustrations were in harmony with the type. That harmony was lost when the pages were reduced for reproduction here, the nature of the illustrations being such that the interior white space was lost and they became almost solid blacks.

Harmony of Type. The use of harmonious types will aid in securing a pleasing effect. Tone, form, and design must be considered to achieve harmony when combining types. It was pointed out in a preceding paragraph that types often become darker in tone as they become larger in point size. In a given size of a type, lines of all capitals, all small capitals, and capital and lower case lines of italic or roman, may differ in degree of blackness.

Often, the easiest way to achieve harmony of the type is to use but one form (and one design) in the entire composition. In Figure 86-B, the page is set in italic, except for one minor line. Figures 86-C and 86-D are composed in all capitals. It would be well to leave the mixing of the various forms, as in Figure 86-A, to the expert typographer. Simplicity in type arrangement is always good taste.

Harmony of Color. The novice in printing should limit himself to a safe color combination such as vermillion and black; and the vermillion should be used sparingly. There is no color as strong in tone as black. Therefore, the line to be printed in color should be set in a type of a heavier weight to prevent a weak appearance due to lack of tone harmony.

Proportion. 2:3, 3:4 and 3:5 have been found to be pleasing proportions in printed matter. The sizes of the title pages shown here are very near one or another of these proportions.

Position. The position most easily seen in a given space is said to be about two-fifths down from the top and slightly to the left of the horizontal center. Slightly less prominent is the top, while the bottom is regarded as third best. On the pages shown, the book title has been placed in either one or the other of the two most prominent spots, while the publisher's imprint occupies the third position.

The positioning of a rectangular block of type on a page requires that equal margins be put at the two sides, and the same or a little more at the top. The bottom margin should be the greatest of the four. Often the top margin is in proportion to the bottom as 2:3. A page placed in exact center vertically will appear too low, as the optical center is actually slightly above the exact center.

Contrast. Some form of contrast should be used to cause the principal points to stand out in the composition.

Contrast of size and contrast of tone cause the titles to stand out in the title page examples. It is recommended that the use of bold face types to secure contrast of tone be limited to advertisements, as these types are less pleasingly proportioned than the roman design after which they are patterned.

Contrast of form is also present in Figure 86-B, the italic capitals contrasting with the italic lower-case used for the major part of the page. Decorative types are widely used to achieve contrast of form, but when this device is resorted to there also should be present a harmony between the decorative type and some part of the composition.

Balance. The most pleasing effect, from the standpoint of balance, seems to be achieved when the center of mass of the type group is placed about two-fifths down from the top of the page. See especially, Figures 86-D and 86-C. The addition of a small group near the bottom of the page often seems to add to the stability of the design as a whole.

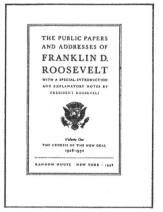

Fig. 86-C. Title Page
by William A. Kittredge

Fig. 86-D. Title Page
by Joseph Blumenthal

Unit 87

How to Use Modern Typographic Style

Centered arrangements, such as the illustrations in Unit 86, in which the contour is similar on each side of a centered vertical axis, are known as symmetrical layouts. Arrangements in which the parts on the two sides of the axis are dissimilar (see Figure 87-A) are known as asymmetrical layouts. They have been avoided by most printers because of the difficulty of achieving a pleasing effect with the irregular contour. In recent years a so-called "modern" style of typography has developed which is based on the application of fundamental principles to the asymmetrical arrangement, rather than on the use of any particular form or design of type, as some seem to believe.

The fresh, clean streamlined look which is evident in most good contemporary work, whether "modern" or conventional in arrangement, is usually the result of a simple, logical presentation of the display elements with a careful apportioning of the white space — a massing of the white space at spots where it will be most effective.

An analysis of Figure 87-A, a "modern" arrangement, follows:

Basically it is a rectangular arrangement. If a rectangle is drawn so that the lines touch the edge of the type on the four sides, it will be found that the margins are conventional — equal at the sides, with possibly a little more at the top, and with the bottom the largest.

White space has been massed and aids in emphasizing the heading. The heading has been "stepped" in order to lead the eye to the firm name. Compare the harmonious effect achieved by interspacing the heading in the large field of white, with the effect present in the interspaced lines of condensed caps in the crowded advertisement shown as Figure 87-C.

The proportion between the widths of the areas occupied by the heading and the text group approach one of the accepted ratios.

The composition is unified around a vertical axis which is off the center. Order is achieved by starting the text, without indention, on that axis and by directing the motion from the illustration and the heading to the junction of the axis and base. Turn to Figure 83-B and note the similarity in handling of the units around the vertical axis; also pay special attention to the handling of the important phone number — it is centered on the axis, and placed at the bottom, which is one of the most effective display positions.

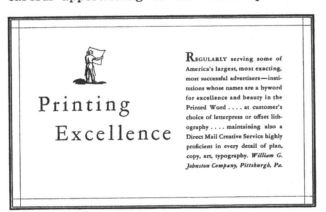

Fig. 87-A.

Fig. 87-B   Fig. 87-C.

Unit 88

How to Choose a Type Face

Not only are there hundreds of type faces available, but some of the faces can be obtained in families or groups including bold, medium, and occasionally extra bold, in both basic roman and italic, as well as other special variations. Thus, one family of a type face may include various point sizes in different associated renderings of lower-case and capitals, as well as roman small capitals in the smaller point sizes. Hence, only a specialist could possibly know all of the type faces, their variations, and the founder producing a particular face. Fortunately, most commercial plants confine themselves to a few different faces and fonts (and school shops, usually fewer) which makes the problem of type recognition and familiarity a relatively simple one in actual practice.

To some extent, the choice of a type face is restricted by the method of line construction used. Faces available for hand-setting are not always available for slug-casting by Intertype and Linotype, or Ludlow. Likewise, Monotype matrices can be obtained only in certain faces. None of the faces available for hand-setting and slug-casting are precisely the same as those available for use in preparing typewritten copy with justifying typewriters.

The best sources of information on type faces are specimen sheets obtainable through the founders, or distributors, of printing types. The leading distributors in the United States are American Type Founders, Inc., Elizabeth, New Jersey; Baltotype, Baltimore, Maryland; and Bauer Alphabets, Inc., New York City.

Matrices for use in producing machine-set slugs are manufactured by Intertype Corporation and the Mergenthaler Linotype Company. Matrices for hand-set slug-casting are manufactured by Ludlow Typograph Company. Matrices for machine-set lines of individual pieces of type are manufactured by Lanston Monotype Machine Company. Monotype matrices may also be used for casting individual pieces of type to fill cases for use in hand-setting.

Practically all founders or manufacturers produce types of the following groups: (1) Venetian, or Jenson style faces; (2) Caslon and oldstyle developments derived from Caslon; (3) Garamond, and variations such as Garamont and Granjon; (4) Bodoni and related faces; (5) Baskerville and allied faces such as Bell, Bulmer, and Scotch Roman.

All producers of type cast sans serif and square serif faces of one sort or another. These faces resemble each other in certain respects, but have special features that distinguish them. Names of these type faces vary with the producer, each seeking to distinguish his face by a special name. Black Letter or Old English faces are not in great demand because their use is restricted to special kinds of printing needs; however, most of the founders and manufacturers produce such faces.

A wide variety of script and special display types are featured by founders who cast type for hand-setting. Some of these faces are also available in Intertype, Linotype, Ludlow, and Monotype matrices. The distinguishing characteristic of these special decorative types is that they contrast sharply with the regular body type ordinarily used in a printed form. They are not intended for continuous reading, and anyone who uses them in such manner is insulting the intelligence of his readers.

Publishers of books have long sought a general-purpose type face and manufacturers and founders have tried to meet this demand. Among the faces more commonly in use are Antique, Bookman, Century, and Cheltenham. However, within recent years efforts have been made to introduce faces that vary somewhat from the conventional book types. Among the faces which have gained popularity are Caledonia, Centaur, Cochin, Deepdene, Egmont, Electra, Fairfield, Times Roman, Waverley, and Weiss Roman. These type faces are the product of contemporary designers including Frederic W. Goudy, W. A. Dwiggins, Rudolf Ruzicka, and Emil Weiss.

Because of the conditions under which newspapers and magazines are produced, Linotype, Monotype, and Intertype have developed special faces for that purpose. The point size in newspaper faces is frequently smaller than the point size used for other printing. Consequently, special attention must be given to readability in small sizes. The facts that newsprint is relatively a rough-surface paper, that oil solvents are used in newspaper inks, and that printing is done from stereotypes moving at high speeds, are matters of consequence in the experimental development of newspaper faces. Except as a matter of information, these faces are of no special interest to the person working in a commercial plant because he will not ordinarily be called upon to use them.

On pages 118-121, showings of several type faces are presented for study and reference. The faces included are but a few of the many hundreds which are available, and were chosen because they illustrate points made in this and preceding units. Units 81 and 98 will be found to be extremely helpful in studying these specimens.

Caslon   **10 point**

ABCDEFGHIJKLMNOPQRSTUVWXYZ

ABCDEFGHIJKLMNOPQRSTUVWXYZ

abcdefghijklmnopqrstuvwxyz   1234567890

[]%†§‡¶*()$,.-;':'!?&⅛¼⅜½⅝¾⅞

Special No. 3   Old Style

g j p q y J Qu   1234567890

Special No. 4 Small Caps

ABCDEFGHIJKLMNOPQRSTUVWXYZ

Caslon Italic   **10 point**

ABCDEFGHIJKLMNOPQRSTUVWXYZ

abcdefghijklmnopqrstuvwxyz   *1234567890*

[]%†§‡¶()$,.-;':'!?&⅛¼⅜½⅝¾⅞*

Special No. 3   Sp. No. 2   Special No. 5

gjpqyJQu   *g*   *ABCDEFGJLMNPTY*

Special No. 4 Small Caps   Old Style

ABCDEFGHIJKLMNOPQRSTUVWXYZ   *1234567890*

Caslon — Intertype

GARAMOND No. 3 with ITALIC and SMALL CAPS   10 Point

ABCDEFGHIJKLMNOPQRSTUVWXYZ&

ABCDEFGHIJKLMNOPQRSTUVWXYZ&

ABCDEFGHIJKLMNOPQRSTUVWXYZ&

abcdefghijklmnopqrstuvwxyz   fiflffffiffl

abcdefghijklmnopqrstuvwxyz   *fiflffffiffl*

1234567890 [($£,.:;'-'?.,!*†‡§¶)] 1234567890

1234567890 {($£,.:;'-'?.,!†‡§¶)} 1234567890*

⅛ ¼ ⅜ ½ ⅝ ¾ ⅞ ⅓ ⅔ ⅕ ⅖ ⅗ ⅘ ⅙ ⅚

⅛ ¼ ⅜ ½ ⅝ ¾ ⅞ ⅓ ⅔ ⅕ ⅖ ⅗ ⅘ ⅙ ⅚

Available: 6, 7, 8, 9, 10, 11, 12, 14 pt.;
18, 24 pt. with Italic; 18 pt. Roman

TYPOGRAPHIC REFINEMENT CHARACTERS

Two-Letter Small Caps, Special No. 5

ABCDEFGHIJKLMNOPQRSTUVWXYZ&

ABCDEFGHIJKLMNOPQRSTUVWXYZ&

Available: 6, 7, 8, 9, 10, 11, 12, 14 pt.

Recut Italic, Special No. 5

abcdefghijklmnopqrstuvwxyz

Special No. 5 Logotypes

*f fi fl af aff ef eff hf if iff kf lf mf nf of off pf
rf sf tf uf uff yf If Of Off*

Available: 6, 7, 8, 9, 10, 11, 12, 14 pt.

One-Letter Roman Logotypes, Special No. 5

fa fe fo fr fs ft fu fy ffa ffe ffo ffr ffs ffu ffy
f, f. f- ff, ff. ff- f ff

Two-Letter Logotypes

Ta Te To Tr Tu Tw Ty Va Ve Vo Wa We Wi Wo Wr Ya Ye Yo

Ta Te To Tr Tu Tw Ty Va Ve Vo Wa We Wi Wo Wr Ya Ye Yo

fa fe fo fr fs ft fu fy ffa ffe ffo ffr ffs ffu ffy f, f. f- ff, ff. ff- f ff

fa fe fo fr fs ft fu fy ffa ffe ffo ffr ffs ffu ffy f, f. f- ff, ff. ff- f ff

Garamond — Linotype

No. 1 with ITALIC and SMALL CAPS   10 Point

ABCDEFGHIJKLMNOPQRSTUVWXYZ&

ABCDEFGHIJKLMNOPQRSTUVWXYZ&

ABCDEFGHIJKLMNOPQRSTUVWXYZ&

abcdefghijklmnopqrstuvwxyz fiflffffiffl

abcdefghijklmnopqrstuvwxyz fiflffffiffl

1234567890 [($£,.:;'-'?!†‡§¶)]

1234567890 [($£,.:;'-'?!†‡§¶)]

⅛ ¼ ⅜ ½ ⅝ ¾ ⅞ ⅓ ⅔ ⅕ ⅖ ⅗ ⅘ ⅙ ⅚

Old Style No. 1 — Linotype

Janson   **12 point**

ABCDEFGHIJKLMNOPQRSTUVWXYZ

abcdefghijklmnopqrstuvwxyz   fiflffffiffl

$1234567890   .,-'':;!?()[] $1234567890

ABCDEFGHIJKLMNOPQRSTUVWXYZ&

ABCDEFGHIJJKLMNOPQRSTUVWXYZ

abcdefghbijklmnopqrstuvwxyz fiflffffiffl

$1234567890   :;!? $1234567890

Special Kerned Characters

TV WY   *ATVWY*

Long Descenders in 8, 9, 10, 11, 12 Point sizes—For
Specimens see following page

g j p q y   *f g j p q y*   fi fl ff ffi ffl

Janson (Hess) — 12 Point — Monotype

Cloister Old Style   **10 point**

ABCDEFGHIJKLMNOPQRSTUVWXYZ

ABCDEFGHIJKLMNOPQRSTUVWXYZ

abcdefghijklmnopqrstuvwxyz   1234567890

[]%†§‡¶*()$,.-;':'!?&⅛¼⅜½⅝¾⅞

Cloister Old Style Italic   **10 point**

ABCDEFGHIJKLMNOPQRSTUVWXYZ

abcdefghijklmnopqrstuvwxyz   *1234567890*

[]%†§‡¶()$,.-;':'!?&⅛¼⅜½⅝¾⅞*

Special No. 5

ABCDEGJMNPRTUV

Cloister Bold   **10 point**

ABCDEFGHIJKLMNOPQRSTUVWXYZ

ABCDEFGHIJKLMNOPQRSTUVWXYZ

abcdefghijklmnopqrstuvwxyz   1234567890

[]%†§‡¶*()$,.-;':'!?&⅛¼⅜½⅝¾⅞

Special No. 7 Small Caps

ABCDEFGHIJKLMNOPQRSTUVWXYZ

Cloister Old Style — Intertype

Baskerville   **10 point**

ABCDEFGHIJKLMNOPQRSTUVWXYZ

ABCDEFGHIJ KLMNOPQRSTUVWXYZ

abcdefghijklmnopqrstuvwxyz   1234567890

[]%†§‡¶*()$,.-;':'!?&⅛¼⅜½⅝¾⅞

Special No. 7 Small Caps   Old Style
ABCDEFGHIJKLMNOPQRSTUVWXYZ   1234567890

Baskerville Bold   **10 point**

ABCDEFGHIJKLMNOPQRSTUVWXYZ

abcdefghijklmnopqrstuvwxyz   1234567890

Old Style
[]%†§‡¶*()$,.-;':'!?&⅛¼⅜½⅝   1234567890

Special No. 4 Small Caps
ABCDEFGHIJKLMNOPQRSTUVWXYZ

Baskerville — Intertype

ABCDEFGHIJKLMNOPQRSTUVWXYZ

abcdefghijklmnopqrstuvwxyz   fiflffffiffl   .,-'':;!

$1234567890%   ¼½¾⅛⅜⅝⅞ $123456

ABCDEFGHIJKLMNOPQRSTUVWXYZ&

ABCDEFGHIJKLMNOPQRSTUVWXYZ

abcdefghijklmnopqrstuvwxyz   fiflffffiffl

$1234567890   ,-'': ;!? $123456789

Bulmer — 12 Point — Monotype

ABCDEFGHIJKLMNOPQRSTUVWXYZ

abcdefghijklmnopqrstuvwxyzæœ   fiflffffi

$1234567890   .,-'':;!?[]()   ctst $1234567

ABCDEFGHIJKLMNOPQRSTUVWXYZ&ÆŒ

ABCDEFGHIJKLMNOPQRSTUVWXYZ

abcdefghijklmnopqrstuvwxyzæœ   fiflffffi

$1234567890   :;!?   ctst $123456789

Kennerley Old Style (Goudy) — 12 Point — Monotype

A B C D E F G H I J K L M N O P Q

T U V W X Y Z & a b c d e f g h i j k l m n o

r s t u v w x y z . , - ' : ; ? l " ") $ 1 2 3 4 5 6 7 8

Nicholas Cochin Bold — 14 Point — Baltotype

A B C D E F G H I J K L M N O

R S T U V W X Y Z & a b c d e f g

j k l m n o p q r s t u v w x y z . , -

? ! ; fi ff fl ffi ffl $ 1 2 3 4 5 6 7 8

Bodoni Bold — 14 Point — Baltotype

SCOTCH No. 2 with ITALIC and SMALL CAPS   10 Point

ABCDEFGHIJKLMNOPQRSTUVWXYZ&

ABCDEFGHIJKLMNOPQRSTUVWXYZ&

ABCDEFGHIJKLMNOPQRSTUVWXYZ&

abcdefghijklmnopqrstuvwxyz   fiflffffiffl

abcdefghijklmnopqrstuvwxyz   fiflffffiffl

1234567890   [($£,.:;'-'?'!'*†‡§¶)]

1234567890   [($£,.:;'-'?'!'†‡§¶)]*

⅛ ¼ ⅜ ½ ⅝ ¾ ⅞ ⅓ ⅔ ⅕ ⅖ ⅗ ⅘ ⅙ ⅚

⅛ ¼ ⅜ ⅛ ⅝ ⅔ ⅜ ⅛ ⅔ ⅓ ⅓

Available: 8, 9, 10, 11, 12 pt.
(Also: Scotch with Italic and Small Caps: 6, 11½, 14 pt.)

TYPOGRAPHIC REFINEMENT CHARACTERS
Two-Letter Small Caps, Special No. 5
ABCDEFGHIJKLMNOPQRSTUVWXYZ&

ABCDEFGHIJKLMNOPQRSTUVWXYZ&

Scotch — Linotype

Century Catalog   **18 point**

MAGNIFICENT GARDEN

CHILDREN enjoy outdoor count

quieted nerves brought content

14 Point

HUMBLE PEASANT FOUND TRE

PLOUGH brought farmers unexpected

anticipate tremendous real estate dev

12 Point

ROMANTIC PRINTER ENTHUSIASTIC

BEGAN life among lowly inhabitants of dismal

and through intelligent reading learned rudin

10 Point

GIGANTIC WORLD EXPOSITION DELIGHTS

MODERN display electrified audience of graphic arts

attending magnificent advertising exhibition held in

8 Point

QUANTITY PRODUCTION OF FINE PRINTING REQU

BEAUTIFUL examples of modern trend in typography and col

produced like so much hash. They require intelligent planning

6 Point

MANUSCRIPT BOOKS WRITTEN AND ORNAMENTED BY ANCIEI

RARE gems of the typographic art were produced nearly five hundred years ag

of years before the invention of movable type every book had to be written a

Century Catalog — 6 to 18 Point — ATF

ABCDEFGHIJKLMNOPQRSTUVWXYZ&
abcdefghijklmnopqrstuvwxyz   fiflffffffffl
$1234567890   .,-'':;!?

ABCDEFGHIJKLMNOPQRSTUVWXYZ&

ABCDEFGHIJKLMNOPQRSTUVWXYZ&
A B C D E G M P T   gy gg ct
abcdefghijklmnopqrstuvwxyz   fiflffffffl
$1234567890   :;!?

Deepdene (Goudy) — 12 Point — Monotype

A B C D E F G H I J K L M
Q R S T U V W X Y Z
a b c d e f g h i j k l m n o p q
v w x y z   fi fl ff ffi ffl
$ 1 2 3 4 5 6 7 8 9 0 ., -':;

Della Robbia — 14 Point — Monotype

AAABCDEFGHIJKLMNOPQRRSTU
WXYZ&
aabcdeffghijklmnopqrrsttuvwxyz
$1234567890   .,-":;!?

CDEFGHIJKLMNOPQRSTUVWX
abcdeffghijklmnopqrrstuvwxyz
$1234567890   .,-'":;!?()

Stymie Bold — 12 Point — Monotype

A B C D E F G
J K L M N O P   C D E F G H I J
S T U V W X Y   M N O P Q R S
$ 1 2 3 4 5 6 7   V W X Y Z &
                     2 3 4 5 6 7 8 9 0
a b c d e f g   c d e f g h i j k
j k l m n o p   n o p q r s t u v
s t u v w x   w x y z
. : , ; - ' ! ?   , ; - ' ! ? —

Square (Sans Serif) Gothic and Condensed Gothic — Ludlow

ABCDEFGHIJKLMN
OPQRSTUVW
AXYZ ✠ ABC
AEFGHIK

Lombardic Initials — Baltotype

A B C D E
F G H I J K
L M N O P
Q R S T U
V W X Y Z
a e k m n
l v w

Goudy Hand-Tooled Italic Swash — Baltotype

ABCDEFGHIJKLMNOPQ
STUVWXYZ&abcdefghiklmn
qrstuvwxyz.,-':;?!fiflflffffiffl$12345678

Goudy Text — Baltotype

ABCDEFGHIJKL
NOPQRSTUVWXYZ
abcdefghijklmnopqrstuvwx
st nd rd th or .,-';:!?$12345678

Wedding Text — Baltotype

ABCDEFGHIJKLMNOPQRS
ABCDEFGHIJKLMNOPQRS
Bank Gothic — Linotype

ABCDEFGHIJKLMabcdefghijklm $1
Trylon — Baltotype

PREVIEW FASHIONS
Stellar — Ludlow

LOCAL COLUMN
Ultramodern — Ludlow

I Am the Leaden Army that
Valiant — Monotype

Debated several important iss
ATTENDING THE OPEN FOR
Lydian Bold — ATF

MANSION RESTORED
Cartoon — Bauer

Zero exists only
Studio — ATF

A LUDLOW QUA
Umbra — Ludlow

AHIJKLaghijkl4
Stymie Shaded — Baltotype

ABCDEFGHIJKLM
Stymie Bold Open — Baltotype

ABCDEFGHIJKLMNOP
Narciss — Linotype

I Am the Leaden
Cooper Tooled — Monotype

Flower Show in
Lilith — Bauer

ABCDEFGHIJKLMNO
PQRSTUVWXYZ 1234567890
Nova Script — Intertype

Golden Wedding Celeb
Coronet — Ludlow

I am the Leaden
Artscript — Monotype

Issues Pamphlets
Mayfair — Ludlow

Quality Silverware, antique
Tango — ATF

Journey through Scandinav
Bernhard Cursive — Bauer

Modern Interior Decor
Trafton — Bauer

Old Mahogany Bookcase
Stradivarius — Bauer

Fifth Anniversary Celebration and
Keynote — ATF

Representative Appointment Conf
Gillies Gothic — Bauer

June opens up a seaso
Rondo Bold — ATF

System proves its
Hauser Script — Ludlow

Unit 89

How to Make a Layout

In complicated jobs involving special type arrangements, irregular breakup of copy, or variations in placement and quantity of text on the different pages, a plan showing what the finished job is to be like is ordinarily prepared. This plan also shows the manner in which illustrations, decorations, or ornamentation are to be used; in a sense, the procedure is analagous to the preparation of architectural plans for houses, and models or mock-ups for industrial products. A preliminary plan of a printing job is called a layout. Its purpose is to indicate to the typographer, typesetter, stoneman, pressman, and the bindery superintendent, the manner in which the work in the several production divisions is inter-related.

When accompanied by specifications, the layout serves as a production guide. Specifications may be indicated on the layout, or may be shown separately on a work ticket. Frequently, specifications are written on a large envelope especially prepared for the purpose, in which all the copy and the layout are placed. The envelope, or work jacket, serves to protect the copy and layout as the job is routed through the plant to each production division. At each station along the route, the copy and layout are removed from the jacket for reference, and then replaced upon completion of the part of the job being done at that point. In this manner, each department is able to check on work of other departments and obtain complete information on all preceding steps as the job progresses through the plant.

In many cases the layout, complete in all details, including special instructions, is fastened together to show page arrangement, and thus serves as a complete working dummy. In other instances, that part of the work requiring special treatment is laid out and attached to a page make-up dummy, consisting of several sheets carrying only general notations to show the final arrangement of the completed material as it will appear when made up into pages. In all instances, the purpose of the working dummy is to guide the production departments in the step-by-step assembling, printing, and finishing of the job.

In preparing the layout, the layout man must have full information about the job and be able to visualize its appearance as a finished product. He must also be familiar with type faces and their availability in different sizes, must understand printing operations, printing materials, artists' media, and relative costs, as well as how to produce desired effects. He need not be an artist or typographer, but must be familiar with the contribution which they can make in the final preparation of copy and translation into type.

After assembling all needed information relative to the purpose and nature of the job to be planned, the layout man takes into account the amount of display, text material, and illustrations in relation to each other, and prepares a series of small sketches as the initial step in determining the design elements to be used in planning the printed piece.

After having determined the general arrangement, a rough layout is made in which the various elements are blocked out to show the position which they will occupy on the pages in the dummy. For some jobs, this rough

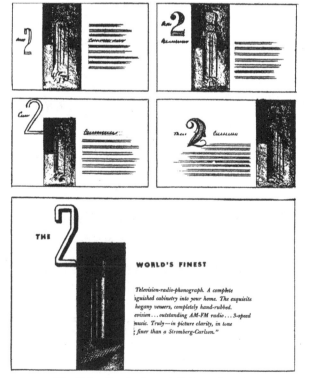

Fig. 89-A. Thumbnails and Paste-up Layout

layout with marginal notes may serve as a production guide with no further elaboration or refinement. On other jobs, it may be found necessary or desirable to prepare a more elaborate facsimile or visual of the job (comprehensive layout). In connection with either of these—rough or comprehensive—the layout man may require that sample pages be set and made up for his inspection and approval before giving an "O.K." to go ahead with the job.

In a visual, the areas to be filled with display, text, and illustration are carefully marked out to exact size. Display lines are frequently hand-lettered to resemble the type to be used, initial letters are specified, and text material is indicated by lines of exact length, spaced and arranged in the manner in which they are to be set. Illustration areas are blocked out with lines and rough sketches, or "doodles," which are placed within these frames to indicate the nature and size of the illustration.

A closer facsimile of the job may be prepared by using scissors and paste. By searching through magazines or other printed jobs, samples of type faces to be used can ordinarily be found in both text and display. These may be cut out and pasted in the appropriate spots on the layout. The fact that the message contained in these cutouts is not the same as that which will appear in the finished job is of no consequence, because their purpose is to show the general appearance of the job. The same procedure may be used for illustrations, and any illustration similar to that actually to be used will serve the purpose of the layout man.

It can readily be understood that paste-up layouts have an advantage over layouts containing hand lettering, pencil lines to represent type, and sketches to designate illustrations, because the paste-up layout will have the same general appearance as the finished job. Another advantage of the paste-up method is that different arrangements can easily be tried for effect before making a final choice of the design of the job.

Thumbnail sketches and paste-ups are the research laboratory of the designer in search of a satisfactory layout. By these methods all experimentation can be done before type is set and cuts made. The four pencil sketches in Figure 89-A represent solutions to a problem involving a tall picture, a paragraph of copy, and the use of a large numeral suggested by the customer, who prefers a "modern" design. The paste-up of one of the sketches at the bottom of Figure 89-A shows how closely the final printed piece can be simulated with a few odds and ends clipped from a magazine. Actual copy can be substituted, and accurate specifications for sizes and placement can be determined from the paste-up.

As a means of verification and checking, and to show the layout man or the customer what the finished job will look like, a finished layout is sometimes made before the job is run. This is done by pasting proofs of the type, along with proofs of the illustration plates or photoprints, on the sheets of a dummy. A finished layout may also be used to guide the make-up man in imposing the job.

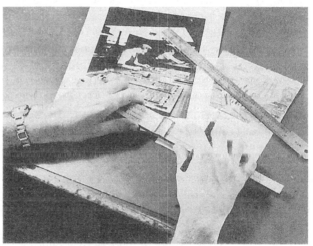

Fig. 89-B. Preparing a Rough Layout

Fig. 89-C. Preparing a Visual or Finished Layout

Unit 90

How to Prepare Manuscript

Composing a job for printing is greatly facilitated if the copy is appropriately prepared for the printer's use. When "good" copy is received from the customer, it may be sent to the composing room in its original form after being edited and marked up to provide specifications for setting. However, if the customer's manuscript is not in suitable form it should be redrafted before being sent to the composing room, because "bad" copy creates confusion, causes loss of time, and thus frequently adds to the cost of producing a job.

Good manuscript consists of clear typewritten copy in the original. Carbon copies are not suitable, because they are often difficult to read at the outset and become more so in use through smudging. Copy should be double-spaced and positioned to provide margins of an inch or more all around. Only one side of the sheet should be used. All pages should be numbered, and inserts appearing on supplementary sheets should be clearly marked and cross-referenced. If new material is to be added after the pages have been typed, it is better to cut the sheets apart and paste them up in a manner to provide continuous sequence, rather than attach fliers to already prepared sheets. The ideal to be sought in a manuscript page is an arrangement which permits continuous and uninterrupted setting by the compositor.

Consistency in style in copy should be sought editorially. Therefore, most plants adopt a style manual for the guidance of all concerned, including customers. The manual most widely used in book plants is the University of Chicago *Manual of Style*. This manual must be supplemented for special copy and, in some instances, a plant manual is prepared. For example, practically all large metropolitan newspapers have their own style manual.

Accuracy, consistency, and exactness as to fact are objectives to be sought in both copy and proof. Editing of the manuscript should occur before it is sent to the composing room, because the compositor should not be expected to do otherwise than follow copy. Consequently, if copy is not properly edited, expensive alterations in composition may be necessary after the job has been set in type. This fact should be made clear to the customer, because it is standard practice to charge for authors' alterations, i.e., composition changes arising out of corrections on the proof that vary from the original copy.

Editing as it occurs in a printing plant does not include rewriting. The printer should not make changes in copy that encroach upon the author. However, manuscript copy should be examined and corrected to avoid misspelling, faulty punctuation, improper compounding of words, grammatical errors, and other obvious structural defects. On the matter of capitalization, use of figures, italics, quotes, use of bold face, and other matters of style in which alternative practices are sometimes followed, it may be desirable to confer with the customer to determine the style he prefers. In such instances, the printer should advise and make appropriate recommendations but leave all decisions to the customer.

Specifications and instructions to the compositor should be entered on the manuscript before the copy is sent to the composing room. In general, specifications are either furnished by the customer or agreed to by him and supplied by the layout man. These instructions and specifications should be complete and explicit in order to relieve the compositor of the necessity of making arbitrary decisions of his own choice.

Specifications should identify the type, its point size, the page and sheet size, and length of line in picas. Paragraph indentions should be clearly indicated and the kind of indention desired specified. The manner of handling of heads, sub-heads, and special display should be indicated both as to position on the page in reference to text material and the kind and size of type face to be used. Breaks for color, if any, should also be designated.

The fitting in of illustrations should be shown by a layout and the manner of handling captions and legends indicated. Captions and legends are often typed on separate pages to accompany the illustrations. If plates for illustrations are available, they may be sent to the composing room with the copy. If they are to be ordered separately, the date on which they will be available should be stated.

Unit 91

How to Copyfit

In laying out a job, copy must be fitted to the page areas. All methods of copyfitting depend upon character count in one form or another. The number of characters in typewritten copy can be computed by measuring the average line length and multiplying the number of inches by the number of typewritten characters to the inch. Elite typewriter type runs 12 characters to the inch, and pica typewriter type runs 10 characters. After computing the number of characters in typewritten copy, it is possible to determine the length of the typeset line and the number of lines necessary to accommodate the copy.

Since different characters in type occupy different amounts of space, and since the spacing of words in several lines of type will vary, no two lines in the same type face are likely to contain exactly the same number of characters. Therefore, an average must be used. The simplest method of determining this average is that of counting the number of characters in several lines of type and dividing by the number of lines involved. Spaces between words and punctuation marks should be counted as characters.

Tables showing the average line count for different type faces in lines of different point sizes are frequently prepared for reference by the layout man. As basic information in preparing these charts, he may use a sample paragraph or he may use alphabet length. This and other information may be obtained from the manufacturer of mats used on the typesetting machine, or from the founder if the type is to be composed by hand-setting.

Before beginning work on a book or booklet of straight matter, it is usually necessary to know the least number of pages which will be required to accommodate the copy which is to be set, or to know the line length, type size, and leading which will be necessary to get the copy to fit a predetermined number of pages. Accuracy in copyfitting is important, because if computations are not correct, expense is likely to be involved in resetting the type or making a new layout or plan which will accommodate the copy.

Unit 92

How to Mark Copy

Copy should be marked up throughout to show the manner of setting and to make corrections in the copy. For this purpose, printers' marks should be used as shown in Unit 35, page 50; however, the procedure to be followed in marking copy differs from the procedure for marking proof.

While proof marks are placed on the right and left hand margins of proof, copy marks should be written within the copy and punctuation marks inserted at the appropriate points. Special instructions for composing and arranging the type on the page should be written in the margins.

Customer's copy should be followed except where obvious errors of spelling, punctuation, capitalization, and grammar are observed. Such errors should be corrected, and the approval of the customer obtained, before the copy is sent to the compositor for setting. Copy marks commonly used include the following:

Marking in Copy		Meaning
small	three line underscore	set in capital letters
Small	diagonal cross out line	set in lower-case
¶	paragraph mark	start new paragraph
no ¶	no paragraph	run together
ever will	coupling parts of text	no break
lb.	circled abbreviation	spell out
5	circled figure	spell out
pound	circled word	abbreviate
five	circled figure	abbreviate
small	single underscore	set in *italics*
small	two line underscore	set in SMALL CAPS
small	wavy line underscore	set in **bold face**
small	cross out	do not use
small	transposition loop	change order
?	query to author	verify accuracy of copy
1/	figure or letter in chevron	footnote designation
stet	for crossed out material	let it stand
∧	caret	insert marginal material
□	em space	indent one em
□□	two-em space	indent two ems
□□□	three-em space	indent three ems
⌒	ringed word or phase	to indicate position

Fig. 92-A. Standard Copy Marks

Unit 93. The Alphabet as a Means of Communication

When you set type in a stick, you are really bringing together various characters of the alphabet to form words and sentences. Without the simple twenty-six letter alphabet which we use, printing would be a discouragingly difficult process. Therefore, the story of the origin of the alphabet is one which should be known by all who wish to understand fully the art of printing.

The alphabet in handwritten form paved the way for handwritten books. The first examples of printing of which we have knowledge resembled hand-drawn letters. The evolution of the alphabet is shown in the illustration on this page. Modification of the design of letters in the alphabet is shown by examples in the illustration on page 127.

Printing is an important art because the exchange of ideas is necessary for the existence of social and business life in the world today. However, printing as a means of communication has been in general use less than five hundred years. For about 1500 years prior to the invention of printing, handwritten books and manuscripts were used to record and convey ideas. But primitive men four or five thousand years ago had to resort to simpler devices.

Piles of stone, crude monuments, marks on trees, and other objects of nature are believed to have been the first means of recording events and discoveries. Drawings and inscriptions on stones were the next step. Such means were used by the early Egyptians, Assyrians and Chaldeans. Later, baked clay tablets replaced the somewhat cumbersome ones made of stone. Not satisfied with either of these inscription surfaces, the ancients continued to experiment with other materials. From their efforts came papyrus (a rough-surfaced mat made of the fibers of a reed-like plant which grew on the banks of the Nile), parchment (prepared skins of sheep and goats), and vellum (made from skins of young calves).

Pictures were probably the first devices used for conveying thoughts. By gradual modification a sort of shorthand method of writing evolved. These symbols, best illustrated by the early Egyptian hieroglyphics, did not represent sounds found in the spoken word but presented ideas in a meaningful arrangement.

Gradually, pictorial and symbol writing were displaced by phonetic characters which were eventually combined into an alphabet. Fragments of pottery, recently discovered in ruins being excavated in Palestine, have given rise to the theory that an alphabet was in existence as early as 2000 B.C. However, the alphabet as we know it today was founded on the early Phoenician system which was adopted by the Greeks about 1000 B. C. With the passing of the center of civilization to Rome, the Latin alphabet, based on the Greek, became the world standard and survives today in our roman letter forms.

Over two hundred alphabets have been known to exist, and about fifty are in use today. These vary in the number of letters and sounds. One,

ORIGINS OF LETTERING ⁊ I

A presentation of its evolution

1 Paleolithic pictographs on caves and tools were a prehistoric form of recording thoughts and deeds. Drawings in France and Spain still exist

2 Egyptian hieroglyphics, a decorative form of picture writing, developed into a system of lettering symbols in which each represented a word.

3 Cuneiform, or wedge-shaped symbols of the Babylonian epoch; a syllabic "shorthand" version of hieroglyphics, simplified for easy inscription on clay

4 Chinese ideographs are brush signs based on pictographic methods, with each character representing a definite idea and a sound ...

5 Greek script on wax or papyrus evolved its alphabet from the Sinaitic adaptation of Egyptian hieroglyphics ...

6 Roman capitals that show the "serifs"—chisel-made endings to stone-cut letters—and the fine design of the letters (TRAJAN COL) UMN)

Fig. 93-A. From Pictographs to Roman Capital Inscriptions
(Courtesy, Graphic Design, by Friend and Hefter)

the Italian, contains as few as twenty-one letters, while the Polish uses forty-five. The Japanese language contains seventy-two sounds for which forty-eight characters are required. Chinese, of all languages, more nearly resembles the ancient pictographic form of communication. In Chinese some 30,000 characters exist, of which number about 500 are in common use.

English letter forms are based on the Latin alphabet. Our capital letters are almost exact copies of letters used for inscriptions on public buildings in Rome in the time of Cicero. The lower-case letters in our type fonts are imitations of minuscules used by the Carolingian scribes of about 700 to 900 A.D. Minuscules were handwritten variations of the Latin capitals. The basic model of present letter forms was the handwriting of Alcuin, an English scholar employed by Charlemagne to conduct the palace school in Tours (now in France) about 800 A.D. The Caroline minuscule can be traced back to the early uncials of about 300 A.D. Uncials were rounded, handwritten corruptions of the Latin capitals.

In this brief sketch we have reviewed the development of the means of communication which is the foundation of printing. This story of the growth of graphic means of conveying ideas closely parallels the growth of civilization. Some historians, in fact, assert that the beginning of civilization dates from the invention of writing. Printing as the successor to the written word as a means of disseminating information has become the agent of progress. Because of this fact, workers in the field of printing may be justly proud of the industry which they serve. The printing industry is the heart of modern civilization. Without printing, commerce would become paralyzed and our way of life would change completely.

Some things to think about: Why is an alphabet more efficient in written communication than a character for each word? Why did primitive men use objects of nature to record events? Why were clay tablets used before skins of animals in making records? Which would be more efficient as a means of communication: pictographs (graphic presentation of ideas by pictures) or ideographs (graphic presentation of ideas by symbols)? Are ideographs ever used today? Could a language be developed with only ten letters in the alphabet? Why are upper-case letters called capitals? Why did scribes finally develop rounded letters? Why is writing necessary to civilization? The culture of some early civilizations has been lost. Would this have been likely if printing had been in existence? Why is printing so necessary to modern civilization? Why has the change in letter forms been one of gradual evolution? Why are unique or unusual letter forms more frequently used for display purposes than for composing straight text material? In what ways does ordinary typewritten copy differ from copy which has been set in type? Why have manufacturers of justifying typewriters designed characters for use on such machines so that they resemble standard type faces? (See page 127.)

NOTE: See Unit 96, "Roman Letter Development," page 132, for the illustration showing the gradual change of the letter "g" in script and type.

ORIGINS OF LETTERING · II
Showing the art and the artist

Fig. 93-B. From Roman Pen Letters to Modern Handscript and Typewritten Characters
(Courtesy, Graphic Design, by Friend and Hefter)

Unit 94. The Evolution of Printing

Fig. 94-A. Page from the "Diamond Sutra"

Fig. 94-B. "Saint Christopher" Woodcut — 1423

Most history books state that printing from movable types was originated by Johannes Gutenberg, at Mainz, Germany, between the years of 1435-1445. Some students of history have said that the credit for the invention of printing should be shared with Laurens Coster, who is alleged to have printed Latin schoolbooks in Haarlem, Netherlands, about the same time. These are interesting facts that you should remember, but printing was in the process of development before either of these men was born. Printing, as an art, did not suddenly burst upon the world in the middle of the fifteenth century. Instead, printing came into existence through a long process of development.

Early printers like Gutenberg were trying to use type to produce books to imitate bound manuscripts which were really hand-lettered books. Folded manuscripts were used as books for more than a thousand years before printing was begun in Europe. Manuscripts folded in sheets like books are known to have existed as early as 200 to 300 A. D. These folded manuscripts may not have been bound as books when they were first used, but there is evidence to indicate that manuscript binding was well established by the eighth century.

Handwritten scrolls were forerunners of folded manuscript books. Scrolls made of papyrus were used by the early Egyptians. Ptolemy I founded a library in 300 B. C. in which scrolls were written across the sheet, but gradually the writing was placed on the scroll in separate sections or pages running lengthwise. This change made the reading of the contents easier and paved the way for the introduction of folded manuscripts.

Manuscript books were produced in the Middle Ages by scribes who were members of religious orders. Since such men dedicated their lives to the work of producing manuscript books, great skill was developed; and remarkably beautiful examples of these documents are still in existence. Many were illustrated by hand-drawn designs and sketches, and some were profusely ornamented. The inscribing of large, decorative initial letters in color at the beginning of paragraphs was a favorite method of enlivening the appearance of manuscripts after about 600 A. D. By the end of the four-teenth century, manuscript writing had become a fine art in Europe. It was not unusual, there-fore, that early printed books were imitations of famous manuscripts.

To one not familiar with the development of printing, it might seem that the use of en-graved wood blocks would be the natural step between manuscript books and those later print-ed from movable types. However, printing from wood engravings is known to have occurred in Japan as early as 770 A. D., and there is some foundation for the belief that the process orig-inated in China about 400 A. D. The art of printing from wood blocks flourished in the Orient for several centuries before being intro-duced into Europe. One of the most pretentious block printing undertakings, the production of the Confucian classics, was completed in China in 953 — a task that required twenty-one years of labor.

Single-page block prints, presumably pro-duced in 1418 and 1423 in Germany, are in existence today, but the oldest known European block-printed books were produced in 1450. Gu-tenberg is believed to have printed from wood blocks in a small way; therefore, it may be that his work in this connection impressed him with the possibilities of printing from movable type. In general, however, the making of books from engraved wood blocks developed in Europe side by side with typographic printing, for the ma-jority of the early block-printed books are dated after 1470.

In making possible the important transition from hand-lettered manuscripts to books print-ed from type forms, Gutenberg and the other early printers needed: (1) a supply of single letters cast in type which could be assembled to make words; (2) a method of locking the type into a solid form; (3) a surface such as paper to receive the impression; (4) an ink to register the impression of the type on the paper; (5) a method of bringing the paper and type form to-gether under pressure. In one manner or an-other, all of these needs had been met long be-fore Gutenberg began his experiments. But we must credit Gutenberg with the insight and in-genuity necessary to co-ordinate all of these factors into the art of printing.

Printing from movable types had been tried

Fig. 94-C. Manuscript Book Lettering

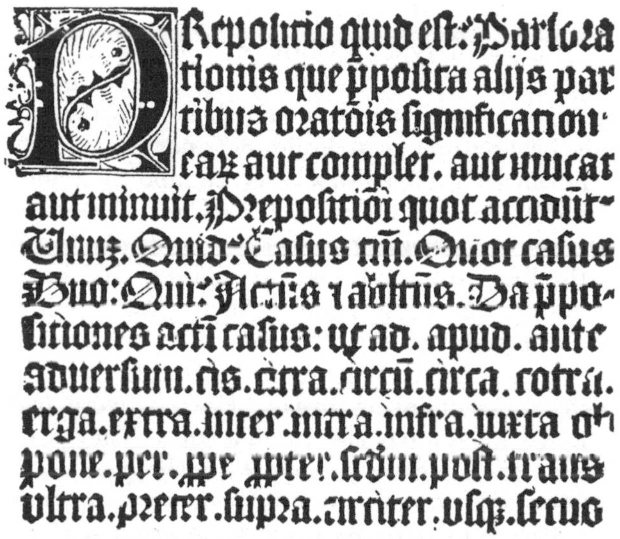

Fig. 94-D. Block Letter Book Specimen

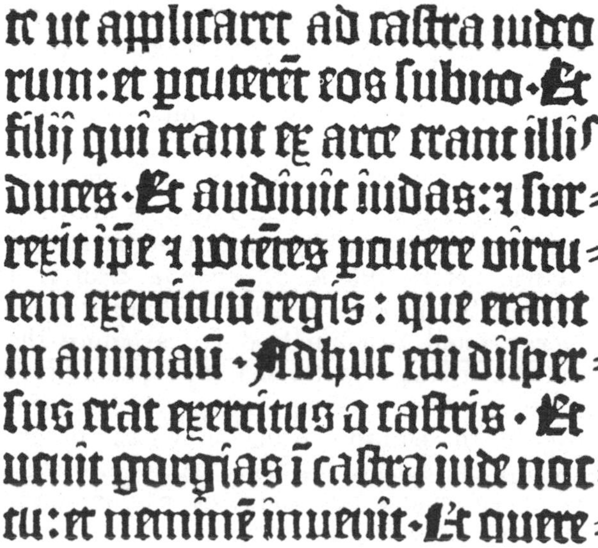

Fig. 94-E. 36-Line Bible (Gutenberg Specimen)

in China and Japan many years before Gutenberg's time. The use of separate characters in printing was probably invented by Pi-Cheng, a Chinese, between the years 1041 and 1049. His types, reputedly, were cast in porcelain and were not wholly successful. In 1314, Wang Cheng, another Chinese, published a description of a method of printing from movable wood types locked in a chase in somewhat the same manner as that used today. Type cast from metal in Korea, in 1392, was widely used in China and Japan; and in 1403, the King of Korea established a foundry for casting type in bronze. However, printing from separate characters was apparently not commercially successful in the Orient.

The use of type in China and Japan may not have been known to Gutenberg, but the use of molds and punches was known to him through his occupation as a lapidary and silversmith. The casting of metals was commonly understood by men in his calling. The use of separate letters in embossing, stamping, and inlaying of title lines on bindings for manuscript books was most certainly a procedure with which he was acquainted.

Where did Gutenberg get the idea for the use of the printing press? Presses were used for various purposes in his time. They were used for domestic purposes in the making of wines, and for commercial purposes in bookbinding and papermaking. The press was not new, but its use for printing was probably original. The Chinese and their European followers employed the planer method, hand-and-block, and secured an impression on but one side of the sheet in making prints from wood blocks and other relief surfaces.

Paper and printing ink were not new when Gutenberg began his work. Paper is known to have been made in China from tree bark, rags, and fish net in 105 A. D. by one Ts'ai Lun; however, the process of papermaking was discovered about two hundred years before that date. Paper was used for many purposes by the Chinese and was being extensively manufactured by the eighth century. Even the process of sizing or coating, for the purpose of making the paper opaque or producing a more desirable surface, was known to the early Chinese papermakers. Papermaking was a well-developed industry throughout the known civilized world by the time Gutenberg was born in 1400, and paper mills existed in Spain, France, Italy, and Germany at that time.

In the making of ink for printing purposes, the Chinese also led the world in discovery. Wei Tang perfected an ink for block printing, using lampblack, as early as 400 A. D. Viscous inks, essential to printing, were in use in Germany for block printing and for stamping titles on manuscript book bindings, before Gutenberg's time. Heavy paints, somewhat similar to printing inks, were also used by artists at that time. Doubtless, Gutenberg and other early printers experimented to secure an ink of suitable body and consistency, although the pigments and vehicles for such inks were widely known.

The early history of type, paper, ink, and presses has been given to show how a new commercial process gradually develops and then seems suddenly to come into existence. The history of steel, airplanes, radio, automobiles, television, and many other inventions — which we make use of daily — would show the same remote beginnings. When we use these things which make life more convenient, comfortable, and happy, we should remember that we are enjoying the benefits of the applied intelligence and effort of many men.

To Gutenberg we must attribute the envisionment of the commercial and cultural possibilities of printing as a process of graphic reproduction. To the cumulative effect of the inventions of many minds in a growing civilization, we must attribute the evolution of printing as a graphic art.

Questions for thought: Why was the Bible so often the document printed by early printers? Why is it unlikely that printing was invented in any particular year or short period of years? Why did the early scribes write cross-wise on scrolls? Why do you suppose manuscript writers of the Middle Ages added decorations to their hand-written books? Why was not typesetting used more extensively by the Chinese? Why did early printers try to substitute movable type for block pages? Was printing an invention or several inventions? To what extent did the fact that Gutenberg was a silversmith have a bearing on the development of printing from movable type?

Unit 95. The Genesis of Type Faces - Early Gothics

Our common type faces are based on hand-written letters used in producing manuscripts before books were printed. They are either imitations of early handwritten letters or represent a modification of early type faces which, in turn, were modeled after the lettering found in manuscript books.

The standard *roman* lower-case letters and capitals assumed their present form about 1470 in a face cut by Nicholas Jenson. While Jenson, a Frenchman, learned printing in Germany, he did his first printing in Venice, Italy. The letters inscribed in manuscript books by Venetian monks were Jenson's models. Jenson's types served as the pattern after which later types have been created. Jenson was not the first to use roman letters, but to him must go the credit of having developed a serviceable and beautiful face upon which no later designer has been able to improve significantly. Type faces designed after the Jenson model are often referred to as Venetian types.

First books in Europe were not printed in the roman face. Gutenberg's types were black-letter or *gothic*. They were constructed to imitate the style of letter used by religious scribes living in the vicinity of Mainz, Germany, the center in which Gutenberg began his printing activities. John Fust and Peter Schoeffer, who entered the printing field through business relations with Gutenberg, continued to use the gothic letter form. Thus, the gothic letter became firmly established in Northern Europe.

To avoid confusion, it must be pointed out that "gothic," as used by some modern type-founders to designate sans serif types, has no relation to gothic when used to describe first types. Nor does gothic when used to describe first types have any relation, except indirectly, to the Goths, the Teutonic tribe which overran the Roman Empire in the second century. Gothic, as a term applied to architecture and other forms of art, designates the style characteristic of Northern and Western Europe from the twelfth to sixteenth century. It is in this sense that gothic is also applied to letter forms. The gothic style differed so markedly from the classic styles of the Greeks and Romans, that the term was originally applied as an epithet of

Fig. 95-A. Gothic Type of Fust and Schoeffer — 1457

Fig. 95-B. Semi-Gothic Type of Mentelin — 1460

Fig. 95-C. Modified Gothic — Fust and Schoeffer — 1485

derision, meaning crude, barbarous, or in low taste. That, of course, was contemporary opinion and does not necessarily represent current appraisal, although roman types are preferred today. They are considered to be more legible.

Tradition governed the use of the gothic letter by early printers. Styles of these first types were not created by the punch cutter, and it is probable that their use lasted for a considerable period because the only way to make pages that could be read by persons accustomed to manuscript books was to imitate them. As soon as the roman types were cast, the use of gothics decreased by degrees until today their only descendents familiar to us are *Old English* types Although Black Letter types are still used to some extent in Northern Europe, they are gradually being superseded by roman faces.

Historically, it is difficult to trace the origin of the gothic letter forms, as used in inscribing manuscripts. It is definitely known that they sprang from the common source of all letter forms, the capital letters used in inscriptions on public buildings in Rome, which in turn were derived from the symbols used in the early Phoenician alphabet. But the gothic forms varied considerably from other classic forms of letters which sprang from the same source. Some students of paleography (the study of ancient writing) have offered the theory that gothics developed as a style through the attempts of scribes to conceal their lack of skill by ornamentation. In any case, this letter form persisted in Northern Europe in handwritten manuscripts from about the twelfth century until after the time of Gutenberg.

Since Germany was the point of origin of printing and the center from which printing spread to other countries in Europe, it is not surprising that gothic letters were also used in the first books printed in France, England, and the Netherlands. However, their use in those countries declined rapidly after the sixteenth century.

Study these questions: Why were first printing types gothic? Why have roman types become more common than gothic types? Why did the art and culture which developed in Northern Europe differ from the Greek and Roman culture in the early Middle Ages? Why did early scribes use black or heavy letters? To what extent does the tool or implement (chisel, brush, stylus, quill, pen) govern the appearance of the letter drawn by the artist or scribe?

Unit 96. Roman Letter Development

The manuscript hand of the Venetian scribes, which Nicholas Jenson followed as his model, developed apart from the gothic. It, too, was an evolution of roman capital letters. In formal writing and inscriptions the early Romans used square capitals which have come down to us, with slight modifications, in the form of our upper-case alphabet. For correspondence and documents not requiring formal writing, cursive or running capitals were used. These letters were large and, as noted, were originally pen drawn. By slow degrees, these characters

| UNCIAL | ENGLISH | CAROLINE | ENGLISH | ENGLISH | ITALIAN | ITALIAN | F. W. G. |
| 7TH CENT. | 8TH CENT. | 9TH CENT. | 10TH CENT. | 11TH CENT. | 12TH CENT. | 16TH CENT. | 20TH CENT. |

Fig. 96-A. Development of Lower-case "g" from Roman Uncial

assumed forms differing somewhat from pen drawn imitations of stone-cut inscription letters. Nine of the letters, A, D, E, G, H, M, T, Q, and V, particularly, had been modified by the seventh century, apparently to make their production easier and speedier. These modified script renditions of roman letters, known as *uncials*, represent about the half way mark in the transition from capitals to lower-case. But for rapid production of books even these letters could not be made speedily enough. Therefore, a smaller and more rounded letter form gradually evolved. These letter forms, known as *minuscules*, are the precise basis of our present day roman lower-case letters. (See Figure 96-A.)

Many national styles in writing developed as learning was carried from Rome throughout the rest of the known world. The influence of the roman characters might have been lost, however, had not Emperor Charlemagne taken an interest in the revival and spread of learning. Charlemagne encouraged the establishment of a school at Tours by an English scholar named Alcuin. The calligraphy of this school became the model for the rest of Europe. By the tenth century the use of letter forms from which we derive our lower case was quite universal. However, not until these letters were cast in types by Jenson did they assume the fixed form with which we are familiar.

In crediting Jenson with our style of roman type face, it would be unfair to overlook other early printers who experimented with roman letter forms, or who modified the early gothic letters. The first German types were angular and pointed, but later German types became more rounded. Even Gutenberg's later types show this influence. A semi-gothic face, tending distinctly toward roman, was used in 1460 by John Mentelin, the first Strassburg printer. Mentelin's son-in-law, Adolph Rusch, used a crudely cut roman face in a book published in 1464. Later, other roman faces appeared in Germany, but gothic predominated.

Even in Italy, roman types antedated Jenson. Conrad Sweynheym and Arnold Pannartz, two fifteenth century German political refugees, were welcomed at a monastery located at Subiaco, near Rome, where they engaged in printing activities. Their first type, which appeared about 1465, was roman in shape and arrange-

Fig. 96-B. Venetian Manuscript Letter

Fig. 96-C. German Roman Type — Rusch — 1464

Fig. 96-D. Second Type of Sweynheym and Pannartz — 1468

iiti uoluut:qui neque a corporibus ieparatione
mortales colere uideantur: nec beatitudinis pri
fateantur. Non ergo ad beatitudinem cōsequen
pora: sed corruptibilia: grauia:moribunda:non
bonitas dei:sed qualia esse compulit peccati poei

Sed necesse est inquiunt: ut terrena corpor
teneat:uel cogat ad terram: & ideo in caelo esse
illi homiēs in terra erant nemorosa atque fruc
obtinuit.Sed quia & ad hoc respondendū est:u
quo ascendit in caelum:uel propter sanctorum
sunt: intueantur paulo attentius pondera ipā
efficit: ut ex metallis quę in aquis posita contir

Fig. 96-E. Specimen of da Spira Type — 1469

qui omnibus ui aquarum submersis cum filiis
mirabili quodā modo quasi semen huāni generi
utinā quasi uiuam quandam imaginem imitari
quidem ante diluuium fuerunt:post diluuium a
altissimi dei sacerdos iustitiæ ac pietatis miracul
brǣorū appellatus est:apud quos nec circuncisi
ulla mentio erat . Quare nec iudǣos(posteris eni
gentiles:quoniam non ut gentes pluralitatem de
hebrǣos proprie noiamus aut ab Hebere ut dicti
transitiuos significat.Soli qppe a creaturis natu
nō scripta ad cognitionē ueri dei trāsiere:& uolu
ad rectam uitam puenisse scribunt:cum quibus
totius generis origo Habraam numerādus est:cu

Fig. 96-F. Specimen of First Jenson Type — 1470

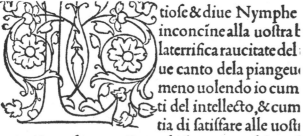
tiose & diue Nymphe
inconcine alla uostra
laterrifica raucitate del
ue canto dela piangeu
meno uolendo io cum
ti del intellecto,& cum
tia di satiffare alle uosti
non ristaro al potere.Lequale semota qualūque
si congruerebbe altronde,dignamente meritano
eloquentia,cum troppo piu rotunda elegantia &
tura di pronūtiato,che in me per alcuno pacto no
il suo gratioso affecto.Maauui Celibe Nymphe
tūche & confusa & incomptaméte fringultiéte ha

Fig. 96-G. Aldus-Roman Type — 1499

ment but massive like the gothic. It is probable that many Italian printers developed roman faces about this time; but the only one resembling closely our roman types was used about 1469 by John and Wendelin da Spira, reputed to have been the first printers of Venice.

The relation of Nicholas Jenson to Sweynheym and Pannartz and to the brothers da Spira is not fully recorded by history. It is known that Jenson was a Frenchman, Master of the Mint at Tours, and that he went to Mainz, Germany about 1458 to learn the new art of printing which had not yet reached France. Like Sweynheym and Pannartz, he seems to have fled to Italy after the sack of Mainz in 1462. He is supposed to have been employed by John da Spira and may have cut the da Spira types. Whether this be true is not highly significant, for the type face that became the model for succeeding type designers appeared in a book printed by Jenson in 1470.

The *humanistic* manuscripts, that is, manuscripts of classical literature produced by Venetian scribes, were Jenson's models. He did not copy the handwriting of scribes, letter for letter, but created a font of related letters that are legible and pleasing in effect. He clearly recognized that mechanical perfection is not as desirable as the composite appearance of the page. Commenting on the contribution of Jenson, D. B. Updike states: "Jenson's roman types have been the accepted models for roman letters ever since he made them, and, repeatedly copied in our own day, they have never been equalled."

Can you answer these questions? Why did scribes modify the roman capital letters? Why has the writing used in state documents influenced letter forms? Why did the writing of religious scribes of the medieval period have such a marked influence on letter forms? Why did Jenson use roman letter forms instead of gothics? Why do you suppose Jenson's types were so nearly perfect? Why was classic literature printed more extensively in Rome than in medieval Germany?

NOTE: A chart showing the various forms of the letter "D" appearing on page 136 illustrates several of the points covered in Units 95 and 96. Compare that chart with the one on page 132 showing the development of the letter "g."

Unit 97. Italics and Display Types

Practically all roman type faces in common use today have accompanying *italics*. This was not true of the first roman faces. Jenson, for example, did not produce *cursive* type, for italics were a separate development.

Italics were first used to print small, compact books. Early books were large and cumbersome. The gothic types used in early books were large. When roman type came into use, they were gradually cast smaller, and letters and lines were fitted more closely. But even this economy in page size did not satisfy Aldus Manutius, a Venetian printer of the period about the turn of the fifteenth century. Aldus, sensing a growing demand for cheaper books, tried to meet the demand by cutting a font of type to imitate the informal handwriting or vernacular cursive of his time. Aldus called this type *Chancery*. By the Italian contemporaries of Aldus, his type was called *Aldine;* but in the rest of Europe, the face was called *Italic* and this latter designation has continued in use to the present time.

An interesting characteristic of the Aldus books, printed in italics, was the use of roman capitals. In this he followed a practice common in handwritten documents of the time. This style is frequently encountered today in display lines in advertisements, but it is safe to say that most persons currently following the style are not familiar with the history of its origin.

Display types of today are difficult to trace historically. All, in some manner or another, are derived from hand-drawn letters. They may be specifically drawn as a type-design or developed from a letter drawn for another purpose. The type face known as *Trafton Script* is a specifically created design, originated for use as a display face. One sans serif display type, in common use, was suggested to the designer by hand-drawn letters found in cartoons. Some *modern* display faces are not modern at all but revivals of faces found in print, half a century or more ago, which have been sufficiently forgotten to be considered new. The origin of some of our display faces is not difficult to trace if sources are investigated. The upper case *G*, for example, in the face called *Legend* bears a close resemblance to a seventh century roman uncial,

and the lower case of this face shows even closer identity with a tenth century English minuscule. Starting with one or more letters suggested in this manner, the designer develops a new face. But even so his task is not an easy one, for he must develop a complete alphabet which harmonizes throughout the series.

Here are some more brain teasers: Why would a page of italic type be harder to read than a page set in roman? Why did first users of italics use roman capitals in the same book? Why do designers use display types which are different from the text types for advertising? Why does a special display type go out of style quickly? If a designer gets an idea for a display type from ancient handwriting, is he being original? Why can't type be designed in a purely mechanical fashion?

Fig. 97-A. Aldus-Chancery-Venetian — 1501

The changes that have occurred in the development of our present roman alphabet provide many interesting variations in letter forms. This was illustrated in the plate appearing at the bottom of page 132 showing the development of the lower-case "g" from the roman uncial. That plate and the one on this page were prepared by Dr. Frederic W. Goudy and appear in his interesting and important book, *The Alphabet*.

The plate showing the development of the letter "d" is a rendering of different interpretations of the letter as it appears in stone inscriptions, manuscripts, books, and type. The large "D" designated as 1 is a reproduction of the letter from an inscription on the base of the Trajan Column at Rome and dates back to A. D. 114. It is obviously the model for our roman capital letters.

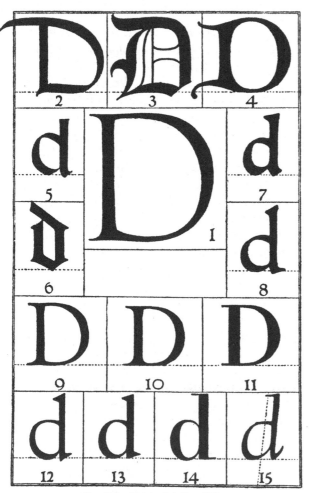

Fig. 97-B. Chart of Letter "D"

Number 2 is a hand-drawn capital originally produced by reed or quill pen which illustrates the effect of the writing implement on the letter form. This type of letter was in common use in the 7th and 8th centuries.

Number 3 illustrates the gothic or black-letter development which was commonly used in the 15th century manuscripts produced in Northern Europe. Such letters were the models which Gutenberg and his followers imitated; and their counterparts are present in our modern types in faces known as Old English. Number 6 is a lower-case "d" of the gothic manuscript form of the 15th century, and was used as a model for Gutenberg's first type.

Number 4 is a manuscript Lombardic gothic versal capital letter. Such letters were used by manuscript writers in the southern part of Europe during the 10th and 12th centuries. Number 5 is a hand-lettered lower-case "d" from an Italian manuscript and illustrates the roman form of letter of the 14th century. Number 7 is a lower-case "d" from the second type of Sweynheym and Pannartz (1468). Number 8 is a reproduction of the letter as it appears in the type of Nicholas Jenson (1470).

Numbers 9 and 12 are specimens of Kennerley type designed by Dr. Goudy. In it, Goudy attempted to restore some of the qualities which characterized Renaissance roman types. Number 15 is Kennerley italic, also designed by Dr. Goudy. It will be noticed that there is considerably less slant in this italic than in the original Aldus italic shown on page 134.

Numbers 10 and 13 are reproductions of letters appearing in the type designed by William Caslon in 1724. Caslon's types were the first to gain distinction in England and have been widely used. Dr. Goudy's comment on Caslon is significant: "This letter presents the perfection of unassuming craftsmanship, but lacks any artistic pretension; it is straightforward legible, with a quality of quaintness and even beauty that secures for it a general favor."

Numbers 11 and 14 are Bodoni specimens cut about 1771. Note particularly the distinction in serifs in the Bodoni face as compared to Caslon. Also note that the hairlines are thinner and stems thicker in the Bodoni type. Caslon is an informal type face while Bodoni has more formal characteristics. (See Units 81 and 82.)

Unit 98. Type Designing - Past and Present

Type designing is an art to which few people have devoted their entire attention; yet, thousands of faces have been designed and used. A few of these have found wide acceptance and have continued in use over a long period of years. It is not possible to list here all of the faces that have become classic, but a few of the better known ones can be mentioned. Faces known by the names of the following designers or founders are still used today. (Dates are approximations and are used only to indicate the period in which the types were first used.)

Face	Date	Designer or Founder	Country
Jenson	1470	Nicholas Jenson	Italy
		(Jenson was French)	
Garamond	1540	Claude Garamond	France
Fell	1672	Voskens Brothers	Netherlands
		(Brought to England for use by the Oxford Press by John Fell, an Englishman)	
Romain du Roi	1693	Philippe Grandjean	France
Caslon	1734	William Caslon	England
Modern	1750	S. P. Fournier	France
Baskerville	1757	John Baskerville	England
Bodoni	1768	Giambattista Bodoni	Italy
Bell	1785	John Bell	England
Didot	1775	Francois Didot	France
Golden	1892	William Morris	England

NOTE: Many italic types are patterned after the faces produced by Aldus Manutius, Italy, 1501; Ludovico Arrighi, Italy, 1524; Robert Granjon, France, 1550; and Philippe Grandjean, France, 1690.

The best known contemporary type designer of recent years was Frederic W. Goudy. During his lifetime, Dr. Goudy designed more than a hundred faces which have enjoyed varying degrees of popularity. Of these, a few have attracted greater attention and have gained greater distinction than others—Kennerley, Newstyle, Deepdene, Modern. The esthetic principles underlying the designing of type have been very clearly set forth by Dr. Goudy in the following statement: "Type to be fine must be legible, not merely readable, but pleasantly and easily legible; decorative in form, but not ornate; beautiful in itself and in company of its kinsman in the font; austere and formal, but with no stale or uninteresting regularity in its dissimilar characters; simple in design, but not the bastard simplicity that is mere crudity of outline; elegant, that is, gracious in line; fluid in form, but not archaic; and, above all, it must possess unmistakably the quality called *art* which is the spirit the designer puts into the body of his work, the product of his study and of his taste."

The five-hundredth anniversary of the invention of printing from movable type is being celebrated in 1940 by international precedent. Perhaps we should be celebrating the thousandth anniversary of printing from separate characters, an art invented by Pi-Sheng in China about a thousand years ago. Or, perchance, it is the invention of the printing press that we should be

Fig. 98-A. Modern Version of Jenson (Ludlow)

illuſtrioráque, vti ab omnibus recep
tentíque erimus inſigni memoria H
uanii nepotis , qui eximia cum laude
uilíſque prudentiæ, Mediolani prin
nuerunt.Incidit Galuanius in id tem
lanum à Federico AEnobarbo delet

Fig. 98-B. Early Garamond Face — 1540

regnum tuum : fiat volunt
in cœlo, ita etiam in terra.
ſtrum quotidianum da n
Et remitte nobis debita n
& remittimus debitoribu

Fig. 98-C. Fell Type of 1672

tuum : fiat voluntas tua, ſic
etiam in terra. Panem noſtr
num da nobis hodie. Et rem
bita noſtra, ſicut & remitti
bus noſtris. Et ne nos induc

Fig. 98-D. Fell Italic

cauld, il fit faire un logeme
mefme, 25 d'Aouft, le Gouve
Comte demeura aux enviro
bre, & cette entreprife n'aya
ou pour les attirer à un com

Fig. 98-E. Romain du Roi — 1653

Les quatre premières planches de l'Hiftoi
par médailles ont figuré au Salon de 175.
i'a pas été publié. Il exifte à la bibliothèque
'preuve des neuf pièces que nous publions au
font accompagnées du texte qui s'y rapportai
in-fol.). Les encadrements entourent ce texte
pages; il eft refté à l'état d'épreuves, toutefoi:
tion indique que ces épreuves n'étaient pas enc

Fig. 98-F. Specimen of Grandjean Italic

Quoufque tandem
Catilina, patientia n
Quoufque tandem abi
tilina, patientia noftr

Fig. 98-G. Caslon Roman and Italic — 1734

de fouvenir que vous r
de tous les ennuis que
fur lefquels je compte
dans mon voyage de F

Fig. 98-H. Fournier Type Used by Didot — 1750

Questions: Why are all type faces, in some
respects, imitations of the early type designs?
Would readers like a type face that was distinctly new or different? How do serifs on the
various type faces differ? Why have types designed by English founders greatly influenced
types commonly used in America? Why is a
simple design in type to be preferred to an
ornate design? What is the meaning of the
statement that a Caslon type page is like a man
in everyday clothes, whereas a Bodoni page is
more like a man in a dress suit?

no one which I have purfued
fteadinefs and pleafure, as that o
ing. Having been an early admire
of Letters, I became infenfibly o
tributing to the perfection of tl
to my felf Ideas of greater accu
yet appeared, and have endea

Fig. 98-I. Baskerville — 1757

deantur . Quae enim ref
genda natio , quae nova
ta cum diffitiffimis regioi
quirenda demum remot
haec laboribus majorique

Fig. 98-J. Bodoni — 1768

quiring or staying for the people':
possessed himselfe of the kingdom
panyed with his sonnes and othe
Rome, to besiege Ardea, during v
principall men of the Army meeti
at the tent of Sextus Tarquinius th
in their discourses after supper ever
ded the vertues of his owne wife:

Fig. 98-K. Morris Golden Type — 1892

Unit 99. Early Printing in England

We are interested in early printing in England because it was through England that printing came to the American colonies. Printing was introduced in England in 1476 or 1477 by William Caxton. As a representative of English merchants, Caxton spent thirty years of his life traveling in various countries in Europe. Along with his mercantile activities, Caxton found time to study the literature of the countries visited. As a pastime he undertook the translation into English of a French work, *The History of Troy*. The Duchess of Burgundy, sister of King Edward VI, expressed an interest in the translation, whereupon Caxton secured the assistance of a printer at Bruges, Netherlands, in publishing the book.

In 1476 Caxton brought printing equipment to England from the Netherlands and established a press at Westminster. That he actively pursued his new interest is shown by the fact that some thirty books were printed during the first three years. Among the books issued from Caxton's press were Chaucer's *The Canterbury Tales*, *Fables of Aesop*, and many other works of popular appeal.

English translations of the Bible were prohibited by the Church and State in Caxton's time. To get around this restriction, Caxton inserted various parts of the Bible into other books which he printed. In one volume, *The Golden Legend*, a book translated from Italian and printed by Caxton, there appeared practically all of the Old Testament as well as parts of the New Testament.

Not until 1525 was the New Testament (Tyndale's) printed in English, and not until 1535 was a complete Bible printed in English (Coverdale's). Both of these works were printed abroad and smuggled into England. The first English Bible printed in England was the second Coverdale Bible, published in 1537. Bible printing, which was encouraged in other countries and which accounted for the excellence of the work of Gutenberg and his successors, was so completely hampered and restrained in England that England became a backward country so far as printing was concerned. Freedom of the press did not reach England until the period following the war with the American colonies.

Caxton was not an outstanding printer if

Fig. 99-A. Caxton Type from the First Book Printed in English

Fig. 99-B. Later Caxton Type

Fig. 99-C. Type of Richard Pynson — 1494

his work is measured by standards of mechanical excellence. He was influenced by printing practices in the Netherlands, which did not, in the early period, reach the heights attained in Germany, Italy, and France. But Caxton's work was the beginning of literacy in England. Not only did Caxton publish several hundred books which gained wide circulation, but he encouraged interest in the development of a national literature. His efforts also left a lasting influence on English as a language. When Caxton began to print, there were no standards of spelling, punctuation, or capitalization. In setting standards of style for the printing of English, Caxton greatly assisted in transforming several barbaric dialects into a national tongue.

In 1491, upon Caxton's death, his printing materials came into the possession of Wynkyn de Worde, who had been Caxton's assistant and, in general, carried on the traditions of the founder, printing some 800 books during his lifetime.

During the last quarter of the fifteenth century, several presses were established throughout England. About 1485 a press was installed at Oxford. Unfortunately for historical continuity, the Oxford press did not operate uninterruptedly. From 1519 a long period of inactivity occurred. Not until 1585 was the predecessor of the modern Oxford University Press established. However, since that date the press has operated continuously, probably the longest period of operation of any printing establishment in history.

Richard Pynson, who printed in England during the latter part of the fifteenth and early sixteenth centuries, is believed to have been the first to introduce roman types in England. Pynson brought roman types and ornaments from France, and in their use was influenced by Italian and French typography. He is rated by authorities as "the most tasteful of the fifteenth century English printers."

Pynson's predecessors, Caxton and de Worde, used fonts of type which had been cast in the Netherlands. These contained crudely cut alphabets resembling the gothic letters of the first German printers. It is from these Low Country gothic models, which were used by the early English printers, that we have derived modern black face types known as Old English. They have been modified to provide legibility but still closely resemble in form the types first used for printing in English.

John Day, born in 1522, worked for other printers in early life, but began printing on his own account in 1546. He was the first English designer of a roman type face. It is not known whether the types he designed were produced in England or were cast by Flemish type founders. Day's work as a printer warrants recognition as being of good quality, but he did not produce work of the degree of excellence that characterized printing which was being done in France and Italy during this period.

Following the middle of the sixteenth century, English printing declined still further in quality, partly because the State sought to control the press by censorship and by restricting the number of presses permitted to operate. By 1557, restrictions were so far-reaching that no presses were permitted to operate outside of London except one each at Oxford and Cambridge universities. Naturally there were numerous efforts on the part of printers to evade the restrictions of the government monopoly. This brought drastic governmental action which led to the execution, in 1584, of William Carter as an object lesson. Thus it may be observed that the very conditions which caused men to seek freedom from English political and religious repression by emigrating to the American continent, likewise stifled the art of printing which flourished in the other nations of Europe.

Questions related to this unit: Why was first printing in England concerned with non-religious literature, whereas the Bible was the most widely printed book in Europe? Does censorship aid or retard the development of printing? Why do you suppose more care was exercised in printing the Bible than in printing ordinary literature? In what tongue were Bibles first printed? Why does Old English resemble gothic type? Which was more legible to readers in Caxton's time, gothic or roman type faces? Why did printing tend to standardize language forms when first introduced into England? Radio broadcasting stations are licensed by the federal government. Should printing presses likewise be licensed? Has there ever been a period in the history of America during which printing was restricted?

Unit 100. Two Famous English Type Designers

Along with their restriction of printing, English rulers also controlled type founding. Even when greater freedom of the press was allowed toward the latter part of the seventeenth century, much of the type which was used was imported from the Dutch countries. Typefounding, therefore, was a little known art and those types which were produced were of poor quality. But, in 1692, there was born, in Worcestershire, a child who was destined to completely change the appearance of English printing through the designing and casting of a new type face. His name was William Caslon. Not only is Caslon type still used, but his style of printing is still consciously or unconsciously followed by many contemporary English and American typographers.

In early life William Caslon was apprenticed to an engraver. In 1716 he set up a shop in which he did silver-chasing and cut tools and dies for bookbinders. During the ensuing years, Caslon learned letter-founding at the type foundry of Thomas James. By 1720, Caslon had established a foundry of his own and, over a period of fourteen years, developed various fonts which were offered for general sale to other printers in 1734. Caslon died in 1766, but his descendants continued to operate the foundry until 1874. Even today the foundry is in operation, although in other hands.

Caslon types and their present day imitations have been used extensively for printing in English. Oddly enough, Caslon's letters are not perfect in themselves, but a page of Caslon type produces a balanced, simple, and pleasant effect. At the same time, the letters of Caslon are legible, and they possess a quality which has sometimes been described as "friendly to the eye" or "comfortable." There is an everyday ease of dress in the Caslon types. Commenting on the work of Caslon, Lawrence C. Wroth states that his types have been in "continuous use for two hundred years lacking a single generation. That is why William Caslon, more than any single individual, is the most significant figure of his century in the history of the printed book."

The English printer and type designer, John Baskerville, born in 1706, is regarded by some

sandth anniversary of printing from separate characters, an art invented by Pi-Sheng in China about a thousand years ago. Or, perchance, it is the invention of the printing press that we should be celebrating. At any rate, the five hundredth birthday of printing, as we now understand the art, is being celebrat-

No one knows precisely the events that transpired five hundred years ago, for the historical evidence is obscure. But we do know that somehow the mechanics of bringing movable type, paper, and ink together to produce multiple records became known sometime before the middle of the fifteenth century. We know, also,

Fig. 100-A. Modern Version of Caslon (Monotype)

The five-hundredth anniversary of the invention of printing from movable type is being celebrated in 1940 by international precedent. Perhaps we should be celebrating the thousandth anniversary of printing from separate characters, an art invented by Pi-Sheng in China about a thousand years ago. Or, perchance, it is the invention of the printing press that we should be celebrating. At any rate, the five-hundredth birthday of printing, as we now understand the art, is being celebrated.

No one knows precisely the events that transpired five hundred years ago, for the historical evidence is obscure. But we do know that somehow the mechanics of bringing movable type, paper, and ink together to produce multiple records became known sometime before the middle of the fifteenth century. We know, also, that Johannes Gut-

Fig. 100-B. Modern Version of Baskerville (Monotype)

students of the history of printing as the father of fine printing in England. Baskerville, after having accumulated a fair-sized fortune in other fields, established a paper mill, printing office, and type foundry at Birmingham in 1750. Baskerville spent several years experimenting with designs for types; he also tried various methods of improving the surface of sheets of paper by pressing them between hot plates after printing; and he mixed special inks which he used in producing his first book. Consequently, when he offered his first printed works to the public in 1757 and 1758, they gained wide acclaim as excellent pieces of workmanship. Other books of excellent quality followed. As a result, both his printing and the types which he designed have greatly influenced typography and type design. Baskerville frankly admitted that his type designs were influenced by Caslon, but he introduced a greater lightness and refinement in English types. The types designed by Baskerville are usually considered to represent a half-way step between the *old-style* roman letter which Caslon type so clearly exemplified and the *modern* style of roman letter which is best illustrated by the face developed by the Italian printer, Bodoni.

England's contribution to the development of printing was not as great as that of those countries which comprise Continental Europe. However, it was through English printers that the early traditions of printing in America were established. The first printing equipment used in the colonies, and the printers who operated it, came from England. Benjamin Franklin, who led all others of his time in promoting the printing art in the American colonies, was greatly influenced by the work of Caslon and Baskerville.

Extend your knowledge by seeking the answers to these questions: Why was typefounding so slow in starting in England? How did Caslon's early experience aid him in type designing? Why were Caslon's types popular in the American Colonies? Why did the fact that Benjamin Franklin was acquainted with the work of Caslon and Baskerville have an influence on early American printing? What is the difference between "fine printing" and ordinary commercial work? Why did Baskerville plate his paper *after* printing rather than *before*? What was the difference in the serifs of the types of Caslon, Baskerville, and Bodoni? Why are Bodoni types still called *modern*? Why are Caslon types called *old style*? How do you account for the fact that Caslon type (or modified forms) are still widely used in both England and America?

Unit 101. Early Printing in America

Interestingly enough, printing played a part in assigning the name "America" to the western continent. If the story of the voyages of Columbus had been printed and widely circulated, the name of our continent might have been different. For it was the printing of the story of the voyage of Americus Vespucci to what is now South America that gave the newly-discovered country its name. In 1507 one of the monks of the College of St. Die, located in the Vosges mountains, wrote a preface to an account of the voyage of Vespucci which contained the statement: "I do not see what is rightly to hinder us from calling it (Vespucci's discovery) Amerigo, or America, i. e., the land of Americus, after its discoverer, Americus, a man of sagacious mind . . ." Having gotten into print the name stuck. Today, because of that circumstance, we live in a country known as America.

Printing was used to promote colonization of the New World. There is on file in the New York Public Library a copy of such a promotion piece, dated 1609. It is entitled, "Offering Most Excellent Fruites by Planting in Virginia." It is believed that this printed prospectus influenced people to continue to come to the New World, even in the face of the hardships and disaster which confronted the early settlers. One historian, observing the fact that 750 of the first 900 settlers in the Virginia Colonies died during the first winter, marvels at the force of the printed word which not only induced new settlers to come to the New World, but influenced the 150 survivors to remain. "The tired planters, with the smell of death still upon them, were induced to return to their miseries by a lot of ignorant adventurers whose sole information came from high-powered printed salesmanship. In all history there can be no more arresting evidence of the new force which had come into the new world."

The extent to which printing was used in promoting the New England colonies is not known. But it is known that a printing press made its appearance in Massachusetts soon after the first settlers established themselves. It is possible that the press and printing materials, brought from England in 1638, were to be used for producing religious and political tracts to be circulated in the mother country. Suggestive of this probability is the fact that the first piece printed on the new press was *The Freeman's Oath*. However, conditions changed in England and the press which might have been intended as a propaganda machine was turned to service for the Colonists. The *Bay Psalm Book*, eleven copies of which are in existence today, was produced for home use on the press in 1640.

This early colonial press was procured in England by Reverend Jose Glover. The Reverend Glover died on the voyage over, but his wife assumed responsibility for setting up the press in Cambridge. Stephen Daye, who had been indentured by the Reverend Glover to operate the press, was placed in charge by Mistress Glover. Stephen Daye and his son, Matthew, continued to operate the press until 1647. In the meantime, the widow of Glover married again, this time to President Dunster of Harvard College. Upon her death the press was moved to Harvard College and, during a period of years, was used in close association with the college. In a sense, this represents the beginning of Harvard University Press, the oldest continuously operated printing activity in America.

The printing press, itself, is still in existence and is known as the Stephen Daye Press. In 1939, a special stamp was issued by the United States Post Office Department commemorating the 300th anniversary of the establishment of printing in the American Colonies. A pictorial reproduction of the Stephen Daye Press appeared on the stamp.

Samuel Green took over the task of operating the Daye press about 1649, following the death of Matthew Daye. He continued to print for about thirty years, producing in that time some 300 titles. His most famous book was an "Indian Bible" printed in the native tongue, Algonquin.

In passing, it should be noted that printing in the Massachusetts Colony was not the first on the American continent. Spanish records indicate that the first press to be operated in the New World was established in Mexico in 1539. Printing seems to have flourished in this Spanish settlement, for there are known to have been thirty-three printers in Mexico at various periods between 1539 and 1700.

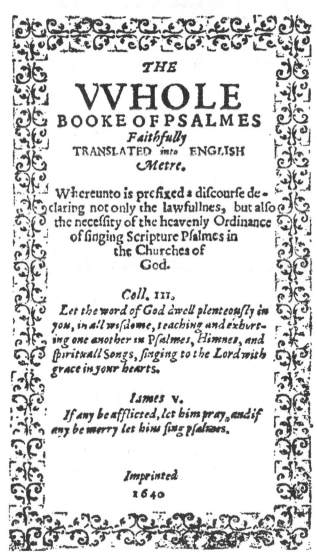

Fig. 101-A. First Book Printed in the Colonies

Fig. 101-B. Stephen Daye Press

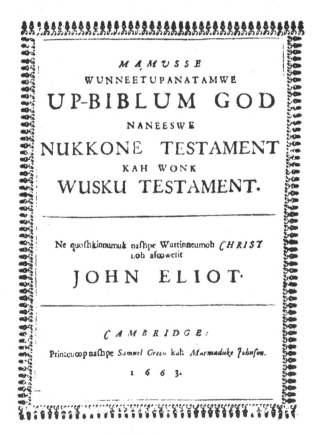

MAMUSSE
WUNNEETUPANATAMWE
UP-BIBLUM GOD
NANEESWE
NUKKONE TESTAMENT
KAH WONK
WUSKU TESTAMENT.

Ne quoſhkinnumuk naſhpe Wuttinneumoh *CHRIST*
noh aſoowefit

JOHN ELIOT·

CAMBRIDGE:
Printeuoop naſhpe *Samuel Green* kah *Marmaduke Johnſon.*

1 6 6 3.

Fig. 101-C. Indian Bible Printed on Stephen Daye Press

Printing did not make headway in the southern colonies to the extent that was true of the Massachusetts Colony. A printing venture undertaken by William Nuthead in Jamestown, in 1682, was suppressed by the King's governor. In 1685 William Bradford began printing in Philadelphia; but, after several unpleasant conflicts with colonial officials, he was forced to abandon his work in 1692. However, he was permitted to move to New York where he again engaged in printing. Other ventures at printing followed the expansion of population and colonization. By 1700 there were a dozen or so printers in Boston. By 1763 there was a press in operation in Georgia, the last of the thirteen colonies to be settled. In 1786 a newspaper was started at Pittsburgh, Pennsylvania, which has been published continuously and is now known as the *Post-Gazette*. Printing came to Kentucky, Tennessee, Ohio, and Michigan in the 1780's and 1790's. In 1808 printing had moved west of the Mississippi to St. Louis. Thus, as migration continued, printing was in evidence.

Direct your thinking along these lines for a while: Why do you suppose the story of the voyages of Columbus was not printed immediately after his discovery of the new continent? How long would it take to get a book on a great discovery into circulation today? What was the difference in motive in colonization in the South as compared with the New England settlements? Why were the New England Colonists anxious to print tracts to be circulated in England? Why were university presses, such as the Oxford Press in England and Harvard Press in New England, among the first to be established? Since printing was established in Mexico about a hundred years before the Stephen Daye press was brought to New England, why did not printing spread from Mexico to North America? Why was the printing of a Bible in Algonquin a remarkable accomplishment? Does printing create literacy (the ability to read and write), or does literacy create a demand for printing? No industry had been honored by the issuance of a commemorative stamp until the Stephen Daye stamp was issued in 1939. Why do you suppose this exception was made? Why was printing discouraged in some of the early colonies? Why did printing follow closely the settlement of the West and Middle West?

Unit 102. Two Printer Patriots

Benjamin Franklin, believed by some to have been the most important American citizen of his time, was born in Boston in 1706. As a boy he learned printing in the shop of his brother who was publisher of *The New England Courant*. In 1723 he quarrelled with his brother and went to New York. Unable to find work, he continued on to Philadelphia where he worked for a French printer, named Keimer. At the suggestion of the governor of Pennsylvania, Sir William Keith, young Franklin went to England to buy a printing outfit. Money which he had been promised was not forthcoming; so for two years he worked in famous English printing plants, including that of William Watts. In 1726 he returned to Philadelphia. By 1732 he had his own printing office and became the publisher of the *Pennsylvania Gazette*. Among the publications which Franklin printed, *Poor Richard's Almanack* became the most famous. Publication was begun in 1732 and continued for twenty-five years, with an average yearly sale of 10,000 copies — the most widely circulated document of the colonial period in which Franklin lived.

As a printer, scholar, author, scientist, and statesman, Franklin exercised a marked influence on colonial thought and political activities. It is difficult to estimate the full effect of his forceful personality on the life of his period. In commenting on this question, Richard Burlingame, in his book, *The March of the Iron Men*, states: "If we were required to point out a precise moment at which our special American culture began . . . we could hardly do better than to mark the appearance of Franklin. If we must give credit to an inventor for our American civilization, it must go to him.

"He was a product of the unspecialized age we have just examined in that he was a jack-of-all-trades. He violated the proverb by becoming master of at least half a dozen. Some of them he created. In the course of his life he was a printer, journalist, columnist, writer, salesman, advertising man, promoter, publicity expert, civic organizer, fireman, postmaster, librarian, military architect, quartermaster, soldier, legislator, diplomatist, and statesman. He was also a scientific discoverer, a practical inventor, an amateur mathematician, a philosopher, an innovator in navigation, transport, hygiene and sanitation, city planning, streetlighting, paving and cleaning, hospitalization, and higher education. He was a wit, satirist, humorist, and hoaxer; a political agitator, a maker of slogans, maxims, and wall mottoes; a promoter of clubs, associations, secret societies, lodges; a good mixer, a vulgarizer of the arts and sciences, a lobbyist, and a politician. He made considerable contributions to meteorology and medicine; he introduced an ideal of cleanliness into an era when bathing was still a lick without a promise; and he was an athlete in a sportless age."

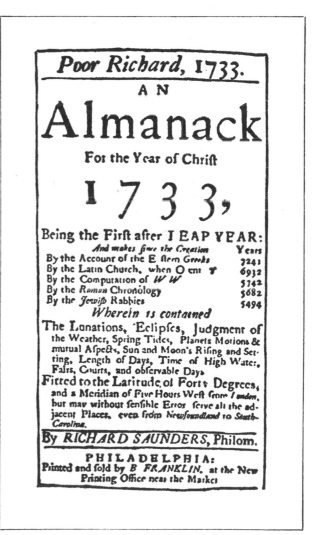

Fig. 102-A. First Issue of Franklin's "Almanack"

Throughout his life, Franklin was active in promoting printing. Although he disposed of his business in Philadelphia in 1748, to devote his time to literary, journalistic, and civic activities, he assisted in the establishment and promotion of forty or more printing plants in the Colonies during his lifetime. While he was serving his country as special minister to France from 1776 to 1785, he operated a private press in his home at Passy, France. Franklin's high regard for his craft is revealed by the words with which he began his will: "I, Benjamin Franklin, Printer . . . "

Franklin is not the only printer of the Revolutionary Period who is celebrated as a great patriot. There are several; but outstanding among them is Isaiah Thomas. Thomas, born in Massachusetts in 1744, was actively engaged in printing from early life. In 1770 he began publication of the *Massachusetts Spy*, a newspaper in which he supported the cause of the patriots. He rendered service during the Revolutionary War as printer for the Massachusetts House of Assembly. Following the war, he re-established, in Worcester, his business which had been almost completely destroyed. As a printer he prospered and became the leading publisher of books in the period following the Revolution.

In 1810 Isaiah Thomas published a two volume *History of Printing in America* which, even today, remains the best source book on colonial printing. Before his death he actively promoted the establishment of the American Antiquarian Society. Upon his death, Thomas bequeathed to the Antiquarian Society his personal library and a fair share of his fortune. This society, which continues in existence today, has been an important organization for preserving source material for the study of American history. Because of the foresight and interest of this famous printer, many facts about early life in America, contained in your history textbook, might not be known. Isaiah Thomas clearly recognized the fact that printing is not only a means of communication, but also is important as a means of record and historical evidence.

Food for thought: Why did Franklin, who had so many other talents and attainments, retain an interest in printing? Why was an almanac a very widely circulated printed piece of the colonial period? Why do you suppose Franklin included literary material in *Poor Richard's Almanack?* Why did he invent the character of "Poor Richard"? Why is Franklin called the "inventor of American culture"? How could Franklin have been recognized as an outstanding man in so many fields in his time?

Who were other great printers of the Revolutionary Period? Who was the leading publisher of books during the period following the Revolution? What is the best source of information on Colonial printing?

THE

HISTORY OF PRINTING

IN

AMERICA.

WITH A

BIOGRAPHY OF PRINTERS,

AND AN

ACCOUNT OF NEWSPAPERS.

TO WHICH IS PREFIXED A CONCISE VIEW OF

THE DISCOVERY AND PROGRESS OF THE ART

IN

OTHER PARTS OF THE WORLD.

IN TWO VOLUMES

BY ISAIAH THOMAS,
PRINTER, WORCESTER, MASSACHUSETTS

VOLUME I.

PRINTING dispels the gloom of mental night—
Hail! pleasing fountain of all cheering light!
How like the radiant orb which gives the day,
And o'er the earth sends forth th' enlight'ning ray!

WORCESTER:
FROM THE PRESS OF ISAIAH THOMAS, JUN
ISAAC STURTEVANT, PRINTER.
1810

Fig. 102-B. Published by the Son of Isaiah Thomas

Unit 103. Development of the Printing Press

In the composition of type by hand there is much in common between printing today and printing as it was practiced by the followers of Gutenberg. The general appearance of type, its casting, and the procedures used in putting it together to form words, lines, and pages have not radically changed. The only major departure from early typesetting has been the introduction of composing machines.

In transferring the impression to paper by the use of printing presses, however, radical changes have occurred. The crude wooden hand presses of the early printers, capable of turning out 300 to 500 sheets in a day, have been replaced with power driven machines which can produce that number of impressions in a few minutes (in newspaper printing, in a few seconds). But this change did not take place rapidly. Like all other modern developments in printing, high speed printing is a development of the last century.

No one knows what Gutenberg's press looked like. By piecing together bits of evidence, it is possible to arrive at a good guess. Presumably it resembled presses used in medieval times for household purposes in making wine, cheese, or finishing linen cloth. Too, it may have resembled presses used in papermaking. Probably it was built around a wooden frame fastened to two heavy upright posts. Pressure was applied by turning a wooden screw. The type form was held in some manner on a table or bed in a box or frame below the point where the screw pressure was applied. Whether this bed could be moved forward to permit the sheet to be laid on the form and then moved back to receive pressure is not known. Nor do we know how the platen was packed or cushioned to avoid crush-

Fig. 103-A. Old Wooden Hand Press — 1508

Fig. 103-B. Early English Hand Press — 1750

Fig. 103-C. First Iron Press

Fig. 103-D. Washington Hand Press

Fig. 103-E. First Power Press — London 1814

ing the type form. Ink was probably daubed on the type form by hand with a leather-covered, half-round device fastened to a wooden handle.

The first illustration of a printing press appeared in a book printed at Lyons, France, in 1499. It resembles, in general, the foregoing description, but details of operation are not clearly depicted. Thirty-four sketches of presses appeared in other books published in the sixteenth century, but all the drawings were quite crude. However, these illustrations show progressive developments in the printing press. From them we can trace improvements, such as the introduction of the iron screw, general use of tympan and frisket with special rests and supports, and carriage for sliding the form back and forth. The extent to which improvements in presses had taken place is indicated by a printers' ordinance passed in Frankfort, Germany, in 1575, which mentions 3,600 impressions as the average for a day's work of fifteen hours.

Improvements in the upright, wooden-frame press continued and reached their greatest degree of refinement about the beginning of the eighteenth century. Franklin worked on such a press in the printing office of William Watts in London in 1724-1726. This press used a torsion screw and was provided with a clever mechanical arrangement devised to provide the proper pressure on the form. The Stephen Daye press, brought to Cambridge from London in 1639, was similar in construction but less perfect mechanically. Further changes in press construction came about slowly during the eighteenth century; none were worthy of note except for addition of metal, in constructing parts and frames, which permitted the use of larger type forms.

The first all-metal press was built by the Earl of Stanhope in the first part of the nineteenth century. This press still used a screw device, but less exertion was required to force the impression on the sheet. Efforts to apply the principle of the lever to the iron press resulted in the development of several presses which came into common use. Among these were the Columbian press, built by George Clymer, of New York; the Albion press, invented by R. W. Cope, of London; the Washington press, perfected by Samuel Rust (somewhat after models patented by John J. Wells, of Hartford, and Peter Smith, of New York). Each of these presses was developed during the period from 1800 to 1825. The Washington press became quite popular in the United States, and by 1900 over 6,000 had been manufactured and sold. Many are still in use as private presses and for pulling press proofs. The Albion press was equally popular in England.

The idea of the printing press, as conceived by Gutenberg, reached its highest development in the Washington and Albion presses. The modern job press and the cylinder press are distinctly different machines. However, the first power press did have some of the features of the hand presses. The Adams press, patented by Isaac Adams in 1830, raised and lowered the form by means of a cam, powered by steam, which operated a toggle joint. In appearance the Adams press has been described as "an old-fashioned hand press turned upside down."

These questions will give you a broader understanding of printing presses: Why was high speed production, as we think of it today, less important in Gutenberg's time? Why must the pressure on the printing form be "cushioned"? Why would not a "kiss impression" have given satisfactory results on Gutenberg's press? Why were first presses made of wood instead of iron? Why do you suppose first presses used a screw? Why do we sometimes apply the nickname, "Inkball," to printing shop apprentices? Why weren't detailed sketches made of Gutenberg's press at the time he invented it? Do you imagine the *Mainz Psalter* was printed in signatures or a page at a time? Why were power presses so long in developing? How did it come about that several "improved" hand presses were developed about the same time? Why do you suppose the Adams press raised and lowered the *form* instead of the *paper?* Has quality of printing improved with increased speed of production? What advantage does automatic inking serve besides speed? Were first platens hand or automatically fed? Why is "fine printing" still sometimes done on an old style hand press?

Unit 104. Modern Printing Presses

The modern job, or platen press is the direct descendant of a machine perfected in 1858 by George P. Gordon, of New York. In this machine, the platen and form were turned on edge. Of the models manufactured today, some employ a rigid bed, and the platen is drawn up against the form. In others, both the platen and bed move with a sort of clam-shell action. Hand lever, foot treadle, and power models can still be secured; however, the majority being produced today are motor powered. Production capacities vary from 1000 to 3600 per hour, depending on the type of job and whether they are fed automatically or by hand.

The modern cylinder press was first conceived by William Nicholson, of London, who secured patents in 1790. But no press was ever built exactly according to his specifications. The first cylinder press actually to be constructed was built in London under the supervision of a German named Friedrich Koenig, who seems to have known something of Nicholson's ideas for perfecting such a machine. The press was first used for printing the London *Times* in 1814, and was capable of turning out eleven hundred sheets per hour. William Cowper and Ambrose Applegarth worked on improvements on the *Times* press and developed a machine which printed 4,000 to 5,000 impressions per hour. By further modification they produced a press, in 1848, capable of delivering ten thousand sheets an hour. In the United States, Richard M. Hoe developed a type-revolving cylinder press, the first models of which produced eight thousand impressions per hour. Later models of the original Hoe press had a capacity of twenty thousand per hour.

All of the presses just described were sheet fed and used type forms. During the first part of the nineteenth century, methods of making stereotypes, invented a hundred years earlier, were being improved. The introduction of stereotypes in newspaper printing, in 1856, by the London *Times* and by the New York *Tribune*, in 1861, paved the way for the web-fed newspaper presses used today. The Earl of Stanhope, who perfected the iron hand press, also invented a method of making stereotypes.

Fig. 104-A. Heidelberg Automatic

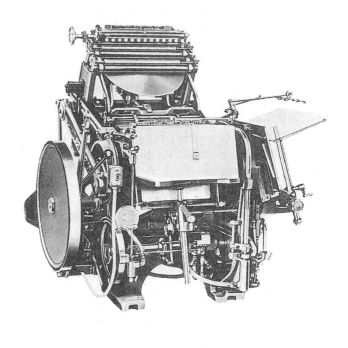

Fig. 104-C. Chandler and Price Automatic Platen

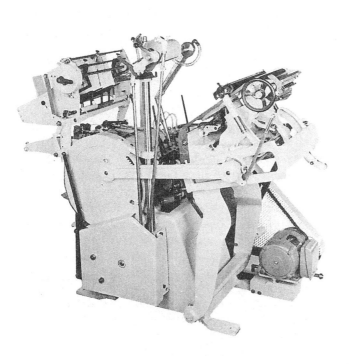

Fig. 104-B. Kluge Automatic

Fig. 104-D. Miehle Vertical

Fig. 104-E. Miehle 29

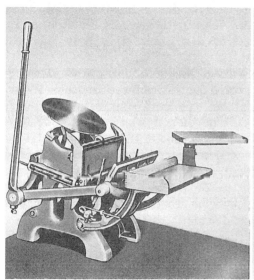

Fig. 104-F. Two Chandler and Price Hand-fed Platen Presses As Used in Schools

Fig. 104-G. Miller TW Two-Color

The first web press was developed by an American, William Bullock, in 1856. A similar press was patented in London in 1866 and put into operation in 1868. These early presses delivered fifteen thousand signatures per hour printed on both sides. A device for folding the papers as they came from the press was added in 1875. Newspaper presses have been developed since to a high state of efficiency. The Hoe double octuple press prints 128 pages from eight rolls of paper printed on both sides of the web. It slits, folds, and collects eight-page signatures to make four thirty-two page sections at the rate of 72,000 sections an hour. By duplicating plates and units, newspapers can be delivered at the phenomenal rate of 144,000 per hour. Magazines and catalogs are frequently printed on presses similar to newspaper presses but operate at slower rates of speed.

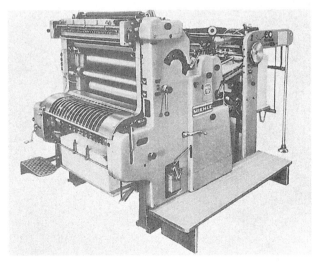

Fig. 104-H. Miehle 29 Offset and Letterset Press

Most modern flat-bed and cylinder presses trace back to Koenig's first cylinder machine. Shortly after Koenig's press was placed in operation in 1814, D. Napier, an Englishman, invented a press using grippers for picking the sheet from the paper table and holding it while the sheet was receiving the impression. This is a feature of all book and commercial presses. Numerous other improvements have been added throughout the years, and the present day cylinder press is a very efficient machine, capable of producing from 2500 to 5000 impressions, depending on the size of the pressbed and the nature of the work being done.

Web-fed rotary and sheet-fed cylinder presses are in use which print two to four colors, successively. By use of separate units for each color in the same frame, a finished job in two or four colors is made possible. The demand for color printing has resulted in increased use of multicolor presses in the past few years.

Offset presses were an American development and were first introduced in 1905. Photogravure, from which commercial gravure methods have developed, was perfected by Karl Klitsch, in Vienna, about 1875. Commercial rotogravure was developed in Germany and dates from 1910. In some respects offset and gravure presses resemble presses for relief printing. However, special features of these presses make them distinctly different.

In addition to inking rollers, offset presses have damping rollers because nonprinting surfaces on the offset plate must be moistened to repel inks. These presses also have three cylinders: one to carry the offset plate, and one to carry a rubber blanket which in turn trans-

Fig. 104-I Miehle 54/77 Six-color Sheet-fed Offset Press

fers the impression to the paper as it is carried through the press on an impression cylinder. Offset presses most widely used in job work are sheet-fed and have a capacity of 3000 to 6000 impressions per hour. However, web-fed offset presses for single and multi-color printing have been perfected which will deliver 12,000 or more printed or folded sheets per hour.

On gravure presses, paper is printed directly from gravure plates attached to, or made on cylinders. Gravure presses differ from relief printing presses chiefly in the method of applying ink on the plate and in the use of a squeegee or "doctor blade" for removing ink from the non-printing surface of the gravure plate. Most presses commonly used in gravure printing are rotary presses, although sheet-fed presses are likely to become more widely used in the future.

More questions on presswork: Why do modern platens carry the form on edge? Which limits the speed of a hand-fed treadle press — the speed of feeding or speed of action produced by the treadle? Why were cylinder presses first applied to newspaper printing? What shape do you suppose the type was on the Hoe type revolving press? Why was web feeding introduced? Why do you suppose stereotypes were used on flat-bed presses before being adapted for newspaper cylinder presses? Why are grippers necessary on a cylinder press? What kind of paper can be printed fastest — extremely thin, average thickness, or heavy? What difference in ink would be necessary on a two-color or a four-color press? Why has web-fed rotogravure been more extensively used than sheet-fed gravure? Why does the rubber blanket on an offset press reduce the necessity for make-ready? Why is a "doctor blade" necessary on a gravure press while not required on an offset press? Why do you suppose high-speed presses were developed more rapidly in England and America than in the rest of the world?

Unit 105. Type and Typecasting Machines

Variety and greater volume in printing became possible when the idea of movable type was first put to practical use. Type, since the days of Gutenberg, has been made by molding printing characters in relief on the end of pieces of metal. The basic principles of typecasting have not changed a great deal in the five hundred years that printing has been practiced. While it is true that some of the processes used in typecasting have been transferred to machines, the casting either of a single piece of type or a line of type on a slug still requires the use of a matrix, an adjustable mold, and molten metal into printing surfaces.

The matrix is a piece of brass or bronze into which the shape of the letter or character has been carved, pressed, or punched. A matrix is a reverse, or female die. The matrix (sometimes called a "mat") is made from the positive die or punch. The first step in designing a type face is the drawing of a pattern of the letters and other characters. Punches for each character are then prepared. These were originally made by carving the letter or character on a piece of hardened steel by hand. Today, punches are usually cut with the aid of a machine.

By using matrices which were fitted into adjustable molds, early typecasters produced type by pouring metal into the molds by hand. Hand casting was practiced until 1838 when David Bruce invented a typecasting machine. By 1862, improvements had been made which provided machines that automatically performed all operations of typecasting. Such machines are used today in casting type for hand setting, known as foundry type.

For more than four hundred years after the invention of printing, all type was set by hand. In the nineteenth century, men began to consider seriously the possibility of creating typesetting machines. Numerous machines intended to replace hand composition have been invented. The first of these was designed by an Englishman, Dr. William Church, in 1822; others followed rapidly. While many of the first typesetting machines functioned satisfactorily, none were sufficiently practical to make them commercially successful.

Many people, including Mark Twain (who, incidentally, was a printer by trade), lost fortunes in seeking to perfect such machines. All made the mistake of trying to develop machines which would set type previously cast and fed into the machine. It was not until the order

Fig. 105-A. Church Typecasting Machine

Fig. 105-B. Barth Typecasting Machine

Fig. 105-C. Ludlow Typograph

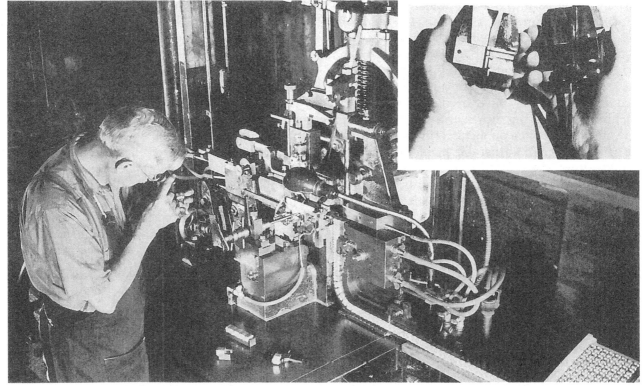

Fig. 105-D. Modern Typecasting of Foundry Type with Hand Mold Shown Upper Right

was changed from casting first and composing later, to composing and then casting, that a satisfactory typesetting machine was finally developed. This is an interesting example of the way in which habits and fixed ideas of doing things often retard mechanical progress. You will recall that it was not until Isaac Adams "turned the hand press upside down" that a power platen press was invented.

Of the various composing machines which have been developed, only two kinds are in general use today. These are machines, such as the Linotype, Intertype, and the Ludlow Typograph, which cast slugs, carrying a justified line of type, molded in one piece; and the Montoype which casts individual pieces of type set in justified lines. The Linotype was invented in 1886 by Ottmar Mergenthaler, of Baltimore. The Monotype was invented in 1887 by Tolbert Lanston, of Washington, D. C. The Ludlow Typograph was suggested by Washington I. Ludlow in 1906 and was later developed by William A. Reade. Intertype, a later development, utilizes the Mergenthaler principle.

Both the Linotype and Intertype are equipped with keyboards which the operator uses to set matrices that are assembled in a line. The line of matrices is fitted into a mold which permits a solid slug to be cast, bearing a line of raised letters. The matrices are automatically spaced before the line is cast and automatically distributed after casting. Slugs are assembled by hand and, after the job is printed, are melted so that the metal may be used over and over.

The Monotype system requires the use of two machines. A keyboard, which resembles a large typewriter, is operated for the purpose of perforating a ribbon or strip of paper while it is being unwound from one spool to another. After the ribbon has been perforated for the desired characters, it is placed on a second machine which casts the type. As the ribbon unwinds on the caster, individual pieces of type are cast and justified in lines as predetermined by the way in which the ribbon has been perforated. The perforations on the ribbon cause a case, containing a complete font of matrices, to shift about over a mold so that the proper character is cast. After a form has been printed from Monotype-cast composition, the type is melted for re-use.

Fig. 105-E. First Linotype — 1886

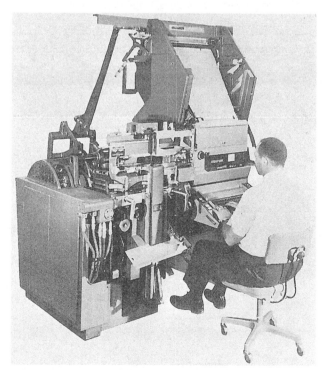

Fig. 105-F. Late Model Linotype

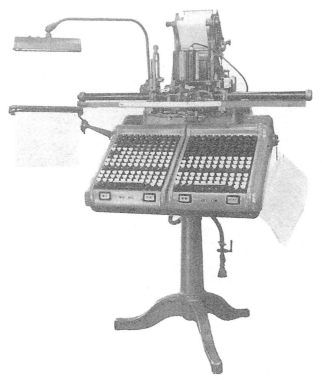

Fig. 105-G. Monotype Keyboard

Fig. 105-H. Monotype Caster

Linotype and Intertype machines can also be equipped with a mechanism by means of which the setting and casting of lines is controlled by a perforated tape. The tape for this purpose is perforated by the use of a separate keyboard. Several machines could, by this method, be operated by duplicates of the tape. Duplicate tapes can also be shipped to different parts of the country so that machines can be operated to cast the same copy from one setting. Tapes may also be perforated by telegraph. By operating a sending device in one city, identical material can be perforated on tapes in any part of the world. News services sometimes use this method literally to set type for several newspapers at the same time. The device is known as a Teletypesetter, even though it is used both for telegraphic transmission of copy and local tape setting of copy.

The Ludlow Typograph is a slug-casting machine. However, the matrices are hand set and hand distributed. This machine is particularly important for special display composition. In a sense, also, the Ludlow provides an "unlimited supply of type" because the matrices can be distributed and set over and over many times without showing wear, which is inevitable in foundry type when subjected to repeated use.

What is your answer? Why must a punch for making matrices be "positive" and the matrix "negative"? Why is an adjustable mold needed in casting type? What is a "pantograph" and how could it be used in cutting punches? Why do you suppose men tried to make machines which would set type that had previously been cast before they hit on the idea of setting matrices, then casting? Why are slug-casting machines, instead of Monotype, commonly used in newspaper plants? Why have type composition plants, which set jobs for others, come into existence in the past several years? Why must a typesetting machine have more keys on it than a typewriter? Why does a typeset page give a better appearance with respect to spacing of letters than a typewritten page? What is the advantage of the Teletypesetter? Why is Ludlow composition frequently faster than setting type by hand? Would hand lettering be more economical in preparing copy for offset printing than setting slugs and taking proofs to be photographed?

Unit 106. Type Metal

It has been assumed that lead, tin, and pewter were among the metals used by the inventors of printing for casting type. Brass, copper, and iron, as well as tin and lead, are referred to in accounts of typecasting printed in 1480. But it is believed that the brass and copper referred to were used in making punches and matrices rather than type itself. Iron wire may have been used to hold the type forms together. Probably the early printers, who operated their own type foundries, discovered the fact that the best type metal is an alloy of lead, tin, and antimony. Repeated experiments have revealed no better combination of metals for the casting of type, so they are still used.

While it is true that all types and type slugs are cast from alloys of lead, tin, and antimony, they are combined in different proportions for different purposes. Lead, when used alone, is too soft as a printing surface. Antimony is added to provide an alloy which becomes harder when the metal is cold. Antimony also makes the metal more fluid when the alloy is in a molten state. It is used, therefore, to provide an alloy which fills the matrix more evenly, giving a better "face." The third element, tin, adds to the fluidity of the type alloy and permits casting to be done at lower temperatures than would otherwise be possible. Tin also adds considerably to the toughness of type metal.

Great care must be taken in refining metals for making type, because impurities, such as copper, zinc, arsenic, and silver, destroy some of the desired characteristics of a suitable type alloy. Care must be exercised in remelting to keep a proper balance of the various component metals. Formulas vary somewhat, but the following combinations are representative:

	For Slug Casting	For Monotype Casting	For Foundry Casting
Lead	84%	72%	50%
Tin	4%	9%	25%
Antimony	12%	19%	25%

Printing plants, nowadays, do not have facilities for casting foundry type. When foundry type becomes worn or nicked, the metal is scrapped and new type is bought. In an average plant the life of foundry type is about four

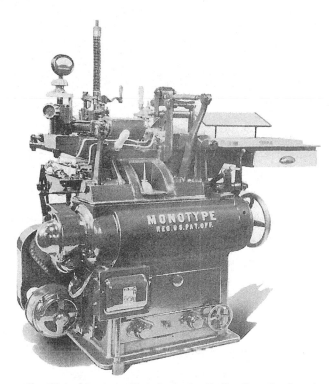

Fig. 106-A. Monotype Giant Caster for Casting Type Quads and Continuous Strip Furniture, 14 to 72 Point

Fig. 106-B. Linotype Equipped for Automatic Tape Operation

Fig. 106-C. Teletypesetter Tape Perforator

Fig. 106-D. IBM Electric Executive Typewriter

Fig. 106-E. Varityper Composing Machine

years (depending, of course, on the use, which varies — popular faces must be replaced frequently, while less used ones merely accumulate dust). Metal used in slug and Monotype casting is melted down in the printing plant in a special furnace and molded into "pigs" for re-use. Loss from remelting averages three per cent, so eventually the metal must be replaced.

Foundry type can be obtained in most fonts in sizes up to 144 points, and some casting machines will produce type of that size. However, because of the weight of metal and casting difficulties, wood is usually used for larger sizes of type. Wood types are available commercially in sizes beginning at 48 point and running as large as ten inches high. Even larger sizes are made on special order. Experiments have been conducted with plastic materials as substitutes for type metal, but types made from such materials have generally been found to be unsatisfactory.

In plants doing a large amount of business, great quantities of metal are kept on hand because several jobs must be in progress at the same time, and because the slugs and type for some jobs are frequently stored in anticipation of reprinting of jobs. Some idea of the amount of metal required for a job may be determined from the fact that slugs for a 6 x 9 page (25 x 38 picas of type) weigh between six and seven pounds.

Extend your knowledge by studying these questions: Why did ancient printers *cast* type as well as *compose* it? Why cannot a foundry type metal be used in Linotype machines? Tin does not reduce the melting point of type alloy but permits casting at lower temperatures. How can that be true? Why is a brittle metal unsuited to use in making type? Disregarding value, why would pure gold be a poor metal for casting type? Could Monotype be used as a substitute for foundry type? How much inactive capital is represented by the type metal in a 64-page, 6 x 9 book, which is being held for reprint, if the metal is worth 30c per pound? A typesetting machine frequently uses 100 pounds of metal per day. If the remelting loss is 3%, and metal costs 30c per pound, what is the loss per month of 24 operating days? Why is copy composed on a justifying typewriter referred to as "cold type"? (See Unit 107.)

Unit 107. New Methods of Copy Composition

Throughout this book emphasis has been placed on the fact that, regardless of the method of obtaining the final impression on paper, printing usually starts with composition of characters, either hand-set or machine-set. These methods are especially adapted to relief printing and are also used extensively in producing originals for printing by offset and gravure. However, since printing by the two latter methods requires the additional step of etching a plate, efforts have been directed toward the elimination of conventional typesetting in the production of originals.

Among the devices developed for producing originals for offset and gravure without typesetting, the justifying typewriter is being used more and more extensively. This method of producing originals greatly reduces production costs; however, reproduced typewritten copy is ordinarily not as pleasing in appearance as the same copy would be if set in type. The primary reasons for this difference which favors hand-set or machine-set type are: (1) except on specially built machines, all typewritten characters are the same width; for example, a narrow character such as "i" occupies the same space in typewritten copy as a wide character like "w"; (2) lack of flexibility in justification sometimes results in open spots or lakes in the finished copy.

These difficulties are being overcome through the development of special machines, such as the Varityper Composing Machine, the Justowriter, and the IBM Executive Typewriter. Consequently, reasonably legible copy of pleasing appearance can be produced. Furthermore, special faces for use in preparing typewritten copy are becoming available in greater variety. Ultimately, this method of preparing originals may replace typeset copy for certain kinds of jobs as machines are improved and as craftsmanship in their use becomes more widespread.

Typewritten copy is ordinarily limited to text material, which means that display characters must either be supplied through typesetting or by some other method. One method sometimes used is that of pasting up copy from already printed letters. Such letters are available either on paper or cellophane. They may

IBM Electric Typewriters b
and speed to today's typing. With on
touch required to release the electric
unnecessary hand and arm motion ha
All operating keys - the carriage ret
shift, and back spacer - are located c
keyboard and are released with the s:
Better quality of typewritten work, in

THIS IS A SPECIMEN OF THE NINE POINT
Tribune News Bold Style (by Coxhead), leaded two points. The Ralph C. Coxhead Corporation of New York makes the announcement of a new invention, a machine which permits type composition in the office by an office typist. The machine resembles a typewriter, both in appearance and operation, but which actually produces finished reproduction copy of type matter ready for use in photo-engraving,

Composition on the Justowriter is the
method of obtaining justified lines of typ
reproduction. A standard typewriter keyl
cally powered type bars combined with a
cates when justification is possible reduc
operator to a minimum. Errors can be
by deleting one or more letters or a who
retyping and justification require no at

Fig. 107-A. Sample Faces of "Cold Type"

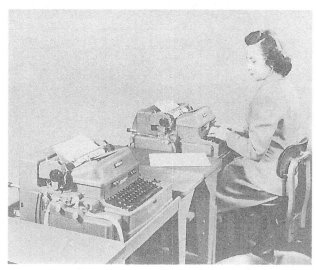

Fig. 107-B. Justowriter. Recorder (right); Reproducer (left)

Fig. 107-C. Fairchild Lithotype

Fig. 107-D. ATF Hadego Photocompositor

be put together to form display lines through a "hunt and pick" system, or they may be assembled in cases similar to those used for individual pieces of type. Alphabets printed on paper are used with printed or typewritten originals. Those printed on cellophane are used with cellophane proofs, which permit the elimination of one step in plate preparation in offset lithography.

A machine known as the Fairchild Lithotype Composer combines typewriter operations with Monotype faces. Characters produced on a Monotype casting machine are mounted on magnesium alloy wheels in two rows, capitals and lower-case, including a full range of numerals. The wheels are interchangeable, providing a full variety of faces. Two wheels may be mounted on the machine at once, permitting the operator to combine light face roman and italics or bold face and light face roman, or any other desired combination. Spacing between words and marginal justification are attained in a second typing of the copy. In the first draft, a justifying scale indicates a justifying numeral after each line. In the second typing, a correspondingly numbered justifying key is used instead of the space bar, which results in automatic right hand margin justification.

Machines have also been developed for photographing type directly, thus eliminating one stage in the preparation of negatives for offset, gravure, and other photomechanical processes. One machine of this type in commercial use is the ATF Hadego Photocompositor. Special type characters of lightweight plastic material, consisting of white letters on a dense black background, are used with the Photocompositor. These types are set by hand in a special composing stick and are photographed line by line. Fonts of 24 or 48 point are used to set the original. By adjusting the machine before each exposure, type images in any size from 4 to 115 point can be produced. Since each line is photographed separately, successive lines may be varied in marginal justification and spacing between words.

For the same reason that efforts have been made to eliminate typesetting and proofing in plate preparation, attempts have also been made to eliminate the camera stage in preparing a photographic negative. A machine known as the Fotosetter, developed by the Intertype Corporation, fixes images of type characters on film instead of casting a slug through the use of matrices and molten metal.

While the principle of the slug-casting machine is used in the Fotosetter, the circulating matrix for each character contains a negative image which is projected onto a film synchronized with a keyboard similar to that found on a conventional Intertype machine. By enlarging or reducing the image, it is possible to set type in a range from 4 to 36 points in size. After composition is completed on the Fotosetter, the film is removed and developed in the same manner as a camera negative. This negative is then inserted into the vacuum frame used in exposing the metal plate. Thus, the Fotosetter encompasses in one operation three stages which ordinarily precede platemaking: (1) setting the copy; (2) obtaining a reproduction proof; (3) photographing the reproduction proof to provide a negative for use in transferring the copy to the plate.

Machines for varying traditional production operations and for introducing substitute processes are developed in response to special needs. Those which meet such needs adequately usually survive and gain in general use. Sometimes their adoption is restricted by natural human resistance to change and the influence of the conventions of craftsmanship — an influence which has historically been extremely pronounced in the graphic arts.

Financial considerations are also involved in the development of new processes and new machines because expenditures of large amounts of risk capital are required on the part of the inventor or the manufacturer of the machines, tools, and auxiliary equipment.

Furthermore, plants which have invested in machines for production by other processes cannot or will not readily sacrifice capital already invested and, in turn, use additional capital for the purchase of machines and equipment necessary in carrying out the new production processes. However, eventually old machines wear out and, in the process of replacement, those adapted to new methods are installed.

Questions relating to changes in production methods, capital investment, replacing of personnel or training existing personnel in new methods, determining relative costs of various methods, seeking to meet competition and render service to customers, are management questions. These questions arise out of problems on which management decisions must be made. The ability to make sound decisions on such matters is the distinguishing characteristic of good management.

In this book most of the operations described relate to craft skills which are essential to the production of printed matter. In the application of such skills, some students who use this book will find highly desirable occupational opportunities. However, it is important for the student to understand also that there are occupational opportunities in the management field to which he may reasonably aspire. Whether the student seeks a vocation as a production worker, a production supervisor, or a production manager in the graphic arts, it is important for him to understand that a knowledge of the processes involved in various methods of graphic arts production is essential to successful employment.

Fig. 107-E. Intertype Fotosetter

Unit 108. Platemaking Before the 20th Century

The first illustrations in books were made from woodcuts. These were tooled out of wood blocks by hand, leaving raised surfaces. This art was fairly well established in Europe before printing was begun by Gutenberg. About that time the cutting of relief printing blocks from soft metal is believed to have been introduced. Such an engraving, dated in 1454, is in existence. However, since wood could be engraved more easily than metal, woodcuts came to be used widely for illustrations in early printing. The earliest known illustrated book, using woodcuts, was printed by Albrecht Pfister at Bamberg about 1460.

Books printed between 1570 and 1770 were usually illustrated by copper-plate engravings; therefore, the making of woodcuts declined. In 1770, however, a revival was started by Thomas Bewick, of England, who developed the technique of using a special engraving tool for cutting *across* the grain of a block of wood, instead of *with* the grain. The revival lasted for about a hundred years and reached its height in this country between 1860 and 1870, during which period woodcuts were used not only for book illustration, but appeared in newspaper printing as well. Today woodcuts are used only to give an "artistic touch" to certain types of printed pieces.

Engraved copper intaglio plates, the forerunner of steel engravings and gravure, were first used in France and Italy in 1476 and 1477, although the method was understood long before that time. Copper engraving did not offer much competition to woodcuts in England until about 1545, and not until 1569 in France. Copper-plate work has continued to be practiced through the centuries and is still used for invitations, announcements, calling cards, and formal letterheads. Since copper is a comparatively soft metal, harder surfaces have been sought for the production of engraved plates. Steel plates are used in printing paper currency at the United States Bureau of Engraving and Printing. Such plates are used, commercially, in printing stock and bond certificates.

The invention of photoengraving is closely linked with the discovery and development of photographic methods. In 1824, Joseph Niepce,
the partner of Louis Daguerre, made the first engraving on metal by photography, the discovery on which all later production of etched printing plates depended. In 1839, Parton, of Edinburgh, developed the sensitizing method, later used in photoengraving. The screen principle was discovered in 1852 by Henry Talbot and practically applied by Berchtold in 1855. Many persons, working on the process in England, France, and America, made photoengraving commercially profitable about 1880.

First halftones were black and white. But the application of color printing to the halftone process was not long in developing after the basic photoengraving process was discovered. Color process work was done successfully in 1892, and today is one of the most widely used methods of graphic reproduction. Thus, colored illustration, which was so prevalent in the era of illuminated manuscripts that preceded the invention of printing, has again come into general use after a lapse of five hundred years. But how marked the change! In the days of the hand-lettered manuscript, an artist-illuminator might spend a year, or more, entering decorations and illustrations in a single copy. Today, high-speed presses turn out, in one hour, 20,000 or more magazines, illustrated throughout with color process reproductions.

Questions on the background of modern commercial printing plates: Why was wood used in making first printing plates? In one of the first illustrated books, the illustrations were printed on top of a type page. Why do you suppose this was done? In another early illustrated book, the same illustration appears several times. Can you think of a reason why this may have happened? Why would a cross-grain woodcut be superior to one cut with the grain? Wood block illustrations, for newspaper printing, were frequently made of several blocks fitted together. Can you determine the reason? Why did copper plates replace woodcuts in printing in the middle period? Why must ink for intaglio printing differ from ink for letterpress? Why is the history of photography important to platemaking? Why is color printing so widely used today? Why is wood engraving considered a fine art today?

Unit 109. Stereotypes, Electrotypes, and Other Duplicate Plates

Newspapers are not printed directly from type and slugs. For this purpose stereotype plates are used. Stereotype plates are sometimes used in printing books and magazines. The first step in making newspaper stereotypes is setting up the copy on Linotype or Intertype slugs. These are then made up into page forms along with Ludlow cast or hand-set heads. In book, commercial, and magazine work, Monotype cast forms are frequently used. Stereotypes are secondary forms because the first form from which they are made must be made up from type or slugs just as the page is to appear when printed.

Stereos are cast solid from papier-mache matrices, formed by pressing the type form into a wet or dry "flong" (the papier-mache substance). Molten metal consisting of lead, tin, and antimony (81%, 5% and 14%) is poured into a mold. In this manner the paper mats can be used to cast a form of one or more pages in one piece. The form can then be used in high-speed printing without danger of slugs, rules, or type working loose.

Stereotypes do not lend themselves to fine work. Therefore, if a form includes halftone illustrations, they must be made with coarse screen (described in Unit 110 on plates and platemaking). They are entirely suitable for newspaper printing, however.

For many long run commercial and magazine printing jobs, electrotypes are used. These, too, are secondary forms made from regularly set and assembled type, slugs, and halftones. In producing electrotypes, a shell is made by electro-chemically depositing copper in a wax or lead mold. The lead or wax mold is made by pressing the primary form into the lead or wax. A matrix results which is submerged in a copper electrolytic bath for several hours. The thin copper shell, which is thus produced, is removed, then filled and built up with molten electrotype metal. This provides a plate with a copper face which can be mounted on a wood block or metal base. Sometimes a thin film of nickel is deposited in the mold ahead of the copper. The resulting plates are called nickeltypes. These are harder and more resistant to wear and chemical action than copper electros.

Duplicate plates molded from rubber are more widely used each year. Initially, rubber plates were developed for use in specialty printing, but within recent years they have been adapted to book work and commercial job printing. Rubber plates are made by using plastic molds which are produced in the same manner as wax molds. (See Unit 110.)

Various attempts have been made to provide some method of printing which would eliminate the necessity of setting type. This is possible in photolithography if the job is to be a reproduction of a previously printed job. In that case, existing printed pieces are photographed and reproduced by transferring the image to offset plates which, in turn, are printed on an offset press. If, however, no printed form exists which can be photographed, then type must be set and a proof made. Of course, a hand-lettered, typewritten, or photo-composed form could be photographed. (These procedures are described in Unit 107.)

Photographic reproduction of reprints and direct photo-composing can be used in offset and gravure printing, but they cannot be used in making stereotypes and electrotypes. Therefore, electrotyping and stereotyping are dependent on the continuance of printing from raised surfaces. Consequently, extension of offset and gravure printing may adversely affect the electrotyping and stereotyping branches of the graphic arts. Such methods would also greatly affect the use of the plates and photo-etched halftones.

Stereotype and electrotype questions: How does stereotype metal differ from Linotype, Monotype, and foundry type metals? Stereotypes for newspapers are curved. Is the mat from which they are made curved or flat when the type form is pressed into the mat? Do stereotypes require make-ready, just the same as type forms, in book printing? In what respect does making an electrotype resemble copper plating? In making nickeltypes, nickel is deposited in the matrix ahead of copper. Why is this a better procedure than nickel plating? Why is offset printing frequently more economical than letterpress in the printing of office forms?

Unit 110. Platemaking for Relief Printing

Current forms of graphic reproduction depend for their effectiveness on the use of a great variety of printing plates. Large newspapers, as has been pointed out in the section dealing with type and typecasting, are printed from stereotype plates. Magazines, and other long run commercial jobs, are usually printed from electrotypes. Stereotypes and electrotypes are secondary plates. (See Unit 109.)

Secondary, or duplicate, plates may also be made from rubber or plastic materials. In manufacturing rubber plates, plastic materials are substituted for wax or papier-mache (used in making stereotypes) because of the intense heat applied in rubber vulcanization. The primary advantage of rubber plates is their durability. Under suitable conditions, runs of more than 100,000 can be printed from these plates. However, special presses are required. In addition to being suitable for use in making the mold or matrix for a plate, plastic materials can also be used in making duplicate plates. Plastic plates can be printed in the same manner as stereotypes. Since they are composed of lightweight material, they are readily mailable.

Primary plates include etched halftones, etched line plates, gravure plates, and offset lithograph plates. In preparing these plates, the first step is the production of a photographic negative by "taking a picture" of the copy which is to be reproduced. From that point on, however, the methods of production and printing of each kind of plate differ considerably as will be explained later.

Halftones are used for reproducing photographs or shaded drawings. The tones of the copy are brought out by "dots" of varying sizes which are introduced into the photographic negative used in making the halftone. These dots are obtained by placing a crossline screen in front of the negative before exposing the copy. The light, reflected through the screen from various parts of the copy, regulates the heaviness or lightness of the dots which result from exposure of the film. The more light that is reflected, the lighter the dots; and, conversely, the less light that is reflected, the heavier the dots and the darker the reproduction. (See also Unit 70.)

To produce the halftone, the photographic negative is reversed and placed in contact with a copper or zinc plate that has been sensitized. The plate is then exposed to light, after which the negative is removed and the plate is etched. The parts not exposed to light will be etched away, leaving the exposed parts as dots of varying weight which stand out in relief, thus giving "tone" to the print.

If copy to be reproduced is black and white, or other solid colors requiring no intermediate tones or shading, line etchings are used. These are photographed on the negative, without a screen. An acid-resisting photographic reverse print is then made on a sensitized piece of zinc which is etched into a relief line plate.

Color printing from halftones is accomplished by making four plates, one each for the three basic colors — yellow, red, and blue — and one for black and white tones. Color process plates are made by photographing the copy successively through filters. Yellow is isolated by photographing through a violet filter; that is, one composed of the other two primaries — red and blue. A green filter prevents the photographing of its elements, yellow and blue, and furnishes a negative for red. An orange filter, a combination of red and yellow, permits the capture of blue in the copy. A black and white negative is then made to provide detail and accentuate highlights.

A halftone color print, like other halftone work, is really an illusion. This can be observed by examining a process halftone reproduction through a microscope. Except in dark areas, or deep tones, the dots produced by the use of a screen neither touch nor lie on top of each other. Rather, they must fall alongside each other, smaller and more widely separated in the light-tone areas, and vary throughout the print with the depth and intensity of the color. Under ordinary observation, however, the original copy appears to the eye to be faithfully reproduced, and is equally as pleasing to look at as the original photograph or painting.

As previously indicated, most primary plates are etched by means of photomechanical and photochemical processes. These procedures are somewhat expensive and also time-consuming.

Therefore, methods have been sought for engraving plates by electromechanical scanning. A machine now available commercially, known as the Fairchild Photoelectric Engraver, produces halftone engravings in six to thirty minutes, depending on the size of the engraving. The maximum size which can be produced on the machine is 8x10″. The printing surface is engraved on plastic material by direct process without recourse to intermediate photography or the use of chemicals.

The mechanical elements involved are a scanning assembly and an engraving assembly. Details of the photograph to be reproduced are transmitted electrically. The machine operates automatically. However, the operator must judge the tonal value of the photograph by observations made through the use of a stroboscopic microscope and meter and, on the basis of these observations, adjust the depth of the engraving stylus to provide gradation in tonal value.

In the process of engraving a part of the surface of the plastic material is burned away to produce halftone dots. A heated stylus on the engraving assembly penetrates the plastic material to varying depths, according to the impulses transmitted from the photoelectric cell as it scans the photograph. Those portions which are penetrated most deeply produce the highlight areas, and those of shallower depth produce the darker tones. The unburned surface of the plastic material forms the dot pattern of the halftone.

The plastic plates produced by this method may be mounted on forms with type for direct printing, or they may be used in making mats for stereotypes. Machines are available for the production of halftones in 65, 85, and 120 line screens.

Platemaking for gravure and for offset lithography will be described in the instructional units which follow. The methods of producing these plates differ radically from the methods used in producing relief printing plates. Furthermore, presses constructed for the purpose of printing relief plates are not adapted to the printing of other types of plates. This is true because the volume of production for each process in most printing plants justifies the installation of press equipment for each method of reproduction if more than one process is used. Multi-purpose presses have been developed experimentally for gravure printing in combination with other processes, but have not been used in competitive production.

It would be possible to develop a machine which would print from any kind of plate surface should need for such a machine arise. In fact, a dual-purpose printing press for printing small forms is available commercially. This machine, known as the Davidson Dual, will print either by the letterpress or by the offset method. The machine will make reproduction from both metal and paper offset plates, or from type surfaces, electrotypes, or rubber plates. Presses are available in two sizes: 10″x14″ and 14″x17¼″.

Fig. 110-B. Davidson Dualith 700

Fig. 110-A. Fairchild Photoelectric Engraver

Unit 111. Platemaking for Offset

Offset lithography uses thin zinc or aluminum (sometimes stainless steel or metal alloy) plates as the printing surface. The basic principle of offset — namely, that ink will adhere to a greasy surface but will not adhere to a moist surface — was borrowed from the original method of lithograph reproduction. Originally, prints were made from porous stones on which designs and letters had been drawn in reverse. That method was discovered by Alois Senefelder in 1796, but has practically been discarded since the introduction of the offset method in 1905.

In printing by offset, either line or halftone negatives are prepared, and these are used to transfer the image photographically to a sensitized zinc or aluminum plate. Plates used in offset printing are grained or roughened, so that nonprinting surfaces will retain moisture which is applied by a special damping roller on the offset press; a grained surface is used because burnished surfaces, such as those used in relief printing, would not retain moisture.

Usually more than one photographic negative is used in preparing an offset plate. Therefore, these negatives must be assembled in a layout which properly positions the type or illustrations on the plate. This layout is made prior to exposing the negatives to the plate by a process known as stripping. This process accomplishes the same purpose for offset that imposition and lock-up achieve for relief printing. For comparison see Units 50-54, 75, 78.

The negatives which are stripped into the layout, or lay-sheet, are positioned on a glass-topped table containing a light. The stripper places the negatives in reverse on opaque (goldenrod) paper which has been cut to the size of the press plate. Areas of the paper are trimmed away with a razor-sharp blade to provide windows and slots that permit the images to show through the negatives. When appropriately positioned, the negatives are then fastened to the paper with opaque cellophane tape. The paper thus serves as a support for the negatives and masks out the areas not to be printed. The preparation of a lay-sheet for offset platemaking is similar to page make-up in letterpress printing. (See Unit 75.)

The plate to be used in offset printing is cleaned, or counteretched, by being placed in a mild acid solution for a few seconds, thoroughly washed under running water, and then sensitized with albumin-bichromate solution. In applying the sensitizing solution, the plate is revolved in a whirler to give an even coating. In deep etch or other special offset platemaking processes, a different sensitizer is used and the stages in plate etching are slightly different than those used in the albumin process.

After the offset plate has been sensitized, the plate and the lay-sheet containing the negatives are placed in a vacuum frame with the negatives uppermost. In this manner, they are exposed to a strong light for the purpose of transferring positive images of the printing surfaces to the sensitized plate. After the plate has been exposed and printed in the vacuum frame, it is smeared or coated with developing ink by hand with a soft cloth, sponge, or wad of cotton. By washing under running water, the developing ink is removed from the nonprinting areas, but continues to adhere to the colloid, or image surface. The plate is then fixed, or gummed, with a coating of gum arabic to protect the image.

In preparing deep etch offset plates, a positive is exposed with the plate to produce a negative image on the plate. When etched, these images are slightly below the surface in the manner of an intaglio plate. The unexposed part of the light-hardened sensitive coating is etched away by means of a special developer, after which developing ink is applied to bring out the printing surface. Deep etch plates provide sharper detail than simple albumin-bichromate plates and also permit the running of a larger number of impressions before changing plates. However, in both processes several identical plates may be made at the same time in order to have extra plates for long run jobs or for quick replacement should a plate become damaged or lose its image on the press.

Regardless of the method used in producing an offset plate, the portion to be printed is a positive in contrast to relief printing plates, which are the reverse of the final print. The reason for the positive printing image on offset plates arises out of the fact that the image of the inked surface of the plate is transferred to a cylinder-mounted rubber blanket, which in turn transfers the image to the paper. Thus the steps in offset printing involve the use of reproduction proofs or originals which are positives, photographic reproductions of originals in the negative, plate image in the positive, rubber-blanket impression in the negative, and a final print as a positive reproduction of the original. The order varies slightly in printing from deep etch offset plates, as explained in the preceding paragaphs.

Offset printing gets its name from the fact that the inked image on the plate is transferred to a rubber-covered cylinder and is then "offset," or transferred to paper. Printing from the rubber blanket eliminates the necessity of doing make-ready as in relief printing (see Units 61-64) to overcome inequality of pressure encountered in letterpress forms. For the same types of jobs on equivalent types of presses, the offset method is ordinarily more rapid than letterpress for the same type of cylinder press jobs, since every revolution of the cylinder provides a printing impression.

Going deeper into the subject of printing plates: Why are halftones, etched line plates, gravure plates, and offset plates considered as primary plates? Are there other forms of primary printing plates? Why are stereotypes and electrotypes classed as secondary or duplicate plates? Why is the photographic negative reversed in making a halftone? Why can a fine screen be reproduced satisfactorily in electotypes but not in stereotypes? How does copy to be photographed for line plates differ from copy for halftones? How is it possible that various hues of the spectrum can be produced by printing three primary colors? Why is a halftone print an illusion? Can gravure supplements be printed in other colors than brown? Why is a photographic positive used in transferring the image in gravure? In what way is application of gravure printing ink similar to the application of paint by an artist? Why do you suppose the use of stone lithography has declined? Why would a polished plate be unsuitable for offset printing? Why is a greasy ink used in lithography and not used in gravure printing? What quality in gravure ink prevents smudging through contact of the printed sheets with each other?

Unit 112. Platemaking for Gravure

Whereas halftone and line plates used in letterpress printing are relief or raised printing surfaces, gravure plates such as those used in printing newspaper supplements are intaglio, or reverse plates. Gravure work is printed from plates containing wells, or depressions, which carry ink that is picked up by the paper. In a sense, gravure, like other forms of intaglio printing, is "painting with ink": the deeper tones are produced by a heavy layer of ink and the lighter tones by a thinner layer of ink, with gradations in between the light and heavy tones. The depth of the wells, or depressions, determines the lightness or darkness of the printing. A very fine screen, 150 lines, makes possible even gradations of shadings, and greater refinement can be obtained by using still finer screens.

The pure white in a halftone is produced by the paper, for, at those points, the relief plate is completely etched away. Similarly, the white portions in gravure printing occur at the spots where the plate surface has no wells, or depressions; that is, the plate has not been etched at all where white appears. Since the gravure plate cylinder is rotated in ink before printing, a special device is required on gravure presses to wipe away the ink from the unetched surface of the plate to provide white areas. This device is known as a "doctor" blade. It consists of a dull knifelike blade, positioned so that it will scrape across the face of the cylinder and remove the excess ink when the cylinder is revolved.

Platemaking for relief halftone work starts with a screened negative, whereas in preparing a gravure plate, a photographic negative is made without the use of a screen. From such negatives photographic film positives are made and assembled, along with reproduction proofs of type matter printed on glassine paper. These are mounted in appropriate position on a masking sheet, which permits light to show through the material to be printed and blocks out light on the nonprinting areas.

In gravure platemaking, a layout is prepared by cutting windows in a masking sheet, and illustrations which have been reproduced on film are mounted on this sheet, along with type printed on glassine paper. A sensitized gelatin sheet mounted on carbon tissue is exposed first to the illustrations and type matter and then to a special screen, which is usually one containing 150 lines to the inch. As a result of these exposures, the sensitized coating on the carbon tissue remains soft where the lines of the screen appear, is hardened slightly in the light areas, and to the greatest degree in the heavy, or highlighted areas. Therefore, when etching occurs, the areas to be printed heaviest are etched deepest and those to be printed lightly are of slight depth.

After exposure, the carbon tissue carrying the sensitized gelatin coating is squeegeed onto a polished copper cylinder. The tissue backing and soft gelatin are washed off in the process of transferring the carbon tissue to the copper cylinder, leaving only the portions of the sensitized gelatin coating which have been hardened by exposure to light, as previously explained. The cylinder is then etched with acid which eats away portions of the cylinder to varying depths, depending upon the extent and hardness of the gelatin coating.

When fully etched, a gravure plate is covered by little cells, or wells, varying in depth depending upon the degree of protection which has been provided by the gelatin coating. These cells, or indentations, are the portion of the cylinder which prints; ink penetrates the cells and as the cylinder turns, the doctor blade scrapes all ink from the unetched or smooth parts of the cylinder. Unetched areas of the plate do not print; on the etched portions of the plate ink is lifted from the wells, resulting in imprints of varying intensity.

Gravure plates are printed by direct contact, in the same manner as letterpress or relief printing. The chief difference lies in the fact that in relief printing ink is deposited on the paper by the raised surface, whereas in gravure, ink is deposited on the paper from indentations in the cylinder. Color printing is achieved with a series of cylinders in the same manner as color process printing is accomplished with halftones in relief printing. Most rotary gravure presses are geared to provide 15,000 or more impressions per hour.

Fig. 112-A. Model 26 Champlain Rotogravure Press

Unit 113. Paper - What It Is

Paper is the largest item of material used in printing. In fact, about a third of the cost of a printed job is the paper used. An idea of the importance of paper in modern life is gained when we consider that about 50,000,000 tons are produced in the world every year. In America, about 300 pounds of paper for every man, woman, and child are used each year. And about half of this amount is used in newspaper, job, and book printing.

Papermaking was invented in China nearly 2,000 years ago. (See Unit 94.) By 1200 A.D. paper was being made in Spain, and 200 years later the art was well established throughout Europe. The first paper mill in England was established in 1494; in the American colonies paper was first manufactured commercially in 1690, in a mill near Philadelphia owned by William Rittenhouse. Paper originally was made for other purposes than printing; but, with the invention of the printing press, changes in the product of paper mills and changes in the methods of manufacturing began to be made.

Ancient papers were made almost entirely from rags and were produced with crude hand-operated devices. Most papers currently used in printing are manufactured by machinery from wood pulp. Only writing and ledger papers are made from rags to any great extent; and even such papers frequently contain a certain percentage of wood pulp. The machine for producing a continuous web of paper was invented by a Frenchman, Louis Robert, in 1798. His invention was financed and developed by an English family, the Fourdriniers. Hence, even today, a papermaking machine is referred to as a "Fourdrinier."

The manufacturing of paper from ground wood pulp was introduced to the world in 1840. Production of cellulose, or wood fibre, by chemical methods, using caustic soda, was perfected in 1854. The use of bisulphite of lime, in the chemical production of pulp, came into use about 1866. Both mechanical (ground wood) and chemical pulps are now widely used in papermaking.

Ground wood pulp is just what the name implies. Paper made from ground wood pulp serves for printing newspapers and cheap grade magazines. By the soda and sulphite processes, lignin and other undesirable elements which remain in ground wood pulp are removed. The resulting cellulose is used for making various grades and weights of book, magazine, and commercial printing papers.

In producing soda pulp, trees such as poplar, chestnut, bass, and gum are used. For sulphite pulp, spruce, hemlock, and other coniferous trees are used, but almost any vegetable fibre can be used in papermaking. Ancient papermakers in China used mulberry shoots; and some of the finest papers are still made in the Orient by the methods used by these first papermakers. Straw from rice, wheat, and other small grains has been used extensively in making certain kinds of paper. Cornstalks have been made into paper experimentally. Esparto grass and other reed plants are extensively used in making paper in European countries.

The more pure cellulose contained in paper, the more permanent and durable it is. About half of the wood from which paper is made is not cellulose. Therefore, ground wood pulp rates only about 50% in cellulose content. Rag pulp, which is 98% pure cellulose, can be produced from new cotton and linen clippings. In between these two extremes stand soda pulps, ordinarily about 75% pure, and sulphite pulps, which usually range between 80% to 90% pure.

The care with which any pulp is prepared, the method used in manufacturing, and other materials added to the pulp in the process of papermaking affect the quality of paper. Therefore, while it is not possible to make good paper unless the pulp is high in cellulose content and free from impurities, some papers are better than others because of the manufacturing methods used.

A great deal has been said and written about the vast destruction of forests likely to result from the extensive manufacture of paper from wood pulp. The paper manufacturers, themselves, have done much to meet this situation by replanting cut-over areas and by starting new forest plantings. It is possible that the fear, sometimes expressed, that our forest resources will eventually be destroyed because of our great demand for paper, is groundless. A movement which may further aid in conservation is the increasing use of reclaimed waste paper in the making of pulp. At least 20% of cellulose going into paper today is made from waste paper. At present waste paper is not used extensively in making printing paper because of the cost of removing ink and other impurities. However, recent chemical developments indicate that a good grade of newsprint can be made from de-inked waste paper.

Get better acquainted with paper: Why is paper a low-cost product, comparatively speaking? How many uses of paper can you think of? Do you suppose the early Chinese used it for different purposes? Why was early paper not wholly suited to printing? Why must rag or highly refined sulphite be used for business papers, while mechanical pulp suffices for newspapers? Why are some cheap grade magazines referred to as "pulps"? Why are magazines like *The Saturday Evening Post* known as "slicks"? Why are reed plants used for pulp in European countries more extensively than in America? Why hasn't the process of making paper from cornstalks been developed commercially? Why do you suppose mulberry shoots make excellent paper? What other things are made from cellulose besides paper? Why are new rags better for papermaking than old rags? Why hasn't de-inking newsprint become a common method of making paper for newspapers?

Unit 114. How Paper is Made

The procedures used in making paper are comparatively simple, but extreme care must be taken in manufacturing printing papers. The pulp for printing papers must be clean and free from chemical residues. The finished sheets must meet definite specifications as to thickness, weight, color, and finish. To maintain uniformity of printing papers, every operation in manufacturing is carefully checked, and the finished sheets are closely examined, inspected, and sorted.

In making paper by hand, the raw substances — rags, mulberry shoots, straw, or reeds — are chopped, ground, or pounded into fine particles. The pulp thus obtained is mixed with water and kept in a floating state. A frame, on which a wire cloth is stretched, is dipped into the floating pulp and quickly removed. The frame is shaken to free the water which drips from the frame or mould and leaves a thin sheet of matted pulp. These sheets are transferred to pieces of felt to be dried. While still moist, they are stacked in piles between felts and completely dried under pressure provided by heavy weights which are placed on boards that are used to cover the stacks.

Paper made by machinery goes through much the same process, but each step is handled mechanically. Pulp is obtained either by grinding or chemically "digesting" rags or wood chips. The pulp is then placed in beaters where revolving iron bars reduce the fibers to the desired fineness. Clay or other substances are added to the pulp in the beaters to fill pores, improve color, and make the finished sheet more opaque. Color is also added at this point; and, just as white clothing is "blued" on wash day, white paper likewise requires the addition of blue tinting pigments or dyes. Just before the pulp is dumped from the beaters, rosin sizing may be added in order to provide a paper which is stiffer, stronger, less given to surface fuzz, and more resistant to ink penetration.

From the regular beater the pulp is dropped into super-beaters, known as "Jordans," where pulp is further refined and mixed. The pulp is then screened or strained, following which a large quantity of water is added. Pulp flows to the papermaking machines in a substance which is frequently 99% water. About 10% of the water drops through the screen which conveys the pulp to the web of the Fourdrinier machine. Pressure removes about 30%, and another 55% is evaporated by passing the paper web over steam-heated cylinders. However, moisture is never completely removed from paper; the finished sheet usually contains 4% to 8% water.

Papermaking machines are long, continuous series of drums, cylinders, felting blankets, calender rolls, and conveyors. One machine has been constructed which produces 150 tons of newsprint in one day. If the daily output of this machine was all in one piece, it would make a web of paper twenty feet wide and 300 miles long. Machines for making book papers are somewhat smaller than those used in making newsprint; but even the smaller machines represent enormous productivity when contrasted with the output of the old plants for making sheets by hand, where a good day's production was about 130 pounds.

During the process of manufacture, paper may be surface-sized or coated. Writing papers, such as bond, ledger, and index papers particularly, require sizing. Application of sizing may be done at some point while passing the web through the Fourdrinier machine, or it may be done after the paper leaves the machine. Starch, glue, or casein are usually used for surface sizing. For certain types of work, particularly the printing of halftones, coated paper is required. Coating is usually applied by passing the paper through a coating machine after it leaves the Fourdrinier, although a method has been developed for spraying a coating on the sheet as it is being made. Clay, satin white, or blanc fixe are the most common coating materials.

Various finishes may be given to the paper when it is being made, or they may be applied later. If the paper is compressed to a smooth finish by chilled iron rolls, it is said to be *calendered* (so called because the smoothing rolls are known as calenders), or *machine finished*. If the calenders are set to produce the greatest possible smoothness, the finish is called *English* finish. A special calender stack or series of finishing rolls may be used to produce a *supercalendered* finish. This is done by moistening the web, usually by steam, and then running the paper between the calenders. *Coated* papers are always supercalendered, but methods have been perfected which make possible high gloss, semi-dull, and dull finishes. Semi-dull and dull finishes provide paper surfaces which reflect less light, therefore, are easier on the eyes.

When the paper web is wound from the papermaking machine without running through calenders, the finish is soft and blotterlike. This finish is really produced by the felt webs between which the paper is compressed in the process of making. Since this procedure resembles the process used by ancient papermakers in the drying of hand-made papers, the finish is

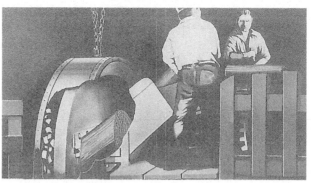
Fig. 114-A. Chipping Pulp Wood

Fig. 114-B. Making Acid for Digester

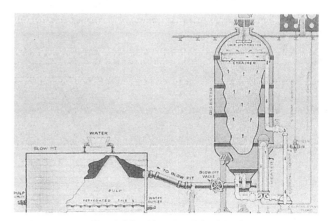
Fig. 114-C. Digesting Pulp Wood

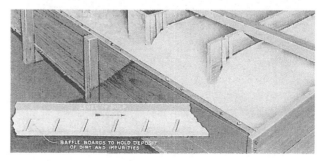
Fig. 114-D. Pulp Leaving Digester

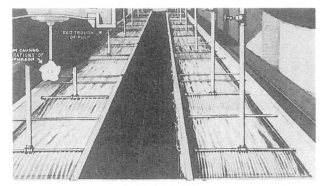

Fig. 114-E. Washing and Screening Pulp

Fig. 114-F. Bleaching Pulp

Fig. 114-G. Reducing Pulp in Beater

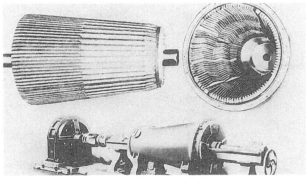

Fig. 114-H. Jordan Super Beater

known as *antique*. By varying the surface of the felt webs, differences in antique finishes may be obtained. Special finishes of this type are sometimes referred to as *felt* finishes. Some book papers are moderately calendered to provide a smooth printing surface without destroying the rough-textured appearance of the paper. Such papers, called *text,* are neither as smooth as machine-finished nor as rough as antique.

Plater finishes and *embossed* finishes are used to provide an extra smooth surface or to give the paper a fancy finish. This finish may be applied by running the paper between rolls, or by interleaving cut sheets between material containing the desired surface design and placing them in a hydraulic press. If, for example, a smooth *plate* finish is desired, the sheets are interleaved with polished metal plates and placed under several tons of pressure in the press. If a *linen* finish is desired, the paper sheets are interleaved with linen cloth and compressed. The hydraulic press method is being rapidly replaced by a machine method in which the paper is fed between two embossing rolls on which the desired design has been inscribed.

If you hold several different kinds of paper to light, you will find other elements of finish which have been built into the sheets. If the sheet has an over-all mat appearance, it is said to be a *wove* paper. Variations in this quality in paper is caused by the mesh (number of wires per inch of the screen over which the pulp flows as it moves onto the Fourdrinier). The mesh of screens varies — 60 to 65 being used for newsprint, and 70 to 80 being used in other printing papers.

If faint water-marked lines appear throughout the sheet, it is said to have a *laid* finish. These laid lines are introduced by wires attached to a cylinder known as a dandy roll, which compresses the paper as it leaves the wire cloth or screen. Special watermarks, as well as laid lines, are produced in this manner. These watermarks serve not only as a means of identification, but also indicate the best printing side. If only one side is to be printed, the side from which the watermark can be read is the best side for printing.

The first handmade papers manufactured by early papermakers showed laid lines because of the kind of screen used. Weak screens were reinforced and the impression of the reinforcement was left on the paper. These laid lines, which were considered a defect in early handmade papers, are sometimes artificially forced into the sheets to add to the ornamental quality of modern papers.

Other special finishes are secured in papers by various processes. These may be obtained in numerous ways: by the *use of special machines*, by the *kind of materials* used or by chemical *treatment* of the materials, and, sometimes, by the *method of drying*. A *deckle edge* is formed on a sheet or web of paper when it is being manufactured. This occurs as the pulp flows against the frame or the border (known as the deckle) which confines the pulp, and a featherlike edge is formed by the falling away of particles of pulp on the outer margins of the web. The deckle edge is trimmed away on most printing papers. However, the retention of an untrimmed deckle edge is considered desirable in certain kinds of printed jobs. In such jobs, the deckle rarely appears at the top of the page, but usually at the fore-edge or at the bottom and, in some cases, at both the fore-edge and the bottom. Various kinds of deckles can be produced by attaching special devices to the edge of the frame of the web conveyor.

Opportunity for thinking: Why is such a vast quantity of water used in making paper? Could you make paper by grinding rags, floating the product in water, and dipping it out with a frame on which a fine screen is tacked? Try it. Why are felts used in drying paper? Why were papers made by ancient producers rough in texture? Why is paper transparent if not filled or coated? Why is surface fuzz objectionable? How does the amount of water in pulp at the time it flows on the machine relate to paper thickness? What changes take place in finished paper when moisture content changes? Why were ancient papermakers not seriously concerned about large quantity production? Why does coated paper give best results in halftone printing? Why have such a vast number of fancy finishes for paper been developed? Which would give a better halftone print, English finish or supercalendered paper? Why is antique paper easier on the eyes than coated paper? How does plated finish paper differ from supercalendered?

Fig. 114-I. Pulp Entering Papermaking Machine

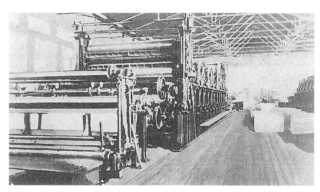

Fig. 114-J. Where Paper Leaves Machine

Fig. 114-K. Converting Paper into Sheets

Fig. 114-L. Trimming to Standard Sizes

Unit 115. Classification of Printing Papers

Paper may be classified in many ways. Sometimes these classes and sub-classes are confusing; therefore, printers usually consider the substance, the finish, and the use to be made of the paper. Newsprint, for example, is a mechanical pulp paper, machine finished, and suitable for newspapers, circulars, and cheap books or magazines. Rotogravure sections of newspapers are printed on supercalendered mechanical pulp papers. Antique papers are chemical pulp papers, bulky and of rough texture, used largely in book printing. They may be unfinished, slightly smoothed or "slip" calendered, or they may have a special felt finish. Antique papers may be made from soda pulp, sulphite pulp, or a mixture of the two. Differences in quality result from the kind of pulp, or mixture of pulps, used.

Bond and ledger papers are used for writing and record purposes and are usually supercalendered or plated to provide a hard finish. They may be made from sulphite wood pulp or rag pulp; or, as is often the case, from a mixture of sulphite and rag pulp. Magazines are usually printed from papers made from sulphite pulp, but paper used for this purpose may be either machine finish, English finish, or supercalendered. Halftones are usually printed on coated papers, but they can be printed on uncoated machine finish, English finish, or supercalendered paper. Cover papers may be produced in any of the forms previously described, but of heavier thickness or weight. (See Unit 114.)

There are many other trade classes of paper. Among the more common ones are *kraft, bristols, boards, manifold, Bible, mimeograph,* and *blotting papers.* Some of these have subclassifications: for example, boards include *binder's board, blanks, cardboard, boxboard, strawboard, chipboard,* and *tagboard.*

Lithograph, or offset, papers are usually considered as a separate class. This is true because the finish on offset papers varies somewhat from papers used in letterpress printing. Bond papers are quite suitable for both types of printing; therefore, many of the papers used in the early development of offset resembled bond papers. It was also found that embossed papers were highly suited to offset. By using special coating materials, coated papers for offset have been developed. In general, paper for use in offset must have two chief qualities: it must resist the effect of water and must be free from fluff or fuzz. If these qualities are present, practically any kind of paper can be printed by the offset method.

The nature of the printing and the process to be used in printing a job, along with such factors as cost, purpose for which the finished job is to be used, and customer preferences, must be taken into consideration in choosing a suitable paper. In printing relief forms consisting of type or line cuts, almost any kind of paper can be used. If halftones are included in relief printing forms, then consideration must be given to the number of lines in the screen. In general, coarse screen halftones will reproduce satisfactorily on newsprint or other papers of rough surface. Fine screen halftones require coated, machine finish, or calendered stock. The size of the screen used in halftone printing by offset is less critical than factors relating to the suitability of the surface of the paper to the process, as described in the preceding paragraph. Gravure printing is ordinarily done on supercalendered or machine finish papers produced from either mechanical or chemical pulp. Heavyweight bond and ledger papers and lightweight bristols are ordinarily used in jobs produced by copper or steel engravings. Special-purpose papers may also be developed for this process as, for example, the paper on which currency is printed.

Questions which the user of paper sometimes asks: What is meant by a 25% rag bond? Why must newsprint be machine finished? Why must paper for rotogravure be soft and flexible? Why are antique papers preferred for book printing? Why is paper made from soda pulp alone less satisfactory than sulphite or a sulphite mixture? What are sulphate papers? How do they differ from sulphite papers? What is kraft paper? What is strawboard? Why must paper used for lithograph printing have different qualities than that used in letterpress printing? What is meant by the word "super," as used in Unit 61 in reference to make-ready?

Unit 116. Specifying, Estimating, and Using Paper

Paper is purchased by the pound, hundred-weight, or ton. Prices fluctuate with economic conditions. In a period of twenty years, newsprint has sold commercially for as low as 2½c per pound and as high as 10c per pound. Prices on book papers have varied from 7c or 8c for the lower grades to 60c or 70c per pound for the highest grades. Average prices for book papers have fluctuated from 12c to 30c per pound. Unwatermarked sulphite bond and ledger papers ordinarily sell at about the same price as the lower grade book papers, whereas the price of 100% rag bond ordinarily exceeds that of the highest grade of book paper.

Sheet size of paper is always expressed in inches. Various sizes are available to meet varying requirements relating to the size of the form to be printed and the press on which the form is to be run. Standard sizes are carried in stock by paper merchants, but unconventional sizes must be obtained on special order from the mill.

Variations in thickness of sheets of paper of the same grade and quality determine its basic weight. Therefore, in selecting paper for a job, the printer thinks in terms of basic weight rather than thickness, which would have to be expressed in thousandths of an inch. For example, he knows that an 80 pound sheet would be thicker and, consequently, stiffer and more opaque than a 60 pound sheet in the same stock. However, in referring to bristols and cardboards, particularly those used in printing mailing pieces, such as postcard stock, thickness is sometimes expressed in point size or thousandths of an inch.

The weights and dimensions of papers have been standardized. Weight is expressed as so much per ream (500 sheets), or as so much per thousand sheets. The weight of the paper per thousand sheets is typically indicated by such designations as "25 x 38, 140 M." This designation means that one thousand sheets of the particular paper in question, 25 inches by 38 inches in size, weighs 140 pounds.

Indicating the weight of paper by thousand sheet count is known as the "new" basis for specifying paper because it is the basis that has been recommended by the American Paper Conference Board to replace the "old," or ream basis. However, printers for several hundred years have been accustomed to think of paper in terms of reams. Therefore, it is common practice in the industry to refer to a paper as a seventy-pound or eighty-pound paper. In referring to "a seventy-pound paper," a printer means that a package of 500 sheets of the paper, in the basic size, weighs 70 pounds. Thus, "140 M" and "70 pound" mean the same thing. Papers used for book and job work commonly range throughout the 50 lb. to 100 lb. weights; i.e., 100 M to 200 M.

Paper may be ordered from a paper mill in any sheet size desired; however, certain sizes may be considered standard because those sizes are usually kept in stock by paper merchants. Common sizes are 22½ x 35, 25 x 38, 32 x 44, 35 x 45, 38 x 50, and 44 x 64. In specifying book papers by weight, however, the 25 x 38 sheet size is the standard by which the weights of other sizes are calculated. This means that 500 sheets, 25 x 38, 70 pound stock, would weigh 70 pounds; but 500 sheets, 35 x 45, 70 pound stock, would weigh 116 pounds. By using arithmetic you can see why that is true. To start in making the calculation, find out how much larger a sheet 35 x 45 is than a 25 x 38 sheet.

The basic size for indicating weights of writing and ledger papers is 17 x 22. The most common weights used in these papers are 16, 20, and 24 pounds per ream; therefore, when someone refers to a 20 pound bond, he means that 500 sheets of the paper, size 17 x 22, weigh 20 pounds. Commonly used sizes in bond and ledger papers are 17 x 22, 17 x 28, 19 x 24, 22 x 34, 24 x 28, 28 x 34.

In cover papers the 20 x 26 size is used as standard; therefore, to refer to a 65 pound cover paper would mean that a package of 500 sheets of 20 x 26 size would weigh 65 pounds. Some cover papers, and practically all bristol and board papers, are sold by the thousand sheets. Likewise, envelopes are usually sold at so much per thousand in sizes designated by number. Two common business sizes are No. 6¾ and No. 10, which measure 3⅝ x 6½", and 4⅛ x 9½" respectively.

In planning the production of a printed job, careful consideration is given to the relation of the size of the form to the size of the sheet to be used, in order that the paper stock can be cut or trimmed without waste from sheets of standard size. Press size and the variety of standard sizes of paper available are also frequently taken into consideration in the original planning or laying out of the job. Unless such planning is done when the job is conceived, waste may occur because the production forms cannot be devised to fit standard pressbed and paper sizes.

The needs of customers have been taken into account by press manufacturers and papermakers in determining standard sizes of their products. Consequently, the range of possibilities which may be considered by the customer in choosing a suitable layout for a job is quite broad. By using ingenuity in planning production, the printer can ordinarily keep waste at a minimum, regardless of the customer's demands. However, it is occasionally possible for the printer to suggest a slight modification in the layout of a job which will bring about a considerable reduction in the cost of production. As an aid in this connection, some paper manufacturers have prepared standard specifications for booklet sizes in relation to sheet size of paper stock for ready reference by the printer in carrying on negotiations with customers. Furthermore, business firms which purchase large quantities of printed products adopt sizes for their printing needs which will permit economy in production, both as to the amount of paper stock used and in relation to utilization of the full capacity of the pressbed.

In planning production, it is also desirable to take into consideration certain characteristics of the paper stock. For example, as pointed out in the preceding units, it is important to select a paper of the type and finish which will give the best results for the particular method of production to be used and the kind of plates included in the form to be printed. The grain of the paper may require consideration in jobs to be folded, because paper can be folded more easily with the grain than across the grain. Consequently, in ordering paper the printer may specify that the grain be with the long dimension or the short dimension of the sheet.

The lay of the grain in a finished job must be anticipated prior to cutting paper for the press run. A finished job such as a book or booklet not only folds better, but stays open more readily, if the grain runs parallel with the binding edge. Likewise, cardboard pieces such as posters stand upright better if the grain is vertical. When moistened on both sides, thin paper will curl in the direction of the grain. Cardboard or cover paper may be tested by tearing—it tears much straighter with the grain than across the grain.

A finished sheet of paper contains 4% to 8% of moisture when it leaves the papermaking machine. Unfortunately, the moisture content of the sheet does not remain constant because changes in atmospheric conditions cause paper to absorb or release moisture. When moisture is absorbed the paper expands across the grain to a greater extent than with the grain and, conversely, the sheet shrinks more across the grain than with the grain when moisture is released.

When a sheet is separated from other sheets, moisture changes may occur in a few minutes. The tendency of the sheet is to assume approximately the same moisture characteristics as the atmosphere of the room in which it is stored or in which it is being processed. For this reason, some pressrooms and cabinets used for storing paper are air-conditioned. Such treatment becomes extremely important where close register must be maintained. The problem is one of holding the moisture content of the sheet relatively constant.

In color process work where separate runs are made to apply each color, production troubles are inevitable if there are marked changes in the relative humidity of the pressroom. Press feeding and bindery work may also be hampered when moisture changes cause the paper to stretch, curl, or become wavy at the edges. These difficulties become more pronounced as the size of the sheet to be processed increases. To meet the difficulties either special means of atmospheric control or paper conditioning must be introduced, or production must be scheduled to permit completion of related operations within time limits in which the paper is not likely to be sufficiently affected to interfere with completion of manufacturing operations.

In addition to printability, the following characteristics should be taken into consideration in determining the suitability of various types of paper, both from the point of view of the printer and that of the customer:

Book papers — a uniform surface which absorbs rather than reflects light, high opacity, bulky or thin as required.

Covers — pleasing texture, attractiveness and permanency of color, strength, durability, good folding quality, freedom from harshness to touch.

Bonds — writing surface adapted to pen and typewriter, durability, strength, snap, pleasant feel and appearance.

Ledgers — good quality, pen writing surface, permits easy erasing without blemish, durability, lies flat without curl, wave, or wrinkle, adequate weight.

Writings — attractive appearance, suitable color, receptivity to ink without tendency to run or blot, good erasing quality.

Offsets — attractive surface with special finish as desired, will not lint or pick, lies compactly flat, free from curl or wave.

Index bristols — surface adapted to pen, pencil, or typewriter, easy erasures, stiff and noncurling.

Weddings — vellum surface, blue white color, sufficient weight to give impression of formality, permits sharp black print.

Blotting and mimeographing — absorbent quality is the primary consideration.

Here are some interesting problems for you to solve in which you can use the information given in the preceding paragraphs. What would be the weight of a twenty-pound, 17 x 22, bond paper if it came in a 25 x 38 size, the same as book paper? What would be the weight of a 65 pound, 20 x 26, cover if it came in book paper size, 25 x 38?

In estimating the quantity of paper required for a job, it is necessary to determine the size of the form which is to be printed, then compute the number of pieces that can be cut from a certain sheet size. Thus, if the form to be printed is made up of four pages, 6 x 9, the outside measurements of the sheet will be 12 x 18 (plus a small margin for trimming if the job is to be bound). By using cancellation as a method of computation, it is possible to determine that four pieces, 12 x 18, can be cut from a 25 x 38 sheet, leaving ample margins to provide for trimming. The trim margin is usually added to the size of the form in making the calculation. If we know that four pieces, 12 x 18, can be cut from a 25 x 38 sheet, and keep in mind that both sides of the sheet are printed, we know that we would get eight printing surfaces, 12 x 18, from a 25 x 38 sheet. If we make no allowance for spoilage, we can print 500 thirty-two page booklets, 6 x 9, from 500 sheets of 25 x 38 paper. If it is 70 pound paper and the price is 24c per pound, the paper for 500 thirty-two page booklets would cost us $16.80. However, it is common practice to make allowance for spoilage. For 500 sheets the customary spoilage allowance is 16%; therefore it would be necessary to order eighty extra sheets in order to allow for spoilage. The amount allowed for spoilage varies; usually it is 10% for 2500 sheets, and 5% for 25,000 sheets or over.

When you have a job to print, ask your teacher to help you determine the following: kind of paper; finish; printing qualities; sheet size before cutting; basic weight; price per pound; allowance for trim; amount of paper required; actual value of paper used on your job, including spoilage. Estimate the paper requirements and approximate cost for runs of 500, 2500, and 25,000 on several direct mail pieces received at your home.

Questions relating to paper problems: Taking the information presented in the preceding unit into consideration, suggest several factors which may influence the price of paper. Why is it necessary to use one sheet size as the standard for specifying weights for different kinds of paper? Why do you suppose 25 x 38 became the standard for book papers, whereas 17 x 22 became the standard for bond papers? Do you suppose the web which leaves the paper machine is the same width of the widest dimension to be cut from the sheet? What size of book paper do you think is most commonly kept in stock by paper merchants? Would it simplify, or complicate, the selling of paper if all stock were sold by the thousand sheets? Must allowance be made for trim if an illustration is printed to bleed off the sheet? Why is the spoilage allowance proportionately greater for a short run than it is for a long run?

Unit 117. Printing Ink

The second most important material used in printing is ink. The amount used on a particular job may vary from a fraction of an ounce for a small run of letterheads or calling cards to as much as 186,000 pounds for a single Sunday edition of a large city newspaper. It is estimated that newspapers, alone, in the United States use between 500,000 and 600,000 pounds of ink in a single weekday. The quantity of ink used daily in printing books, catalogues, magazines, packages, labels, tickets, and an almost limitless variety of commercial jobs exceeds the amount required for newspapers. You can readily understand why inkmaking in itself is a giant industry. In a single year printers now buy more ink than was manufactured in the U. S. during the first 100 years of our history.

In Asia, where the Chinese experimented with printing long before the time of Gutenberg, inks were made from plant substances, mixed with colored earths and soot or lampblack (at least by 400 A. D.). When Gutenberg started printing, inks for various purposes were being made by mixing varnish, obtained by boiling linseed oil, with lampblack. Such inks were used by early printers and continued in use with little modification for 300 years.

With the introduction of web-fed newspaper presses, mineral oils began to be used instead of linseed oil. By the latter part of the nineteenth century, progress had been made in the use of driers, and various new pigments were being used in manufacturing colored inks. (The first patent for making colored inks was issued in England in 1772.) Varnishes of varying degrees of stiffness were introduced to provide inks for different kinds of paper and different kinds of presses. However, the inkmaking methods differed very little from the processes used in the time of Gutenberg. Not until after the beginning of the present century did inkmaking become a complex chemical industry.

Changes in the printing industry within the past quarter of a century have brought about changes in ink manufacturing. Instead of a can of ink being a mixture of linseed oil varnish, carbon black, and an appropriate drier, it is likely to be a synthetic product of a chemical laboratory. It may contain one or more of a hundred newly developed pigments or a specially refined aniline compound. Even the black ink which we use may be free from the old standby, carbon black. It may contain resins dissolved in quick drying solvents which resemble those used in lacquers and enamels. It may be a synthetic compound of glycerin, rosin, and a secretly developed pigment. So vast have been the changes that inkmaking today is a good illustration of the modern miracle of commercial science — industrial chemistry. Because so many developments are recent in origin, only ink manufacturers know the full story.

Many commercial needs have brought about the changes in inkmaking just described. The printing of newspapers at high speeds made necessary the development of inks which would "set" by penetration. Newspapers could not be printed at high speeds with inks which depended on the slow process of surface drying or oxidizing which is characteristic of varnish or other inks of high viscosity.

Gravure printing for newspaper supplements, with its light and heavy spots of color, called for instant setting of deposited pigments without penetration. Solvents that would evaporate almost instantly were introduced. Today, therefore, we have inks which dry by oxidation; by penetration or absorption; and by evaporation. Resinous, or plastic, inks which will dry by hardening when cooled, after they have been applied hot, are in the process of development. Recently, the demands of magazines for instant drying ink for letterpress production have resulted in the development of so-called "vapor" inks.

The growing field of offset lithography has brought additional problems for the inkmaker. He is faced with the necessity of providing pigments, vehicles, and solvents that are not water soluble. He must also produce inks that will not damage rubber blankets and rollers and which permit high-speed production without smudge or setoff on the printed sheets.

In addition to special-purpose inks which are manufactured to order, the inkmaker carries a stock of standard inks which are in general use in printing plants and school shops. As explained in Unit 69, it is important to choose a suitable ink for the paper on which the job is to be run, and the printing surface or surfaces included in the form. The ink requirements of different kinds of paper, as explained in that unit, will ordinarily be satisfactory guides to follow for the general run of jobs. Where there is uncertainty as to the choice of ink to be purchased, the inkmaker can ordinarily make suitable recommendations. The quantity of ink required to produce a job depends upon the kind of paper and the color to be imprinted. A rough stock will require two or three times as much ink as smooth or coated stock, and dark inks may be spread thinner to cover approximately one-third more area than lighter inks.

Adding "dope" in the form of driers or other substances to modify the consistency of the ink to make it "work better" is a practice which should be avoided. Sometimes an advantage in drying can be gained by "doctoring" ink, but generally an apparent need for such treatment indicates that an unsuitable ink has been selected. Different kinds of substances are available to produce different effects, such as speeding up or slowing down the drying, or promoting absorption of ink by the paper. Driers used for these purposes are, respectively, cobalt, special pastes, and japan driers. Where the consistency of the ink is to be changed without modification of drying qualities a reducer, ordinarily a varnish thinner, is used. A student should never try to modify the ink he is using without consulting his instructor. Expert judgment is needed, both in determining the treatment to be given the ink and the proportions to be used.

New commercial developments in printing have greatly expanded the variety of materials which are printed upon. Special kinds of paper are used for packaging, wrapping, and making bags and shipping cartons. These papers cannot always be made so they are easy to print, therefore special inks may be required. Furthermore, the substances contained in the package or wrapper may demand that special ink be used.

Today printing or lithographing may be done on cellophane, wood, tin, glass, plastics, or cloth. In fact, many materials besides paper may be used. Special inks are required for all of these.

From these illustrations it may be seen that printing no longer limits itself to the peculiarities of ink, but demands inks to suit its own problems and needs.

Ink questions: Why must some inks be provided which dry by absorption or evaporation instead of oxidation? How does paint dry? Lacquer? Why is heat in pressrooms frequently kept at 80 to 85 degrees? Could an ink be developed which would set by cooling? What kind of stock requires the most ink? What kind of form requires the most ink? Why have inks changed so rapidly in recent years? Why is printing ink stiffer and heavier than writing ink? What effect does paper sizing have on penetration of ink? On which would ink penetrate most readily, antique paper or bond paper? Why must offset inks differ from letterpress inks? Why must gravure ink be highly fluid? Could water-color inks be used for printing? Why should a press be equipped with an ink agitator? Why is ink which stands in a can for a long time likely to be in poor condition for printing? When should transparent inks be used? What would cause an ink to rub off after printing?

Optional questions: What problem would be presented in selecting ink for a food wrapper? For a soap wrapper? For a package? What do you suppose a double-tone, or duo-tone, ink is? When would it be used? What are aniline inks? Synthetic inks? What is the purpose served by an ink reducer? By an ink dryer? Why would different kinds of ink be required for printing on different materials? How is ink applied in letterpress? In offset? In gravure? Why doesn't the printer mix his own inks? Why are inking rollers for cylinder presses made of glue and glycerine, instead of rubber? Why does the number and size of rollers vary with the size of the pressbed? What would be a good rule for determining the size of the rollers for any particular press? Why are rollers and ink fountains carefully washed after each job? How does the quantity of ink applied affect the color? Why might a sheet printed by artificial light be blacker than one printed by daylight? What things would you wish to know if you were computing the quantity of ink required? Why is more ink required for color printing than in printing black on white?

Unit 118. Binding and Finishing Operations

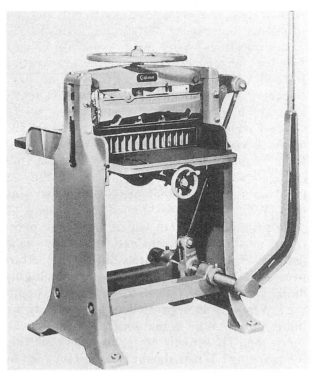

Fig. 118-A. C & P Hand Cutter

In a printed job which has been trimmed to size before running, such as a flat sheet, card, or placard, no further cutting or trimming is ordinarily necessary. The only finishing (bindery) operations involved are inspecting, jogging, and packaging. However, flat jobs are occasionally run two or more to the form and must be cut apart after the press run is completed. Also, in preparation for the running of most jobs, paper sheets of standard size must usually be cut to special sizes, varying with the specifications of the job. Jobs which are to be folded and bound are usually printed on sheets $\frac{1}{8}$ to $\frac{1}{4}$ of an inch larger than actually required for the finished job, to permit a slight trim after folding. Trimming is necessary on such jobs to compensate for irregularities and variations resulting from folding and assembling the printed signatures.

Machines equipped with heavy blades capable of cutting through several hundred sheets with one stroke are used in cutting paper to size and trimming finished flat forms or folded sig-

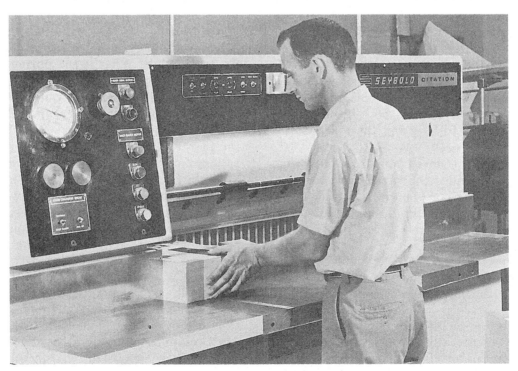

Fig. 118-B. Seybold Power Cutter

natures. Most cutting machines are power driven, although in small commercial shops and in school shops, cutters operated by a hand lever are sometimes used. Special gauges are provided to permit cutting or trimming to precise dimensions. On large cutters the back gauge can be divided into three parts, one for cutting each of three trims on assembled book or booklet signatures. Special cutters are also available for trimming three sides of a stack of signatures with one stroke.

Although the operation of cutting machines appears to be simple, great care must be exercised to avoid injury to the operator. Most cutters are equipped with safety devices. However, special precautions should be carefully observed when such machines are being used. Careless operation of a cutting machine may also result in damage to the top or bottom signatures of a stack of material being cut. To avoid such damage, care must be exercised in placing sheets or signatures on the cutter bed and clamping them in position. If not properly held in position, off angle (slant) cutting will result, because sheets will slip or pull away as the blade moves downward.

In cutting sheets of standard size into smaller sizes, it is usually more desirable to cut to dimensions of which the original is a multiple, and then trim all of the pieces to final dimensions after the desired quantity of blank stock for the press run has been accumulated. The possibility of slight variations occurring because of resetting the gauges on the cutter is avoided by this procedure. In reducing stock sizes to running sheet sizes, careful consideration must be given to the several ways in which the stock could be cut to provide the dimensions desired. By careful calculation and exercise of ingenuity, extra cuts of usable dimensions can sometimes be obtained. The various possibilities can best be determined by spacing off the standard size sheet to the dimensions desired, either by using a ruler and drawing in lines, or by using a templet dimensioned to the size of the sheet to be run.

On certain types of jobs, several finishing operations may be necessary after the job comes off the press before it is ready for delivery to the customer. These finishing operations, which vary from job to job, include

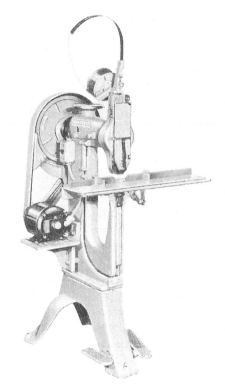

Fig. 118-C. Bostitch #7 Stitching Machine

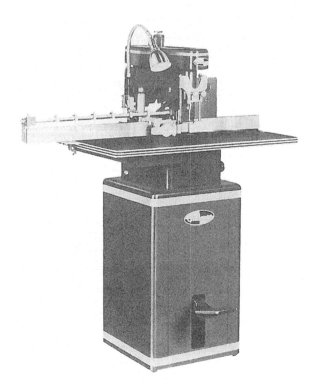

Fig. 118-D. Style E Challenge Drilling Machine

cutting apart forms (if run more than one up), folding, gathering, collating, jogging, smashing, tipping, counting, rounding, backing, marbling, gluing, stamping, inlaying, trimming, punching, drilling, slotting, die cutting, perforating, padding, and packaging. Finishing operations differ in pamphlet binding and bookbinding. Most commercial plants are equipped to do all operations involved in pamphlet binding, but bookbinding is more often a specialty service of commercial binderies.

That part of finishing ordinarily designated as binding refers to various methods of fastening sheets together and attaching covers. Before binding a job, the large printed sheets of the form are folded into sections or signatures. If more than one signature is involved, the sections must be gathered (assembled) in a predetermined order and inspected in the process (collated) to insure that all sections are put together in the right order. Sometimes extra sheets must be inserted after the signatures are gathered.

When all parts of a job which is to be bound are finally assembled, the signatures and inserts are fastened together. The conventional means of fastening or binding are: (1) wire stitching with a machine which cuts and bends pieces of wire from a coil, pushes them through the paper, and completes the fastening by bending over the two ends of the wire; and (2) sewing the signatures together individually and collectively on a special sewing machine.

Most pamphlets are wire stitched, either saddlewise or sidewise. In general, saddle stitching is used for jobs containing fewer than 100 pages, and side wire stitching is used for thicker jobs. However, practices vary, as can be observed by examining a group of magazines on a newsstand. In saddle stitching, the cover and the inside are ordinarily fastened together at the same time. In side wire stitching, the cover may be included with the other pages of the job, or may be attached separately. If attached separately, the cover is double scored down the center on the inside, to give a top and bottom right angle fold, and is then pasted, with or without hinges, to the already stitched inside pages. Side wire stitching holds pages more securely in place, but the finished job is sometimes less satisfactory to the user, because pages do not lie open as readily as they do in a saddle stitched job.

The conventional method of case binding of books, which has been in use for several hundred years, starts with the sewing together of signatures by special sewing machines designed for that purpose. A piece of coarsely woven cloth (super) is then glued to the back of the signatures in such a manner that the cloth extends outward from both sides of the back of the signatures. When glued to an already prepared case, the cloth serves as a hinge for the front and back covers of the book.

Fig. 118-E. Model OS Cleveland (Dexter) Folder

The casing-in process is completed by gluing the end papers of the signatures to the front and back covers. Examples of case binding can be found among your school books.

Greater speed and economy in bookbinding have been sought in various ways. A method which is rapidly increasing in use is known as perfect binding. Many mail order catalogs and telephone books are bound by this method, along with widely circulated novels and other books of popular interest. Machine sewing is completely eliminated in perfect binding and the back of the book is held together with a piece of gauze applied with a highly durable adhesive especially developed for the purpose. Except for the elimination of sewing, this method of binding follows in general the same steps as conventional binding. Various kinds of mechanical bindings are widely used. Perhaps the simplest of these is the ring binder, such as is found in notebook covers. Another simple loose leaf binding is the post binding used on ledgers, record books, price lists, and for similar purposes where the loose leaf feature must be combined with insurance against the sheets pulling out through handling. Other mechanical bindings include spiral wire coils, wire loops, multiple ring bindings of either metal or plastic, as well as tube, clip, and ring plastic bindings. These latter bindings are more suitable for commercial documents than

for library or school books, because books thus bound do not lend themselves readily to racking and storage on shelves.

A wide variety of special machines are found in the modern bindery. One of the more recently developed is a power driven jogging machine. Others commonly found include drills, punches, and perforators. Gathering machines are also widely used in commercial plants and almost universally in magazine and book plants. Some of these machines not only gather signatures, but contain units for stitching and trimming the assembled sections, so that a finished product is delivered without any human handling of the job, except to load the bins from which the signatures are fed to the gathering machine.

While a considerable amount of hand work is still done in some commercial binderies, more and more of the work is being done by machines. In one plant, which produces several million books per year, folded signatures as delivered from the press are handled only once from the time sections are placed in the gathering machine and a finished book is delivered at the end of an intricate assembly of special machinery. The handling occurs for inspection purposes at the end of the assembly line. The book then goes to another special machine, which places books in cardboard boxes and seals and labels the boxes for shipment.

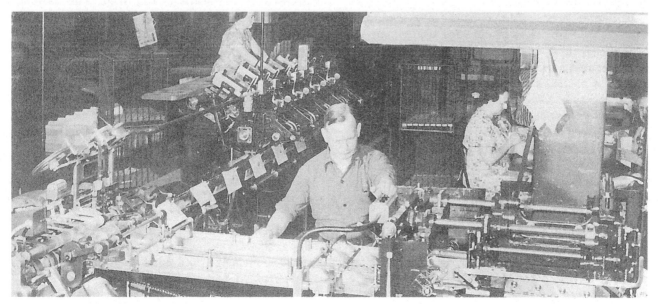

Fig. 118-F. Sheridan Combination — Gathers, Inserts, Saddle Stitches, Trims, and Delivers Finished Booklet

Unit 119. Graphic Arts Occupations

When printing originally began early in the fifteenth century, a craftsman did all of the work of typesetting, presswork, and binding. In many instances he even cast his own type. Today, the only type cast in printing establishments are the slugs and machine-set type units of typesetting machines. Foundry type is manufactured by specialists in typecasting, and is purchased by the printer. Except in the very smallest of plants, today, the worker does not do all of the operations in printing. Workers are specializing to a varying degree, depending upon the kind of equipment found in a particular plant. Therefore, several different occupations exist in the industry. Just what these occupations are can best be indicated by tracing some of the steps in printing.

The first step in printing is composition of the form. If the job requires hand-set type, that work is done by hand compositors. If the type is to be machine set, the work is done by men specially trained to operate the various casting machines — Linotype, Intertype, Monotype, or Ludlow Typograph. In the industry there are men who do nothing but operate Linotypes or Intertypes; others who work only at the keyboard of Monotype equipment; and still others who operate the casting machine for Monotype. Ludlow casting equipment is usually operated by hand compositors.

In some large plants, men are employed whose special work is to care for and repair the typesetting and casting machines. Frequently, plants employ men, known as stonemen, whose task it is to make up and lock up the form for the pressroom. Closely associated with the composing-room workers are others who read and correct proofs. The worker who makes the actual corrections on proof is known as the proofreader and he is usually assisted by someone who reads the copy aloud, who is known as the copyholder. Thus, it will be seen that there are several specialized occupations which relate to the preparation of the printing form alone.

After the type has been set, made up into pages, and locked in the chase as a form for the press, it is taken to the pressroom or press department and printed. The man who operates the press is called a pressman.

In addition to making adjustments on the press and checking the form to secure proper register, or location of the material printed on the sheet, the pressman must also do make-ready to insure a regular and even impression of the form. Make-ready is required to even up certain spots on the form which are too low or too high for clear impression. In make-ready, bits of tissue paper are cut and placed in the packing of the cylinder, or beneath the plates, if any are included in the form.

Some shops have found it more efficient to employ workers who do nothing but assist with make-ready. They make spot sheets, cut out manifold patterns, and paste them up so that they may be used by the pressman. Underlays and overlays, produced by special mechanical or chemical processes, are frequently used instead of hand-cut inlays. Furthermore, various types of gauges and mounting devices, which simplify make-ready, are used in many plants.

A large variety of presses will be found in the press departments of most printing plants. These vary in size and complexity from hand-fed platens to large cylinder presses. For the platens and small cylinder presses only one operator is required; that is, the pressman himself does all the work connected with the running of the job. On the larger cylinder presses an assistant is required. The assistant works under the direction of the pressman, doing a large variety of tasks in preparation for the running, and watching certain parts of the press while in operation. Frequently, the assistant is requred to hand feed the press if it is not equipped with an automatic feeder. On especially large presses it may be necessary to use a press feeder in addition to the pressman's assistant.

Plants that do presswork have finishing departments in which workers perform a large variety of tasks. Mainly their work relates to folding, binding, wrapping, packing, and, sometimes, mailing the printed pieces. In these departments, paper is cut and prepared for the pressroom and the folded jobs are trimmed in preparation for binding.

After a job is completed, it is ordinarily wrapped in packages according to customer's specifications. Neither wrapping nor packing require a great amount of skill; therefore, persons employed to do this work may also be assigned to other jobs, such as hand folding, inserting, gathering, collating, inspecting, and jogging. This type of work is spoken of as bindery hand work, and includes some forty or fifty different tasks to which the worker may be assigned alternately.

A moderate degree of skill is required in cutting paper stock, setting and operating folding machines and other bindery equipment. Persons trained to operate such machines are ordinarily assigned exclusively to this work. There are, however, in most bindery departments several small machines, such as sewing, stitching, perforating, and punching machines. The operation of these devices is easy to learn, and workers may be assigned alternately to small machine work and hand work.

If the bindery department includes bookbinding (making case or hard bindings) as well as pamphlet binding, then other specialized machine workers are required. In most commercial plants a moderate degree of craftsmanship is required in bookbinding; however, where bookbinding is practiced as an art, craftsmanship of a very high order is essential. In the early history of printing, a great deal of care was exercised in the binding of books. Vellum, calf, and other types of leather bindings were common. Beautiful examples of these early bindings are still in existence, some of which are still in good condition after four hundred years or more.

Although plates for use in letterpress printing are not usually made on the premises of printing plants, except in newspaper plants, plate makers are graphic arts workers. A number of the occupations relating to plate making require special skill. In preparing stereotypes, it is necessary to make mats, cast stereotype plates, and trim or finish the plates for mounting. In making electrotypes, various kinds of molds are made which require a certain amount of hand finishing before they are placed in the electrolytic bath. After the electrotype shell has been made, it is necessary to trim the copper plate, fill it with lead alloy, and prepare the plate for mounting. In making these plates, one worker may do a variety of tasks. However,

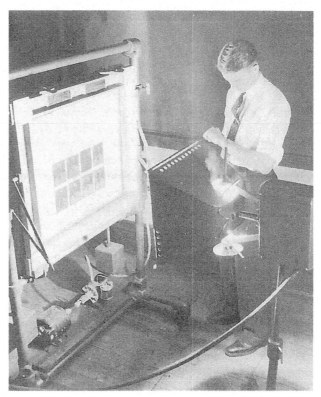

Fig. 119-A. Exposing an Offset Plate

Fig. 119-B. Lettering a Layout

where large quantities of plates are made, a considerable amount of specialization exists.

Photo-engraving plants, specializing in the production of halftone and line engravings, employ men whose tasks are indicated by the job names in common use. Included are photographer, stripper, printer, tint layer, artist, etcher, router, blocker, finisher, and proofer. In such plants the tasks include photographing the copy, fitting together several parts of copy after photographing (known as stripping), exposing the sensitized copper or zinc plates through the photographic negative, doing hand work on the plate before and after etching, handling the metal plate in the etching bath, removing excess metal, squaring the plate for mounting on wood blocks, or preparing the plate so that it can be mounted on metal base, and taking proofs of the engraving.

Similar to photo-engraving workers in some respects, but distinctly different in other ways, are workers who photograph, etch, retouch, and finish copper plates for rotogravure printing. This is also true, to some extent, of workers in offset printing who photograph copy and make plates for photolithography. Usually the plates used in gravure printing and the offset process

Fig. 119-C.   Stripping a Negative

Fig. 119-D.   Routing an Engraving

(photolithography) are made in the plants doing those types of work. In spite of the similarities in work in various kinds of platemaking, the worker trained in one would not be qualified to work in either of the other two without special training.

Men who operate newspaper presses, rotogravure presses, and lithograph presses are known as pressmen, also; however, their work is so distinctly different that specialization is required. A worker who is familiar with platen and job cylinder presses would not be able to enter any one of the other fields without special training and experience. Furthermore, pressmen who are qualified in either letterpress or gravure would be completely lost in attempting to operate an offset press. The same thing would be true of an offset pressman trying to work at letterpress or gravure printing.

There is, today, no such thing as a printing craft in the industry. Rather, there are several crafts. Many of these are highly specialized and often sub-divided. This condition is a product of the machine age in which we live. Craft specialization has its advantages, but there are distinct disadvantages. See if you can determine what they are.

In most manufacturing industries there is a tendency to transfer the skill of the craftsman to a machine. This is done in a limited way, at first, then still more machines are invented until finally the worker requires little skill. He becomes a machine tender instead of a craftsman. It has not been possible to eliminate the need for skilled craftsmen in printing. Even the invention of typesetting machines did not do this. Instead, it created a need for a new kind of craftsmanship.

Can you determine the answers to these questions? Why has it been difficult to transfer the skill of the worker to machines in the printing industry? Do you think it will ever be possible? Why do large plants employ workers who do nothing but proofreading or make-ready? Why is less skill required in bindery work than in composition or presswork? Why do most plants buy plates instead of making them? Why is it not possible for an offset pressman to operate a job cylinder press without special training? Would a Linotype operator be able to operate a Monotype keyboard without special training?

Unit 120. Workers in the Graphic Arts

By far the greater percentage of workers in the graphic arts industries are men. Only about 12% of the total number employed are women. For the most part, women employees in printing plants work as proofreaders, as Monotype keyboard and Teletypesetter perforator operators, or as hand and small machine operators in finishing and binding departments.

Among men workers in printing, the greatest number in any of the specialized crafts are employed as hand compositors or operators of typesetting machines. At least half of the skilled workers employed in printing are engaged in work relating to the composition, make-up, and lock-up of printing forms — five times the number employed as pressmen. About 25% of the total number of men employed in printing occupations fill jobs requiring no special skill or only a moderate degree of skill. These men are ordinarily engaged in work which relates to the handling of stock, cutting, trimming, and binding activities.

The actual number of workers in the two major printing crafts may be of interest to you. There are approximately 200,000 compositors and machine typesetters in the United States and about 40,000 printing pressmen. As a normal circumstance, the printing industry needs about fifteen to twenty thousand new workers each year to fill vacancies created by retirement and changes in occupation. It cannot be said, of course, that 15,000 to 20,000 new workers regularly find employment in the industry every year, because business conditions may change, causing an increase or decrease in the need for workers. However, that there are opportunities for youth in printing is shown by the fact that over 65,000 persons employed in the industry in 1950 were under 20 years of age.

To prepare new workers for the industry, many plants are providing apprentice training courses. These apprentices receive a small wage while learning one of the trades and in four to six years become qualified craftsmen. Ordinarily, there are more than ten thousand apprentices in training; however, business conditions may cause this number to increase or decrease in any particular year. Apprentice-

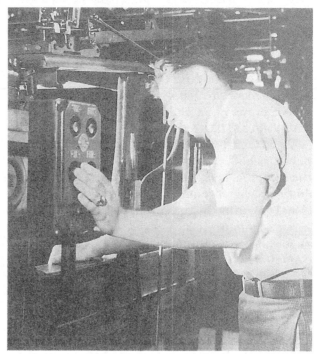

Fig. 120-A. Starting a Printing Press

Fig. 120-B. Operating a Linotype

ship opportunities exist in practically every large city. Information about them can ordinarily be obtained through public school guidance counselors and your printing teacher. One of the outstanding apprentice training courses for printing is operated by the United States Government Printing Office, Washington, D. C. Appointment to the government apprentice school is made on the basis of civil service examinations.

Vocational schools, operated not only by the public school systems but by organizations in the graphic arts, provide training for the industry. The circumstances surrounding vocational training in these schools differ with different communities. Your teacher can tell you about the opportunities that may exist in your community.

Employment conditions in the printing industry are quite favorable in comparison with many other production or manufacturing industries. Employers and workers in the various skilled crafts co-operate closely in seeking to provide pleasant working conditions; and, in general, employers maintain a very close personal acquaintance with their workers.

The rate of pay in the graphic arts is good compared with other industries. Wage studies made by the United States Department of Labor have repeatedly shown that average hourly wages in printing are higher than those in any of the other major industries. This is probably due to the fact that the proportion of skilled craftsmen to other workers is higher in printing than in other industries. Employment in printing is relatively steady. Therefore, comparisons of the yearly income of workers in major industries shows printing at the top of the list.

Not only are there outstanding opportunities in printing for young people who wish to become skilled craftsmen, but also for those seeking office, supervisory, and professional opportunities. Printing employs fewer persons in the classification of unskilled labor and minor operative skills than other industries. On the other hand, the ratio of supervisory and professional employees is three times greater than it is in other industries, and for clerical employees, twice that of other industries.

The need for professional employees in the graphic arts greatly exceeds the supply of qualified personnel. Opportunities lie in the fields of product design, marketing, production planning and control; technical development of materials, processes, and production equipment; along with the application of engineering and science, personnel supervision, financial management, and business administration to enterprise management. Ordinarily, college training is needed to qualify for professional service. Training may vary from a few specialized courses to a four-year college degree program. Your teacher or counselor can give you the names of schools providing such training.

These questions are not answered in the unit you have just studied, but you may be able to reason out the answers. Try them. Why are more men employed in printing than women? Why are there more compositors and typesetting machine operators than pressmen? Why does the number of workers in the printing industry fluctuate from year to year? When should industry have the greatest number of apprentices in training — in good times or slack times? Why do you suppose the United States Government operates the largest printing plant in the world? Why is it not possible for a boy to enter the printing industry as a fully trained craftsman after attending public school printing vocational courses? Why is there a closer relation between workers in the graphic arts and their employers than in other industries? Why is employment steadier in the printing trades than in some of the other crafts? Why is the rate of pay usually lower in smaller communities than large cities?

Study Helps

Helpful Books and Sources of Information

Because there are so many worthwhile books relating to the graphic arts, it is difficult to prepare a list of titles without omitting valuable ones. The references suggested here are those we believe to be most helpful. The most basic ones are starred. Books known to be out of print are omitted here. Many of these older books are important sources of information and are available in libraries. Your teacher or a librarian may be able to suggest additional books. You may also consult bibliographies contained in most of the books in this list.

There are many excellent publications by the Graphic Arts Technical Foundation (formerly Lithographic Technical Foundation), 131 East 39th Street, New York 16, N. Y. Only the most basic have been included in this list. A teacher may join the GATF for a nominal fee, allowing him or his school to purchase these publications at the member price (30% of list price).

Some of the books listed here are rather technical and will challenge mature students with special interests. Several references are very simple explanations which are easily read.

Graphic arts information also can be found in encyclopedias, and by using various indexes such as the card catalog in a library. Following are headings where such information often can be found. (Basic ones are in *italic*).

Advertising (layout and typography), alphabet, *art* (commercial, graphic, prints), bibliographies, block (books, or prints), blueprinting, bookbinding, *books*, cameras, *color* (printing, prints), communication, composition, copying processes, copy reading, copyright, currency (counterfeiting), editing, electrotyping, electronography, electronic data processing, electrostatic printing, embossing, engraving, etching, forms, *graphic* (arts, design, reproduction, technology), gravure, Gutenberg, halftones, history, incunabula, illustrators, information storage and retrieval, ink, intaglio, Intertype, inventors, lettering, letterpress, linotype, *lithography*, marking, monotype, music printing, newspaper (layout and typography), occupations (workers, labor unions), *office duplicating* (or reproduction), offset, optics (lenses), packaging, *paper, photo-* (many combinations), *photography*, pictures, planography, plates, presses, print making, *printing*, (as a graphic art, layout and typography, practical, presses, processes), private presses, proofreading, publishing, pulp, ruling, (silk) screen process (serigraphy), (postage) stamps, stamping, stereotyping, stenciling, textile printing, *type* (founding, setting, typography), typewriter, watermarks, xerography.

Printing Terms

American Paper and Pulp Assn., *The Dictionary of Paper*. New York: American Paper and Pulp Assn., 2nd ed. 1951. 303 pp.
An accurate description of terms and materials.

Hostettler, Rudolph, *Technical Terms of the Printing Industry*. New York: George Wittenborn, Inc., 3rd ed. 1959. 195 pp.
Basic terms in five languages.

Pocket Encyclopedia of Paper and Graphic Arts Terms. Kaukauna, Wis.: Thomas Printing & Publishing Co., 1960. 92 pp.
A pocket manual of terms used in graphic arts.

*Porte, Rhoda A., *Dictionary of Printing Terms*. Salt Lake City: Porte Publishing Co., 5th ed. 1950, 173 pp.
Long a standard reference tool.

Turner, Mary, ed., *Bookman's Glossary*. New York: R. R. Bowker Co., 4th ed. 1961. 212 pp.
Printing and publishing terms in 7 languages.

Layout and Design

Analysis and Design of Office Forms. New York: American Assn. of Collegiate Registrars and Admission Officers, Commission on Office Management and Practices, 1958. 33 pp.

Anderson, Donald M., *Elements of Design*. New York: Holt, Rinehart and Winston, 1962. 218 pp. Paper

Birren, Faber, *Color: From Ancient Mysticism to Modern Science*. New Hyde Park, N. Y.: University Books, 1962. 338 pp.
Color traditions and contributions of art and science.

Birren, Faber, *Color Psychology and Color Therapy*. New Hyde Park, N. Y.: University Books, rev. 1961. 302 pp.

Boughner, Howard, *Posters*. New York: Pitman Publishing Corp., 1962.
Problems of design and outstanding examples.

Bowman, John J. and R. Allan Hardy, *Jewelry Engravers' Manual*. Princeton, N. J.: D. Van Nostrand Co., Inc., 1950.
Design of initials, monograms, special marks.

Dair, Carl, *Design with Type*. New York: Farrar, Straus, and Cudahy, 1952.

De Lopatecki, Eugene, *Advertising Layout and Typography*. New York: The Ronald Press Co., rev. 1952. 165 pp.
Designs analyzed, simplified, and improved.

Feldsted, Carol J., *Design Fundamentals*. New York: Pitman Publishing Co., 2nd ed. 1958. 164 pp.
Basics, patterns, ads, and pictorial design.

*Felten, Charles J., *Layout*. New York: Appleton-Century-Crofts, Inc., 3rd ed. 1950. 122 pp.
Integrating materials, type and photos.

McLean, Ruari, *Modern Book Design*. Fair Lawn, N. J.: Essential Books, 1959, 116 pp.
Design of plain printed pages for reading.

Medlin, C. J., *Yearbook Layout*. Ames, Iowa: Iowa State University, 1960. 132 pp.
Creative layouts of photo pages.

Nash, Ray, *Printing as An Art*. Cambridge: Harvard University Press, 1955.
A history, nicely designed by Bruce Rogers.

Printing Layout and Design. Albany: Delmar Publishers, Inc., 1956. 288 pp.
Type, color, design for typical jobs, 350 layouts.

Copy Reading, Style, Proofreading

Garst, Robert and Theodore Bernstein, *Headlines and Deadlines*. New York: Columbia University Press, 3rd ed. 1961. 237 pp.
Copy editing and headline writing for journalists.

*Lasky, Joseph, *Proofreading and Copy-Preparation*. New York: Mentor Press, 1954. 656 pp.
The most authoritative book on this subject.

Leslie, Louis A., *20,000 Words—Spelled, Divided, and Accented*. New York: Gregg Division, McGraw-Hill Book Co., 4th ed. 1960. 244 pp.
Spelling, hyphenation, punctuation, no definitions.

New York Times, *Style Book for Writers and Editors*. New York: McGraw-Hill Book Co., 1962. 124 pp.
A new style manual by a renown publication.

Smith, Robert M. and Robert A. Steffers, *Practical Exercises in Proofreading*. Glen Ellyn, Ill.: Kenilworth Press, 1957.
Work book of galley proofs with errors.

U. S. Government Printing Office, *Style Manual*. Washington: U.S.G.P.O., rev. 1959. 496 pp.
Compounds, capitalization, punctuations, etc.

*University of Chicago, *Manual of Style*. Chicago: University of Chicago Press, 11th ed. 1949. 497 pp.
One of the most useful, especially for academic use.

Art, Lettering, Copy Preparation

Cardomone, Tom, *Advertising Agency and Studio Skills*. New York: Watson-Guptill Publications, 1959. 125 pp.
Preparation of art and mechanicals for reproduction.

Goudy, Frederic W., *The Alphabet and Elements of Lettering*. Berkeley, California: University of California Press, 1942. 101 pp. Now published in paper by Dover Publications, New York.
Complete well-illustrated discussion of lettering and the alphabet, by our most prolific type designer.

Leach, Mortimer, *Letter Design in the Graphic Arts*. New York: Reinhold Publishing Co., 1960. 227 pp.
The understanding and execution of letterforms.

*Maurello, S. Ralph, *How to Do Paste-Ups and Mechanicals*. New York: Tudor Publishing Co., 1960. 160 pp.
Well illustrated, complete, by an experienced teacher.

Maurello, S. Ralph, *Complete Airbrush Book*. New York: Tudor Publishing Co., 1954.
How-to instruction for beginners or artists alike.

*Wright, Harry B., *Lettering*. New York: Pitman Publishing Co., 3rd ed. 1962.

Type, Typography, Composition

Burns, Aaron, *Typography*. New York: Reinhold Publishing Corp., 1961. 111 pp.
Principles and examples of modern use of type.

Harding, Edwin B., *A Practical Touch System for Line Casting Machines*. Brookings, S. D.: Edwin B. Harding, 1955.
A 10-finger system, maintenance; boxed pamphlets.

Harding, Edwin B., *Line Casting Operation-Machinist*. Chicago: Graphic Arts Monthly, 264 pp.
Emphasizes mechanism, problems and adjustments.

Karch, R. Randolph, *How to Recognize Type Faces*. Bloomington, Ill.: McKnight & McKnight Publishing Co., 2nd ed. 1959. 264 pp.
1693 faces classified with clues for recognition.

*Polk, Ralph W., *The Practice of Printing*. Peoria, Ill.: Chas. A. Bennett Co., Inc., 5th ed. 1962. 324 pp.
Basic letterpress text emphasizing composition.

Tinker, Miles A., *Legibility of Print*. Ames: Iowa State University Press, 1962.
Best type specifications based on extensive tests.

Updike, Daniel B., *Printing Types: Their History, Forms, and Uses*. Harvard University Press, 3rd ed. 1952. 2 vols. 618 pp.
Comprehensive background of alphabet and printing.

Imposition

Warner, H. Wayne, *Planning for Better Imposition*. Chicago: Graphic Arts Monthly.
Basic layouts and techniques for modern equipment.

Photography (general)

Battison, John H., *Movies for TV*. New York: The Macmillan Co., 1956. 376 pp.
The movie making process and selection for TV.

*Eastman Kodak Company (editors), *How to Make Good Pictures*. Rochester, N. Y.: Eastman Kodak Company, 1957. 256 pp.
Covers most phases for the every day enthusiast.

Eaton, George T., *Photo Chemistry in Black-and-White and Color Photography*. Rochester, N. Y.: Eastman Kodak Company, 1957. 124 pp.
For those with little chemistry, physics or theory.

Hoke, John, *The First Book of Photography*. New York: Franklin Watts, Inc., 1954. 69 pp.
A very elementary book for grades 5-10.

Kodak Filters and Pola-screens. Rochester, N. Y.: Eastman Kodak Company, 1961, 48 pp.
Complete technical data for uses of filters.

*McCoy, Robert A., *Practical Photography*. Bloomington, Ill.: McKnight & McKnight Publishing Co., 1959. 291 pp.
A good basic text for beginners.

United States Bureau of Naval Personnel, *Photographer's Mate 3; also 2; also 1 and C*. Washington, D. C.: Navy Department, rev. 1961, 1958, 1960. 3 vols., 447, 696, 400 pp.
Quite complete photo library for naval ratings.

Wolbarst, John, *Pictures in a Minute*. Boston: Photographic Book Publishing Co., Inc., 1958. 176 pp.
The Polaroid Camera, its operation, picture ideas.

Reproduction Photography and Stripping

*Halpern, Bernard, *Offset Stripping Black-and-White (507)*. New York: Lithographic Technical Foundation, Inc., 1958. 360 pp.
Negative manipulation for beginner or journeyman.

Jaffe, Erwin, Edward Brody, Frank Preucil, and Jack White, *Color Separation Photography for Offset Lithography with an Introduction to Masking (509)*. New York: Lithographic Technical Foundation, Inc., 1959. 222 pp.
Advanced work for those adept with halftones.

Jaffe, Erwin, *Halftone Photography (508)*. New York: Lithographic Technical Foundation, Inc., 1960. 210 pp.
Intermediate work using crossline and contact screens.

Kodak Graphic Arts Handbook. Rochester, N. Y.: Eastman Kodak Company.
A continuing source of accurate information on reproduction materials. Booklets revised frequently.

Neal, Harry Edward, *No Pictures, Please*. Washington, D. C.: Harry Edward Neal, 1959. 20 pp.
Laws controlling reproducing of pictures and printing.

*Robinson, Karl D., *Line Photography (503)*. New York: Lithographic Technical Foundation, Inc., rev. 1956. 123 pp.
Basic camera techniques for the beginner.

Platemaking (relief and general)

Flexography: Principles and Practices. New York: Flexographic Technical Assn., 1962. 310 pp.
Comprehensive suggestions and standards for all work from design to drying; also history and glossary.

Line, Halftone and Color: An Introduction to Modern Photoengraving. Chicago: American Photoengravers Assn., 1959. 48 pp.
An illustrated survey of photomechanical methods plus letterpress reproduction. Glossary.

Mertle, J. S. and Gordon L. Monsen, *Photomechanics and Printing.* Chicago: Mertle Publishing Co., 1957. 422 pp.
Complete information on photo platemaking for letterpress, offset, gravure, and screen process.

Presswork (relief and general)

Lichter, William H., *Shop Manual of the Typographical Numbering Machines.* Chicago: Graphic Arts Monthly. 132 pp.

Mills, George J., *Platen Press Operation.* Pittsburgh: Carnegie Institute of Technology, 1953. 150 pp.
Imposition, lock-up, makeready and inks for the beginner and the advanced student.

*Polk, Ralph W., *Elementary Platen Presswork.* Peoria: Chas. A. Bennett Co., 1955. 148 pp.
The platen press, makeready, and simple operations.

United States Government Printing Office, *Theory and Practice of Presswork.* Washington: U.S.G.P.O., rev. 1962. 248 pp.

Ink

Printing Ink Handbook. New York: National Assn. of Printing Ink Makers, Inc., 1958. 55 pp.
Inks, ingredients, uses, and correcting troubles.

Reed, Robert F., *What the Lithographer Should Know About Ink (310).* New York: Lithographic Technical Foundation, Inc., 1960. 219 pp.
Technical information to improve presswork.

Wolfe, Herbert J., *Pressmen's Ink Handbook.* New York: Dorland Books, 1952. 267 pp.
Kinds, testing, buying, problems, remedies, glossary.

Bindery

A.L.A. Library Technology Project, *Development of Performance Standards for Library Binding, Phase I.* Chicago: American Library Assn., 1961. paper.
Test standards for library bindings.

Klinefelter, Lee M., *Bookbinding Made Easy.* Milwaukee: Bruce Publishing Co., rev. 1960. 96 pp.
Simplified binding of books, magazines, and sheets.

*Lewis, Arthur William, *Basic Bookbinding.* Baltimore: Dover Publications, Inc., 1955.
Authentic hand operations explained thoroughly.

Paper

*Hunter, Dard, *Papermaking in Pioneer America.* Philadelphia: University of Pennsylvania Press, 1952.
Authentic history by a lifetime devotee.

Libby, C. E. (ed.), *Pulp and Paper Science and Technology, Vol. 1, Pulp.* McGraw-Hill Book Co., 1962. 436 pp.
Comprehensive instruction by 36 educators and industrialists, tested for teaching.

Reed, Robert F., *What the Lithographer Should Know About Paper (308).* New York: Lithographic Technical Foundation, Inc., 2nd ed. 1959. 166 pp.
Technical information helpful to lithographers, and to papermakers.

*Sutermeister, Edwin, *The Story of Papermaking.* Boston: S. D. Warren Co., 1962. 209 pp.
A basic introduction to the paper industry.

Taylor, Jack W., *Rule of Thumb Tests for Printing Papers.*
Simple tests for finish, formation, opacity, strength, size, bulk, grain, etc.

Offset Lithography (plates, presses, duplicating)

*Cogoli, John E., *Photo-Offset Fundamentals.* Bloomington, Ill.: McKnight & McKnight Publishing Co., 1960. 209 pp.
Complete beginning text in photowork and offset.

Hoch, Fred W. and Carl B. Harris (ed.), *Offset Duplicator Techniques.* New York: Fred W. Hoch Assoc. Inc., 1957. 96 pp.
Platemaking, running Multiliths or other duplicators.

Knowles, Lester, *In Business with a 1250 Multilith.* Colton, Calif.: Lester Knowles, 1955. 195 pp.
Equipping and operating a beginning offset shop.

Tory, Bruce E., *Offset Lithography.* Chicago: Graphic Arts Monthly, Inc., 1957. 331 pp.
A complete review of the lithographic industry.

United States Bureau of Naval Personnel, *Lithographer 3 & 2 and 1 & C.* Washington, D. C.: Navy Department, rev. 1955. Two vols., 584 and 367 pp.
Photomechanicals, style, and glossary, in *3 & 2*; color, presses, bindery and management in *1 & C.*

Intaglio Engraving and Gravure

Cartwright, H. Mills and Robert MacKay, *Rotogravure.* Lyndon, Ky.: McKay Publishing Co., 3rd ed. 1956. 303 pp.
A survey of European and American methods.

Steffens, Robert N., *Engraved Stationery Handbook.* North Bergen, N. J.: The Cronite Co., Inc., 1950. 430 pp.
Complete text for steel and copperplate engraving, etched banknote methods, equipment lists.

Screen Process

Biegeleisen, J. I. and Max Cohn, *Silk Screen Techniques.* New York: Dover Publications, Inc., 1957. 187 pp.
Art and commercial processes, color, stencil methods.

Eisenberg, James and Francis J. Kafka, *Silk Screen Printing.* Bloomington, Ill.: McKnight & McKnight Publishing Co., 2nd ed. 1957. 91 pp.
Six kinds of stencils, art, color, industry, supply sources, projects, bibliography.

Kosloff, Albert, *Photographic Screen Process Printing.* Cincinnati: Signs of the Times Publishing Co., 1962. 235 pp.
Principles, photo stencils, equipment and supplies.

Kosloff, Albert, *Ceramic Screen Printing.* Cincinnati: Signs of the Times Publishing Co., 1962. 97 pp.
Inks, printing, firing, decals, enamels, references.

Zahn, Bert, *Screen Process Methods of Reproduction.* Chicago: Frederick J. Drake & Co., 1956. 252 pp.
Methods, machines, products: cloth, glass, decals, etc.

Printing Technology and Management

Catalog of American Standards. New York: American Standards Assn., 10 East 40th St., 1963. 83 pp.
Available standards for office records, photographic goods, paper, and many others.

Franklin Printing Catalog. Salt Lake City: Porte Publishing Co., revised monthly. 1,252 pp. Leased, but write for training use.
Cost tables, helps, sample jobs for estimating.

Hartsuch, Paul, *Chemistry of Lithography.* New York: Lithographic Technical Foundation, Inc., 1961. 358 pp.
Basic chemistry for the beginner, pH, hydrocarbons, chemistry of platemaking, photography, paper, ink.

Jaffe, Erwin, *Physics for Lithographers (402).* New York: Lithographic Technical Foundation, 1959. 139 pp.
Machines, liquids, heat, electricity, light and optics.

Robinson, Karl D., *Air Conditioning for Lithographers (309).* New York: Lithographic Technical Foundation, 1950. 90 pp.
Properties of air, printing needs, and equipment for conditioning.

Rodier, Harold B., *Establishing and Operating a Small Print Shop.* Washington: United States Department of Commerce.
Basic information, suggestions and standards on establishing and operating a small print shop.

Taylor, Frank A., *Colour Technology for Artists, Craftsmen, and Industrial Designers.* New York: Oxford University Press, 1962. 140 pp.
Practical information with color plates.

U. S. Bureau of the Census, *1958 Census of Manufactures.* Washington 25: U.S. Dept. of Commerce; Printing. Publishing and Forest Products Div., 1959.
Figures, graphs, comparing processes and products.

Von Bosse, Theodore P. and J. H. Borowsky, *Estimating and Pricing for the Graphic Arts Industry.* Philadelphia: North American Publishing Co., 1960. 95 pp.
Cost accounting based on sound successful practices.

Career Information

Aptitudes needed, career opportunities, training, schools, scholarships, etc.

Abel, Charles, *Photography: Careers and Opportunities for You.* Philadelphia: Chilton Co., 1961.

Angel, Juvenal L., *Careers in Design, Decoration and Commercial Art.* New York: World Trade Academy Press, Inc. 2nd ed. 1952. 20 pp.

Angel, Juvenal L., *Careers in the Field of Printing.* New York: World Trade Academy Press, Inc., 2nd ed. 1957. 26 pp.

Angel, Juvenal L., *Careers in Publishing and Printing.* New York: World Trade Academy Press, Inc., 2nd ed. 15 pp.

Biegeleisen, J. L., *Careers in Commercial Art.* New York: E. P. Dutton & Co., Inc., rev. 1952. 255 pp.

Clark, F. E. *Craftsmen in the Graphic Arts.* Scranton, Penna.: International Textbook Co., 3rd ed. 1950. 183 pp.

Institute for Research, *Career as a Newspaper, Magazine, and TV News Photographer (202).* Chicago: Institute for Research, 1961. 23 pp.

Melcher, Daniel, *So You want to Get into Book Publishing.* New York: R. R. Bowker, Co., 1962.

*Pollack, Phillip, *Printing, Careers and Opportunities for You.* Philadelphia: Chilton Co., 1959. 136 pp.

Ryan, Bernard, Jr., *So You Want to Go into Advertising.* New York: Harper and Row, 1961.

*U. S. Bureau of Labor Statistics, *Employment Outlooks in Printing Occupations* (1300-77). Washington, D. C.: U. S. Dept. of Labor, 1962. 24 pp.
Excellent source of trends, figures, and possibilities.

Science Research Assoc., Inc., *Jobs in Publishing.* Chicago: Science Research Assoc., Inc., 1960. 32 pp.

Publications, Advertising, Specialties

Arnold, Edmund C., *Functional Newspaper Design.* New York: Harper & Brothers, 1956. 349 pp.
Design of newspapers: functions, type, heads, etc.

Arnold, Edmund C., *Profitable Newspaper Advertising.* New York: Harper & Brothers, 1960. 136 pp.
A good basic book on advertising.

Dunn, S. Watson, *Advertising Copy and Communication.* New York: McGraw-Hill Book Co., Inc., 1956. 545 pp.
Basics of writing and designing advertising.

Medlin, C. M., *School Yearbook Editing and Management.* Ames, Ia.: Iowa State College Press, 2nd ed. 1956. 212 pp.
Complete guide from the selection of a theme until the books are distributed.

National School Public Relations Assn., *Print it Right.* Washington, D.C.: National Education Assn. 1953.
Preparing, printing, publishing school propaganda.

Strauss, Victor, *Point of Purchase Cardboard Displays.* New York: Presentation Press, 1954. 218 pp.
Planning, constructing, and printing of displays.

Duplicating (except offset)

Cansler, Russell N., editor, *Fundamentals of Mimeographing.* Chicago: A. B. Dick Co., 1957. 87 pp.
Stencil making, machine operation and uses.

*Herrman, Irvin A., *Manual of Office Reproduction.* New York: Office Publications, Inc., 1956.
General text for duplication techniques.

How to Plan and Publish a Mimeographed Newspaper. Chicago: A. B. Dick, Co., 23 pp.
Organizing a simple duplicated publication.

Straub, Laura L. and E. D. Gibson, *Liquid Duplicating Systems.* Dubuque, Ia.: Wm. C. Brown Co., 1960.
Spirit duplicating or Ditto.

Straub, Laura L. and E. D. Gibson, *Stencil Duplicating Systems.* Dubuque, Ia.: Wm. C. Brown Co., 1960.
Handbook for mimeographing.

Techniques of Mimeographing. Chicago: A. B. Dick Co., 1960. 60 pp.
Tips for typing stencils, adding art work and running.

Art Prints, Crafts, Hobby Printing

Briggs, John R., *Woodcuts: Wood-Engravings; Linocuts and Prints by Related Methods of Relief Print Making.* London: Blandford Press, 1958. 176 pp.
History, examples, bibliography, artists, procedures.

Heller, Jules, *Printmaking Today.* New York: Holt, Rinehart & Winston, Inc., 1958. 266 pp.
An introduction to the graphic art processes.

Horodisch-Garman, Alice, *Bookplates in Pen and Ink.* New York: Aldus Book Co., 1954.
A series of 21 bookplates drawn by the author.

Kafka, Francis J., *Linoleum Block Printing,* Bloomington, Ill.: McKnight & McKnight Publishing Co., 1955. 84 pp.
The art of block printing for craftsman and student.

Kafka, Francis J., *The Hand Decoration of Fabrics.* Bloomington, Ill.: McKnight & McKnight Publishing Co., 1959. 198 pp.
Various hand printing and dyeing processes, supply sources, gallery of samples. Well illustrated.

Kauffman, Desire, *Graphic Arts Crafts.* Princeton, N.J.: D. Van Nostrand Co., 2nd ed. 1962. 244 pp.
Block printing and other simple processes for fun.

Lieberman, J. Ben., *Printing as a Hobby.* New York: Sterling Publishing Co. Inc., 1963. 128 pp.
Printing on a private press you can make. Comprehensive instruction by the "Prop." of the historic Kelmscott press used by Morris and Goudy.

History and Culture

Aldis, Harry G., *The Printed Book.* Cambridge: The Cambridge University Press, 3rd ed. 1951. 141 pp.
Essays on the history of printing. Unusual illustrations; bibliography.

Carter, T. F. and L. C. Goodrich, *The Invention of Printing in China and Its Spread Westward.* New York: Columbia University Press, 2nd ed. 1955. 282 pp.
Basic historical reference on earliest printing.

Diringer, David, *The Illuminated Book: Its History and Production.* New York: Philosophical Library, 1955. 523 pp.
A comprehensive history of books, well illustrated.

Diringer, David, *Writing: Its Origins and Early History.* New York: Frederick A. Praeger, Inc., 1962.

Jennett, Sean, *Pioneers in Printing.* London: Routledge & Kegan Paul Ltd., 1958. 196 pp.
Significance of Gutenberg, Caxton, Caslon, Baskerville, Senefelder, Koenig, Mergenthaler, and Lanston.

McMurtrie, Douglas C., *Story of Printing and Bookmaking.* New York: Oxford University Press, 3rd ed. 1943.

Morison, Stanley, *Four Centuries of Fine Printing.* New York: Barnes & Noble, Inc., 3rd ed. 1960.
Design and typography in various periods.

Newhall, Beaumont, *The History of Photography from 1839 to the Present Day.* New York: Museum of Modern Art, 1949. 265 pp.
A complete history of the growth of photography.

U. S. Government Printing Office, *100 GPO Years 1861-1961.* Washington, D. C.: G.P.O., 1961. 164 pp.
History of our public printing office.

General References

Auble, J. Woodward, *Arithmetic for Printers.* Peoria, Ill.: Chas. A. Bennett Co., Inc., 1954. 188 pp.
Problems in estimating, copy fitting, paper, ink, etc.

Carlsen, Darvey E., *Graphic Arts.* Peoria, Ill.: Chas. A. Bennett Co., Inc., 1958. 158 pp.
Simplified activities in each graphic arts area.

Curwen, Harold and J. Brough, *Printing.* Baltimore: Penguin Books, Inc., 1955. 32 pp.
Simple full color story of most printing processes.

Epstein, Sam, and Beryl Epstein, *The First Book of Printing.* New York: Franklin Watts, 1955.
Written for grades 5-7, many illustrations.

Hague, Clifford W., *Printing and Allied Graphic Arts.* Milwaukee: Bruce Publishing Co., 1959. 256 pp.
Elementary and advanced printing, binding, related.

The International Association of Printing House Craftsmen, Inc., *Printing Progress — A Mid-Century Report.* Cincinnati: International Association of Printing House Craftsmen, 1959. 543 pp.
A comprehensive view of new developments.

Jackson, Hartley E., *Printing: A Practical Introduction to the Graphic Arts.* New York: McGraw-Hill Book Co., 1957.
A basic printing text.

Kagy, Frederick D., *Graphic Arts.* Homewood, Ill.: Goodheart-Willcox, 1962. 112 pp.
A broad brief view for the elementary student.

Karch, R. Randolph, *Graphic Arts Procedures.* Chicago: American Technical Society, rev. 1957. 383 pp.
The various processes for laying ink on paper.

Lush, Clifford K., *Junior Letterpress and Lithography.* Peoria, Ill.: Chas. A. Bennett, Co., Inc., 1962. 96 pp.
Simple junior high text for letterpress and offset.

Marinaccio, Anthony, *Exploring the Graphic Arts.* Princeton, N. J.: D. Van Nostrand Co., 2nd ed. 1959. 297 pp.
Graphic communications, and major processes.

Mills, George J., *Sources of Information in the American Graphic Arts.* Pittsburgh: Carnegie Press, Carnegie Institute of Tech., 1951. 120 pp.
Lists films, filmstrips, periodicals and many books.

Pocket Pal for Printers, Estimators, and Advertising Production Managers.* New York: International Paper Co., 7th ed. 1963. 131 pp.
Good survey of history, processes, materials, terms.

Stemp, Lillian, *Safety Manual for the Graphic Arts Industry.* Chicago: National Safety Council and the Education Council of the Graphic Arts Industry, Inc., 1953. 96 pp.
An authoritative program of safety education.

Strauss, Victor, editor, *The Lithographers Manual.* New York: Waltwin Publishing Co., 1958. 2 vols. paged within 19 chaps.
A compendium of photomechanical reproduction with units on other processes, very complete.

Weiss, Harvey, *Paper, Ink and Roller.* New York: W. R. Scott, 1958. (grades 5-9).

Selected Organizations

The following trade associations, labor unions, other organizations and their publications may be sources of current information. Typically these are busy offices not equipped to handle much mail, so if you must write, be brief and ask a specific question.

Advertising Federation of America, 655 Madison Ave., New York 21, N.Y. Career, instructional material.

American Paper and Pulp Assn., 122 East 42nd St., New York 17, N.Y. Film list, information.

American Photoengravers Assn., 166 W. Van Buren St., Chicago 4, Ill.

Flexographic Technical Assn., 157 W. 57th St., New York 19, N.Y.

Gravure Technical Assn., Room 5060, 30 Rockefeller Plaza, New York 20, N.Y.

Intl. Assn. of Electrotypers & Stereotypers, 758 Leader Bldg., Cleveland 14, Ohio

Intl. Graphic Arts Education Assn., 1411 K. St. NW, Washington 5, D.C.

National Assn. of Printing Ink Makers, 39 West 55th St., New York 19, N.Y.

National Paper Trade Assn., 220 E. 42nd St. New York 17, N.Y. Career pamphlet, paper facts.

Packaging Institute Assn., 342 Madison Ave., New York 17, N.Y.

Print Council of America, 527 Madison Ave., New York 22, N.Y. Bibliography for art prints.

Printing Industry of America, 20 Chevy Chase Circle NW, Washington 15, D.C.

Screen Process Printing Assn., Intl., 549 W. Randolph, Chicago 6, Ill. Course of study, instruction.

Technical Assn. of the Pulp and Paper Industry, 360 Lexington Ave., New York 17, N.Y. Test standards.

U.S. Dept. of Commerce, Business and Defense Services, Printing and Publishing Industries Division, Washington 25, D.C. Annual survey by sampling, complete census each five years (1958, 1963) published year following. *Printing and Publishing Industry Report,* monthly ($1 per year).

Amalgamated Lithographers of America, 233 W. 49th St., New York 19, N.Y. Organizes plant wide.

Intl. Brotherhood of Bookbinders, AFL-CIO Bldg., 5th Floor, Lafayette Square, Washington, D.C.

Intl. Brotherhood of Pulp, Sulphite and Paper Mill Workers of U.S. and Canada, Fort Edward, N.Y.

Intl. Printing Pressmen and Assistant's Union of N. America, Pressmens Home, Tennessee

Intl. Typographical Union, Box 2341, Colorado Springs, Colo. (or Indianapolis, Ind.)

2006 Addendum

Resources for Letterpress Printers

This list is current as of mid-2006, and is excerpted with permission from Dave Tribby's excellent website for the American Amateur Press Association. The site includes a much more extensive list of resources for letterpress printers, as well as pages devoted to printing museums, private and professional letterpress shops, local printing groups, typefaces available from U.S. foundries, type lore, ATF and BB&S catalog listings, and graphic arts information. (Mailing addresses and websites change frequently; use an online keyword search to verify current contact information for all resources listed below.)
http://www.aapainfo.org/lpress.html

Internet Resources

Getting Started
David Rose has put together a dandy Introduction to Letterpress Printing that contains an amazing amount of information, all directed toward the newcomer to letterpress printing.
http://www.fiveroses.org/intro.htm

Letterpress Discussion List
To join the "Letpress" e-mail list, send a message to Listserv@listserv.unb.ca with the content of the message the single line *subscribe letpress*. Or visit the "Join or Leave the LETPRESS List" page.
https://listserv.unb.ca/cgi-bin/wa?SUBED1=letpress&A=1

Frequently Asked Questions
Green Dolphin Press has prepared a Letterpress FAQ (Frequently Asked Questions) page.
http://www.greendolphinpress.com/letterpress-faq.html

Yahoo! Discussion Groups
PPLetterpress: A forum and clearinghouse primarily focused on printing with digital type and the photopolymer plate process.
http://groups.yahoo.com/group/PPLetterpress/

SFletterpress: A network of hobby and commercial letterpress printers centered on the U.S. west coast.
http://groups.yahoo.com/group/sfletterpress/

Briar Press
This site is devoted to promoting the art of letterpress, and to preserving some of the familiar and not so familiar graphics and images of letterpresses and the printed image.
http://www.briarpress.org/

Flywheel and Cylinder
Manuals and technical information on letterpress equipment.
http://www.boxcarpress.com/flywheel

Type Foundries

Dale Guild Type Foundry
Proprietor Theo Rehak, formerly a typecaster at American Type Founders, set up shop in 1993 using Barth casters obtained when ATF went out of business. They cast type from 6 to 24 points, ornaments, and borders. Sold by NA Graphics (see next section below).

M & H Type (formerly Mackenzie & Harris)
1802 Hays Street, San Francisco, CA 94129
Hundreds of fonts and borders plus composition and photopolymer.
http://www.arionpress.com/mandh/

Other Type Sources
There are many other type suppliers including Quaker City Type, Skyline Type Foundry, and Swamp Press. See Dave Tribby's online resource list for details.

Printing Equipment & Supplies

Don Black Linecasting
120 Midwest Road, Unit # 5, Scarborough, Ontario, Canada M1P 3B2
Dealer in: handset type; Linotype, Intertype, and Ludlow matrices; and presses, equipment, and parts.
http://www.donblack.ca/

Boxcar Press
501 W. Fayette St. Studio 222, Syracuse, NY 13204
Supplier of photopolymer plates and supplies.
http://www.boxcarpress.com/

Letterpress Things (John Barrett)
55 North Chicopee Street, Chicopee, MA 01020
A warehouse full of printing equipment and supplies.
http://www.letterpressthings.com/

NA Graphics (Fritz Klinke)
P.O. Box 467, 1314 Greene St., Silverton, CO 81433
All sorts of printing supplies: type from ATF and Dale Guild, books, spacing material, border, rule, ink, press parts, leads, slugs, quoins, rollers, etc.
http://www.nagraph.com/

Sterling Type Foundry (Dave Churchman)
P.O. Box 50234, Indianapolis, IN 46250
Letterpress equipment, plus cuts, borders and type.

Classified Ads

Briar Press — Letterpress Classifieds
Includes both "Wanted" and "For Sale" categories.
http://www.briarpress.org/classifieds/

eBay
There's usually lots of letterpress equipment at this online auction service. Browse the Printing and Graphic Arts category or search by keyword.
http://www.ebay.com/

Index

GENERAL PRINTING

The 1963 edition of this book was originally printed by offset lithography. It has been republished in September 2006 by Liber Apertus Press, scanned from the 1963 edition. This reissue is digitally printed and bound by Lightning Source, Inc., in Lavergne, TN. The paper is acid-free.

Liber Apertus Press

P.O. Box 261, Saratoga, CA 95071 USA
www.LiberApertus.com
info@LiberApertus.com

Made in the USA
Coppell, TX
08 September 2020